# SHAY

## THE AUTOBIOGRAPHY

# SHAY

## ANY
## GIVEN
## SATURDAY

### THE AUTOBIOGRAPHY

*With Chris Brereton*

Sport Media

*To my four amazing children, each
as beautiful and perfect as the other:
Shayne (Horse Jnr), Sienna (Mrs Moo),
Gracie (Baby G) and Cassie-Elsa
(Granny Chops).*

*You make my life complete.*

Sport Media

Written with Chris Brereton

First published in Great Britain and Ireland in 2017 by
Trinity Mirror Sport Media, PO Box 48, Old Hall Street, Liverpool, L69 3EB.

www.tmsportmedia.com
@SportMediaTM

Trinity Mirror Sport Media is a part of Trinity Mirror plc.
One Canada Square, Canary Wharf, London, E15 5AP.

1

Hardback ISBN: 9781910335796
eBook ISBN 9781911613077

With thanks to Mark Devlin and Gill Hess Ltd.

Photographic acknowledgements:
Tony Woolliscroft, PA Images, Mirrorpix, Sportsfile.
Shay Given personal collection.
Every effort has been made to trace copyright.
Any oversight will be rectified in future editions.
Cover image: Tony Woolliscroft.

Printed and bound by CPI Group (UK) Ltd, Croydon, CR0 4YY.

# CONTENTS

Foreword by Robbie Keane    9

Foreword by Alan Shearer    12

| | | |
|---|---|---|
| **1.** | Remember, Remember, The Fifth | 15 |
| **2.** | The Donegal Crab | 29 |
| **3.** | Paradise Lost | 47 |
| **4.** | In The Shadow Of Giants | 67 |
| **5.** | Boy In Green | 79 |
| **6.** | Hitting The Big Tyne | 97 |
| **7.** | Ruud Awakening | 119 |
| **8.** | Where's My Future? | 135 |
| **9.** | Mick And Roy | 153 |
| **10.** | Hope And Heartache | 169 |
| **11.** | Zip It | 191 |
| **12.** | Sir Bobby | 203 |
| **13.** | Fight Club | 213 |
| **14.** | World Cup Wannabe | 227 |
| **15.** | The Pain Game | 239 |

| 16. | My Side | 257 |
| 17. | Over And Out | 271 |
| 18. | Noisy Neighbours | 283 |
| 19. | The Madness Of Mancini | 299 |
| 20. | The Hand Of Fate | 315 |
| 21. | Heroes And Villans | 331 |
| 22. | One Sunday | 351 |
| 23. | When Tomorrow Comes | 363 |
| 24. | Go Raibh Maith Agat | 375 |
| 25. | With Or Without You | 393 |

Acknowledgements 413

# *Forewords*

# A manager's dream who loves the craic

*"TWO more minutes Mick, just two more."*

Shay Given is the best goalkeeper I've ever seen in my life and he's also the greatest goalkeeper in Irish history.

*"Two more minutes Mick, just two more."*

This is what I remember most about him.

Not his heroics against Iran or the 2002 World Cup or the way he has saved Ireland a thousand times with his genius.

Not his unbelievable consistency and talent.

*"Two more minutes Mick, I promise, just two more."*

We'd be at Malahide or in Europe – or anywhere in the world, come to that – and it would always be the same.

Mick Byrne would have marched over from the team bus as it was getting ready to leave training for the day but Shay wouldn't be ready to go.

*"Honest Mick, two more minutes, we'll be over then, promise."*

# SHAY

The two of us would be out there in all weathers, knackered, soaked to the skin and we'd have a bag of balls between us, strewn all over the pitch.

After training I always wanted to do extra shooting practice and Shay always, always, wanted to stay behind too, desperate to stop every shot I took. He'd throw me the ball, one touch, bang! Again, one touch, bang! Again and again and again until Mick Byrne had waited long enough and the bus had been stuck in neutral for an hour.

It is Shay's love of hard work and his refusal to ever be satisfied that I remember the most and it is those qualities that have made him the goalkeeper and the man he is.

As a team-mate I've been so extraordinarily lucky to have played with him because you always knew that with Shay Given behind you, you had a goalkeeper capable of single-handedly keeping the opposition quiet. He was that good you felt like you took to the field with an extra man.

When I see young goalkeepers now and they let goals in during training I often shake my head in despair. They seem ok with it, they don't look heartbroken by it. Oh well, it's only training.

Shay couldn't have been any more different. He could let a goal in during shooting practice and it was enough to ruin his afternoon. His head would come off and he'd be trying to fight you. That's what separates the good from the great.

Shay has never stood still and has never been willing to coast.

He is a great lad, we roomed together for a while and became good pals. He knows how to support the group, normally by shouting something stupid from the back of the bus when you're on the phone, and he loves the craic.

# FOREWORD: ROBBIE KEANE

We both go back to the era of big nights out as a team. He loves getting the boys out together as a way of building team spirit and he is the same now as he was when I first met him – friendly, welcoming, funny and just a great man to have around.

His experience has been so crucial to Ireland in recent years and although he may not have played as much as he once did, he has always been open to passing on his knowledge and help to the others in the goalkeeping group. He has no idea, none whatsoever, how much he is respected by others and how much they want to learn from him. Shay is just Shay. Although even at his age – what is he now, 48, 49? – his banter remains as poor as ever. You just have to remember he's a goalkeeper and that's what goalkeepers are like!

We never really spoke about who was going to end up with most caps because I was more interested in goals scored than caps gained and I think Shay was the same. He just wanted to stop goals. It was the same in his 134th match as it was his first. If he was still there now on cap 150 or whatever, his focus and concentration wouldn't be on that, it would be on doing his best for Ireland.

For over a decade Shay Given was his country's first-choice goalkeeper.

For over a decade he always answered the call and always practised and prepared as well as he could to make himself one of the best in the world. He's been a fine team-mate, a better friend, an example to everybody.

Shay Given, he's an Irish legend.

*Robbie Keane, September 2017*

# SHAY

IF I was to sum up Shay Given I would say this – he was a manager's dream.

He was so dependable, he was never late for training, he never caused trouble and he worked and worked and worked at his game every day. Come rain or shine, it seemed that Shay was always there, always trying to improve.

I first got to know him at Blackburn Rovers when he was barely out of his teens but it's fair to say that although some would have been intimidated or overawed by walking into that dressing room, Shay wasn't one of them. A quiet, shy boy he has never been!

Kenny clearly rated him highly at Blackburn and then signed him for Newcastle United as well, which says everything about how good he was. Most people can only dream of impressing a man like Kenny Dalglish once. Shay did it twice.

His work-ethic is what set Shay apart and helped make him the goalkeeper he was. When others walked off the training ground at the end of a session he'd always be there later than anybody else, honing the skills that made him so good and so consistent.

We had some great battles in training and that's the way it should be. We were mates, we liked and respected each other but that meant nothing when we were on the pitch and it didn't stop us from having a pop if we felt it was needed. He demanded the best of himself and everybody around him and that's why he became so important for Newcastle.

There were (many!) times when our backs were against the wall and we knew that we could always rely on him to be there. He was the last line of defence and that is such an important job. In Shay, we had a man who was capable of keeping the opposition out on his own. That helped create and provide so much confidence for the other 10 on the field. We all knew we had someone at the back we could depend on and who could handle the pressure and that certainly helped the rest of us.

He is a great lad to be around, he's a very genuine person, he loves to laugh and he is as trustworthy as they come. Shay hasn't really changed over the years and I like that – and his head definitely hasn't, it's still massive! He's totally the same bloke he was all those years ago, before his career took off.

One area of his life that remains a weak point though is his golf. We used to head to Portugal for a few days at the end of the season and stay at my house, wind down, relax, play a few rounds and have a beer or two. They were great days and heavy days as well! Shay loved his time away with us all. I don't care what he says about me in this book, his golf has never improved, especially after a few beers. We haven't had a game for a while but I've heard he hasn't got any better. He'll tell you differently but don't believe a word of it!

Over a long career you play with and against hundreds of guys but when the time comes to retiring, there's not actually that many you keep in touch with.

I've stayed in touch with Shay and we remain great friends – that says everything about the man he is.

*Alan Shearer, September 2017*

## _1_

# REMEMBER, REMEMBER, THE FIFTH

*I'm four years old.*

*A grand-looking woman of just 41, her glossy, jet-black hair falling across her emaciated shoulders, lies in a bed in a Manorhamilton hospital, slap-bang on the N16 in County Leitrim, surrounded by machines beeping, lines feeding, drugs seeping. There are chewy toffees and drinks on the sideboard, cards littered around the bed, an old newspaper or two frittering around on the spare, hard-worn plastic seats in the ward.*

*She is Agnes Given. My mum. She is dying of cancer.*

*This grand-looking woman of 41 loves a drop of brandy, a dance and a chatter with her five sisters and anyone else who will sit with her for as long as her strength will allow. She's not much of a singer, preferring to leave that to others, but she'll drag you up for a dance or two when the time is right. Or, at least she did. Before the back pains started.*

*Her constant agony has done little to dim her smile and she remains as mentally strong as ever, despite the crippling pain that has overtaken her life.*

*She knows she will not get out of bed again, won't chase me or any of her other five children, will never get to see them grow up. Her days as a midwife in Strabane are over. In fact, most of her days are nearly over.*

*As she lies patiently, crossing herself and praying to God while awaiting the arrival of my exhausted dad, Seamus, racing up from Lifford in his clapped out car every night to comfort his darling wife, the tumour that is silently, relentlessly, thrashing away at the base of her spine grows by the hour.*

*A shabby sideroom at the hospital, a room used for dentistry, has been put aside for six children, mostly clueless, certainly helpless, and they sit there opening their presents. A Rubik's Cube here, a Teddy Ruxpin there – Christmas has literally come early as we're only in the first week of November 1980.*

*The six kids sit looking at each other in misplaced wonder, tripping over the endless gifts handed over by nurses and doctors, all of these professionals hoping that the presents will help solve a problem their medical talents cannot. Tugs-of-war over unopened packages break out left, right and centre as the excited children try and forget what is happening, what is at stake.*

*If only these children really knew. This is to be the last 'Christmas' their mother will spend with them and those wee children will remember little else apart from wading through the mounds of wrapping paper on the floor while looking up at the tear-filled eyes of those medical staff popping in and out, hoping to help, hoping for a miracle, as the children detect the catch in the throat of the ward matron, desperately trying to say something positive, something cheerful.*

*This shouldn't be happening.*

*Not to that grand-looking woman of 41, lying in a bed in a Manorhamilton hospital, slap-bang on the N16 in County Leitrim, surrounded by machines beeping, lines feeding, drugs seeping. Yet it is.*

*Agnes Given, she of the jet-black hair, falling across her emaciated shoulders, has 12 weeks to live.*

*Agnes Given, a mother of six, the eldest 11, the youngest two.*

*Agnes Given, my mum, dying, me aged four.*

*Agnes Given, a woman I can barely remember, a mother I will never forget.*

*****

IT seems strange to miss somebody you hardly knew.

As the second youngest of six; there's Liam – 'The Bear' – who is the oldest, then Kieran, Marcus, Michelle, me and Sinead, plus Jacqueline and Paul from my dad's second marriage to Margaret, I was still nothing but a wee child when mum, Agnes, passed away.

Most people look at footballers and – rightly – see a gilded life, full of money and fame and all the fan worship you could want. You can jump on the average Instagram account for five minutes and see a bunch of young men living a life the rest of the country can only dream of.

Yet in football, as in any other line of work, there are people who have known tragedy, and difficulty, and testing times. I consider myself one such person.

Before Mum took sick in 1980, life for the Givens was as luxurious as it is for any other family not yet cursed with ill health and premature death.

Dad Seamus was a brilliant goalkeeper, in demand by every team in Donegal and beyond, but Monday to Friday he was a higher agricultural officer, a potato inspector for the government, trawling the length and breadth of the country to check yields, keep an eye on any diseases or blights that could affect the crop and generally ensure Ireland was going to remain as one of the biggest potato exporters in the world.

Mum was a midwife before her illness and we were a typically big, Irish Catholic farming family. We lived in a house in Rossgier, Lifford, the county town of Donegal. You may think Lifford is a big place but it's not. Quite the opposite, in fact. It sits right on the border with Northern Ireland, the River Foyle that runs through the town being the natural barrier between north and south.

Lifford, and County Donegal in general, is the kind of place where you'll pop out for a bottle of milk and still be out four hours later. People stop and chat on Main Street, pubs are full of people having a leisurely pint and a catch-up, everybody knows everybody else – and keeps an eye on each other's families. It's a place that has a community, a faith and is all about friendliness and family. I love coming from Lifford. It's been a long time since I've lived there but it will always be home, a place full of amazing memories. And some not so amazing.

At first, Mum got sent for scan after scan because they didn't know what was up with her. Initially they thought it was cancer of the womb and they investigated everything they could but still this mysterious illness did not appear on any of the results. Her own doctor, Dr Coyne, visited Dad one day and let him know how unhappy he was with the treatment Mum was getting. He wanted a second opinion as to why her womb scans were clear but her back was absolute agony.

Of course, cancer doesn't play by the rules and it was actually a tumour growing on her spine that was to take her.

Mum had herself worked in hospitals for years so she knew she wasn't a well lady and needed to get fixed, and fixed quickly. Eventually, Dr Coyne sent Mum to Our Lady's Hospital in Manorhamilton to see a Dr Shannon, an orthopaedic surgeon.

It was November 4, 1980, when Mum saw Dr Shannon. She had deteriorated badly by this stage and the pain down her legs was starting to become unbearable.

"Will you stay in for me Mrs Given?" Dr Shannon asked Mum. "Of course," she said, knowing that being asked to remain in hospital was further sign she needed urgent treatment.

Dr Shannon took her into surgery on November 5, in the early hours, while Dad had returned home, a 90-minute drive back to Lifford. As well as Mum needing nursing, Dad still had to work, still had to put money in the bank and feed six hungry kids. Back in the early '80s, life and time didn't stop for a serious illness and Dad just had to get on with it. He had to try and stay strong as he protected us from the worst.

And it really was the worst.

Dr Shannon did his work on Mum in that operating theatre but the news wasn't good and Dad was needed up in Manorhamilton quickly. In the end, long before the days of mobile phones, the Gardaí had to search high and low around the country fields of Donegal to find him. "Mr Given, you're to go. You're to go right this minute," the police officer said to Dad once he'd been located, a look on his face that spoke enough words for the pair of them.

They had found Dad at 11am and he raced home, packed a bag for himself and Mum and sped up there for 1pm. When he got to the hospital, Dr Shannon was there to greet him.

"Mr Given, follow me," he said, leading Dad straight into his office.

The next thing, he delved into his pocket and took our two chocolate bars, unwrapped the silver foil and rubbed them together, the crumbly bits of chocolate falling all over his desk and stapler.

"That, Mr Given, is what Agnes's back is doing," he told Dad. "That's where the cancer has been all the time. There's nothing we could've done to stop it. She cannot be cured."

"How long has she got?" Dad asked.

"At the very maximum, she's got three months," came the reply.

That was November 5 and she passed away on February 5 – exactly three months to the day. 'Remember, remember, the fifth of November' has a very different meaning in our house.

Liam was only 11, Sinead was just two and there were four more kids in between. Dad was about to become a widower with six children, all under the age of 12.

Before Mum had been taken to Manorhamilton, we'd had a housekeeper in to help Dad and from around July 1980, Mum was getting an injection in her back every night to help her sleep.

Mrs Kerrigan, a heavy-set woman, was about 63 or 64 at the time and lived a good 15 or 20 miles away from us but the key would turn in the back door at 7am every morning, right on the button. She cooked, cleaned and looked after us. She'd get us ready for school, get our lunches ready and basically keep the house running while Mum was sick and Dad was away at work. She stayed until 7pm every day and couldn't do enough for us.

Dad would come in, shattered by work, drained by his wife's imminent passing and put us to bed, a man with the weight of the world on his shoulders. Mrs Kerrigan stayed for two years after Mum died until her own husband got sick and she had to go and nurse him to the end.

*****

I visited Mum every weekend in Manorhamilton during those final three months but Dad never directly told me she was going to die. How do you begin to bring that subject up with your own children? Liam was probably old enough to read between the lines but he never let on to us younger ones what was going on.

When we visited Mum, she couldn't walk or get out of bed. There she was, just 41 – born on the same day as Elvis Presley – and, also, the same age as I am now.

I suppose that brings it home even further.

The hospital was so good to us all. In those days, the matron of the ward was the boss woman and she couldn't do enough to try and make it as easy as possible, trying to lighten the mood. That's what that early Christmas Eve had been all about.

Mum knew she wasn't going to live but nobody had told her outright and she hadn't asked anybody until about a fortnight to go. She knew – of course she knew – but I think that's just something instinctive inside you.

There was a lovely priest at the hospital, he was the chaplain there. Dad visited as often as he could, saying as many prayers as he could think of. We're from a family with a strong faith and it brought him some comfort. Dad spoke to the chaplain about breaking the news to Mum but he just couldn't face it.

Dad actually wanted a different priest, Fr. McConlogue to tell Mum but he was riddled with flu, absolutely full of it, so he couldn't get out of bed and up to Manorhamilton.

In the meantime, this chaplain summoned up the courage, visited Mum, her bed surrounded by flowers and pictures of us all, and told her the news. By the time Dad got up there the next day, Mum had been told what was going to happen. She knew she wasn't going to live and didn't have long left.

As the end approached, Dad sat up every night at Manor-hamilton for 31 nights on the trot. Shuffling around Mum's bed, he'd watch the sun go down and the moon come up from her side, hoping to bring her some comfort, some ease, to let her know how loved she was by him and by all of us.

We went in to see her as well to say our final goodbyes. We were all sat in the little dentist's room again, squashed around this dentist's chair, waiting for our turn to go in and see our mum. They'd tried to make her look like her old self but you could tell she was frail and ill. She could barely speak and was just having her lips wet with a sponge.

That was the last time I ever saw her.

Mum said a few words to each of us, she told Liam and Kieran to be big, strong boys and look after the rest of us. It was tough. Really tough.

We left the hospital and on the way home, Dad did his best to take our minds off it. "You're all getting a present," he said, and our imagination ran wild about what it was. It was his attempt to stop us thinking about Mum and to break the silence in the car that seemed to last forever. As he pulled up the drive, we all got out of the car. The house was pitch black and all locked up. It was dark, it was cold, it was empty, it had no life in it – and that seemed about right.

We got in the house and there were our presents; a pencil case for all of us. Marcus got a Liverpool one, Kieran a Manchester United one – they were thrilled to get a little gift, a little something to remind them that life was not supposed to be like this.

I can't remember what I got because that period is not something I go over too often in my mind. I suppose that's a combination of me being too young when Mum died plus it's not something I want to really explore, even now.

On the evening of February 4, Dad was as close to broken as a man can be so a nurse called Maureen Rooney grabbed him and sent him down to the room set aside for the medical staff to get some sleep.

Dad went down there at about 10pm and fell fast asleep on the bed, barely capable of pulling the covers back. At 1.15am, the door opened.

"Mr Given, Mr Given, you're to get up," Maureen told him. "You're to get down to the ward, immediately."

Mum died at 12.15pm that day.

I was only a wee child and, today, here and now, it feels as if I had no real idea what was going on but one look at our photos on the day of the funeral tells a different story. Six children, dressed in their Sunday best, saying goodbye to their 41-year-old mother.

Five children plus Dad walked behind the coffin into St

Patrick's Church, Murlog, but not Liam. He was head altar boy that year so he carried the cross at the front of the coffin before serving on the altar. That can't have been easy.

After the service, we all surrounded the grave as Mum was committed to earth. You can actually see Mum's grave from our house, that is how close we lived to the church. Uncle Packie is a keen photographer and he took a lot of photos of us all at the graveside, the six of us looking down at Mum's coffin. Dad decided we were going to be at the forefront of the day, and rightly so. Sometimes you do need to confront the way the world works, even at such an early age.

Mum had a massive wake in the home that she had loved; it went steady morning, noon and night for a couple of days with us kids sent over to our neighbours, the McKinneys, for some of it. In those days, you didn't go to a hotel for tea and sandwiches or anything like that for a wake. There was a sit-down meal at the home of the deceased and something like 160 people milling around at ours. The food was served in two sittings at a time, until everybody had been fed.

Men – uncles, friends, brothers, whoever – were all dashing in and out, not knowing what to say, occasionally wandering to the Rossgier Inn down the road to try and find enough courage to speak to us children.

At one stage, towards the end of her life, Mum had made one simple request of Dad. "Seamus," she had told him, reaching for his hand in the hospital bed. "Hold them together, Seamus. You're to hold them together."

Even in her dying moments, Mum was still thinking about us, still worrying about her kids more than herself.

As the wake progressed, Dad's sisters were in the kitchen,

serving the meals along with Mrs Kerrigan, and Dad was so tired he went upstairs and lay on the bed for an hour. He didn't even have the energy to kick his shoes off. He fell fast asleep until Mrs Kerrigan came into his bedroom and roused him.

"Seamus, you're to get up now," she said. "It's your sisters. They want to take a child each." Dad's five sisters had decided amongst themselves that they would all take a child to help lessen the load, leaving him with just Sinead.

Don't forget, this was the 1980s in Ireland, a different time, and it was felt that a man couldn't possibly bring six young children up on his own. Dad's sisters were only doing what was normal at the time, what they thought was best, and the offer came from love, out of the goodness of their hearts. If anything, it shows how close a family we were that they were willing to take an extra child on and I know Dad was extremely grateful for the extraordinary offer.

Dad's five sisters, Susan, Ambrose, Eileen, Kathleen and Mary were stood around in the kitchen when he sprung down the stairs. Eileen began to explain the plans but Dad jumped in. "Eileen, they are not going anywhere, they're staying here," he said, refusing to even consider it. "I'll look after them – they're my children. You're more than welcome to help out as much as you can, but they're staying under the one roof."

Dad had promised Mum that one thing, her words as clear as day to him, even through his grief. *'Hold them together, Seamus. You're to hold them together.'*

And he did. And he has.

That period of my life is not something we really talk about. In fact, I only found out recently that it was cancer of the spine rather than cancer of the womb that took my mum.

I know people who lose their mum at a young age these days get counselling but there was none of that then. It was more about family and the community sticking together. We just had to deal with it and cope with it as best we could.

Keeping the family together – thanks to Mrs Kerrigan's help – was so important. It meant we could grieve together and grow up together. Dad coped so well too, which helped. When Mrs Kerrigan left at 7pm, all he had to do was put us to bed and comfort us, which I suppose we all needed from time to time. Staying together, and getting in scrapes as a family, was exactly what we needed to do.

We had each other, if nothing else, and it would have been one hundred times worse if we had been split up.

When I think of Mum now, I don't think her passing is something I'll ever get over. I think you just learn to live with it and learn how to manoeuvre your way around it so that you don't let it affect you too much.

When I talk about it I still fill up and get emotional and that will probably always be the case. I don't actually think I've fully confronted the death of Mum. I think that's your typical man's perspective – and probably an Irishman's perspective more than most too! We've all got a big carpet at home and we like to sweep all our stuff under it. You never know, one day, I might go and speak to somebody about it – hit it head on – because it is a big burden to carry.

When my own son was four, it really hit home how young he was and how young I was when Mum died. I looked at him and thought, 'My God, it's no age to lose your mum.' And it really isn't.

In recent times, I've not been as regular a churchgoer as I was but I say my prayers every day. In the toilet before a game, I always say a prayer for Mum and that's always been a comfort. To think that she is there, in some way, helping, is a feeling I've always enjoyed.

Now, when I do go home to Rossgier, to Lifford, to County Donegal, I often look up over our land and the acres me and my brothers and sisters farmed ourselves in order to keep a roof over our heads as we grew up.

I'll also look up the valley, up to St Patrick's Church, searching for the gravestone that reads *Agnes Given, Jan 8 1940 – February 5 1981.*

Up there, on the hill, she's looking down at us, checking we're all ok.

# 2

# THE DONEGAL
# CRAB

WELL, that was a laugh-a-minute opening to a book wasn't it?

As tragic as Mum's passing was, and as heart-breaking a sight as it used to be watching Dad doing his best to cope, what I don't want to do is write a book that comes across as nothing but a misery-fest. That's not who I am and neither is that all of my story, plus there's enough sadness in the world without me adding any more to it. But I think it's important to talk about your younger years because they set you up for life.

For weeks after the funeral, we could look up at the church and see Mum's grave and it was just a blur of colour because of all the flowers that had been laid down. It stayed like that for ages until the blooms started to wilt and discolour and people went back to their daily lives, as they must, and we attempted to move on, as we had to.

With the extra help from Mrs Kerrigan, we had to try and get into a routine at our home, which was a mile outside Lifford town centre, right on the banks of the Burn Deele. It's a small river well known as a good spot for catching trout or, if you were unlucky like me, eels that used to make me run a mile.

Dad used the fields around the house as a market garden business, called 'Colehill Gardens', and we were always working in them as well as playing in a big front garden that was the scene of many a brutal game of Gaelic football and soccer as I grew older.

We had three bedrooms – one for Dad, one for my sisters Michelle and Sinead and the last one was for the boys. It was small with two double beds for the four of us. I was in every night with Liam while Marcus and Kieran were in the other. Marcus is very relaxed and Kieran is quieter too so their bed would be peace and harmony while there would be World War Three over in ours.

Me and Liam would have a line down the middle – and you crossed it at your own risk. We were both sparky characters with a temper and there would be a scrap most nights. One night Mark Kelly, who was a mate of Liam's, stayed in the bed with us and we woke up, soaked to the skin. Someone had pissed the bed. I was in the middle and we were all drenched. Mark has since qualified as a lawyer so is good at talking himself out of it and nobody has owned up. Those two blame me because they're big mates but I know it was one of them. *Sluice-Gate* remains a hot topic to this day!

Liam was nicknamed 'The Bear' not because he was the eldest or biggest but a mate from Murlog Primary School, where I would later go, called Liam 'Fozzie Bear' because of his big hair. It stuck instantly and he remains 'The Bear' to this day.

There was one set of wardrobes and a set of drawers in our

bedroom that contained all our worldly goods. As the youngest boy I was at the wrong end of the hand-me-down clothes chain so just lived in whatever gear the others had grown out of.

This was nothing unusual back then and I never thought anything of it. Why would I?

Despite the passing of Mum, I look back on my childhood and upbringing now with a big smile on my face and with plenty of gratitude. That might sound strange to say but the way I was brought up, and the difficulties we faced, helped make me.

To keep us all under the one roof, Dad had to work extremely hard. He also made sure we bent our backs – we 'dipped' – and I cannot remember a time when we weren't all out there with old jute potato sacks around our knees to stop them getting sore, tending the land or harvesting the crops together.

The land that came with the house was put to use – and so were we  spending every minute after school and every school holiday planting lettuces or beans or spuds or turnips or going around the streets of Lifford with Marcus in the produce van, taking orders, racing back to the van and bringing whatever the customer wanted. We grew everything, but spuds were our biggest seller. They were for sale in 7lb or 14lb paper sacks. We would also sell in bulk, by the ton, to other farm-shops and businesses around Lifford.

Me and Marcus would get home from school and immediately jump in the van, which was a kind of horse box trailer pulled by a car. We'd be in it for hours after school and then all day Saturday and Sunday. Once we'd driven around Lifford we'd be off to Ballindrait to do the same there.

We'd leave at 10am and get back at 10pm. It was tough but, being young lads, that didn't mean we couldn't find a way or two to brighten the day up. If somebody was walking down the road and we could get away with it, they'd be pummelled with spuds from all angles while we laughed our heads off on top of the van.

All the vegetables that we grew up on the big field were also available in a little separate field, right next to the house. It was exactly 500 yards long and 40 yards wide and that was the showcase garden, the shop window for everything we were growing. It was there to attract customers, and that meant we had to keep the small field spotless, not a weed in sight or a carrot out of place.

It was my job to do a lot of the weeding in that field and unlike up on the farm field, where you could use ploughs or big spades, it had to be done slowly and perfectly by hand which seemed to take forever. Dad was such a stickler for perfection and God help you if you missed a weed or didn't plant the carrots in a perfectly straight line.

After Mrs Kerrigan left us, we had another housekeeper called Susan McDaid who we nicknamed 'Bottle' McDaid because her surname was the same as the famous soft drink from Ramelton, a lemonade called 'Football Special' that we would all drink as kids because when you poured it, it looked like a pint of lager. We would kid ourselves we were drinking beer.

'Bottle' McDaid was a formidable woman. One time, Kieran had been playing up and she threw him out of the house, breaking a wooden spoon against his arse. I can still hear him howling now as he raced out of the house. We had to smuggle out clothes to him through the bathroom window.

I've got four kids myself now, they all mean the world to me, and when I look back on how Dad coped, I just don't know how he did it. He had a full-time job and had to try and put food on our table while bringing us all up too. It was an amazing achievement. He ran the house with a rod of iron and good on him for it. What choice did he have? Six kids, especially four of them being boys, is never going to be easy unless we knew who the boss was.

And, boy, we knew who the boss was. Every morning there would be a huge bellow up the stairs – "YOU LOT, MOVE, THERE'S WORK TO BE DONE" – and we'd slowly stagger down, shovel in some breakfast and get out into the fields.

Dad certainly made sure we had a decent appetite at lunchtime. There would be piles of sandwiches in the middle of the kitchen table and they wouldn't last long, I can tell you. Thirty seconds and that was it. Dad had a referee's whistle that Michelle or Sinead would blow and that was us off, sprinting back to the house for food. After we'd finished, back out we'd go.

I had to grow up fast. One time when I was about 12, I was watching the shop next to the market garden. Business was dead and times were really tough. This guy in a lorry used to come on a Tuesday, selling wholesale fruit and vegetables, and I bought a box of red apples from him for about 20 quid. I thought our stocks looked a bit low and the old guy sweet-talked me into the deal. I was only trying to do the right thing but Dad came home and he went nuts. He lost the head with me because money was so tight. That's how life was.

I've been told in the time since that our fields were used as a warning to other kids in the area. Mums and dads would drive their children past and say, "Look, if you don't behave then you'll end up like those Given lads in the fields!" Dad would later open a driving range and pitch and putt business – 'Green Acres' – on another field about 200 yards from the house which added to the workload, especially as we had to spend forever picking up sheep wool because it was too similar to the colour of the golf balls.

It wasn't all bad. Working for Dad made us all appreciate the value of a pound note. It made me realise what I've got now and how incredible it is. We were taught what hard work was, where hard work can get you and how there was an honour and a respect to be had in bending your back. Along with sore knees, they were lessons to live by.

*****

Despite the hard work, there was always a laugh to be had in our house. Dad would always sit at the head of a table – it's a habit I've picked up now (mad how you turn into your dad isn't it?!) and this one time, Liam walked in for tea. At the time, he loved *The Smiths* and the cover on one of their singles was Elvis Presley with his hair slicked back in a perfect quiff.

Liam had been to the chemist that day when the house was empty, bought some dye and tried it himself, turning his curly blond hair pitch black. We're all sat there, scoffing away and Dad looked up to see Liam with a cap still wedged on his head.

"Liam, take that cap off, it's bad manners," Dad said. Liam ignored him, knowing he was in for it. "Liam, take that bloody cap off – it's rude," Dad carried on. Still nothing. Next thing, Liam got up and walked out. "I'm finished Dad," he said.

Dad stormed up the stairs after him and yanked the cap from his head. "JESUS CHRIST Liam," he said. "Your mother will be turning in her grave up there." You would've thought he'd had a tattoo of Morrissey on his forehead, the way Dad reacted!

He came back downstairs and none of us would look up from our soup bowls, knowing one look would send us all into hysterics. "There's something wrong with your brother, there's something wrong with him," Dad said, still revved up. "Jesus, the hair his mother give him as well. Ruined – it's ruined."

Another year, Dad bought us this music centre for Christmas. It was state of the art stuff at the time, a massive stereo with a glass front that he had saved up for.

To cut a long story short, this front glass got smashed.

And guess who owned up to it?

Nobody, that's who. Still, 30 years on, everyone's lips are sealed about what happened.

Dad was determined to get to the bottom of it and sat us all around the table, in our pyjamas. "Right, you're to tell me who did it," he said. "Or you're outside." He looked around the table at his kids and there was nothing happening. Next thing, he's thrown us out into the freezing, frosty night. We must've been out in the cold for an hour in our pyjamas, our teeth knocking, nothing on our feet. Nobody would own up and we were all trying to get the guilty party to come clean. (Kieran, now is your chance to do the right thing!)

My Dad has a good heart though, he'd do anything for anybody and he set an amazing example to us all. We walk into a pub and the first thing he wants to do is buy everybody a round of drinks. He did an incredible job with us all and I don't blame him one bit for being as strict as he was.

After some time, he met Margaret. She had such a tough act to follow after Mum but we were thankful for the stability she brought after the housekeepers had gone. To think of it from her perspective, it must have been daunting walking into a house with six kids looking up at her from the kitchen table. That takes some doing and she was a brave lady for taking us all on! I won't pretend it was always easy for us to get used to having a new mother-figure in the house and I suppose we were a 'blended family' before the term was even invented. I'm in the same boat myself these days, I know it can be very difficult for children to adapt and accept a new parent early on and I think we all had our own initial struggles with it.

Margaret moved to Lifford from her home and that can't have been easy for her but Jacqueline and Paul followed soon after and we were then an even bigger family. These days she buzzes around when the grandchildren are there and absolutely loves it.

When I went to my primary school – St Patrick's National School, known locally as Murlog School – I'd be in fights every day. At least one scrap a day, usually more. I've never been in one since but back then I was always up to something. When we'd fight, a big circle would gather and my sisters, Michelle and Sinead would elbow their way to the front to see what was happening – and it usually involved me.

One day I was involved in a fight with a lad called Rory White and we were going for it outside when Dad arrived to pick me up. "Dad, just wait here," I said. I turned around and punched him but he caught me too and gave me a fantastic black eye. I staggered to Dad's car, went home and was straight out in the field – nothing got you out of doing your shift. That day I was pulling carrots out of the ground but the ground was rock-hard and it was that cold my hands were frozen solid. I started warming them on the tractor exhaust but when the blood poured back into my fingers the pain was excruciating – it was agony – and I just stood there crying in the field. But I didn't go back inside, we needed those carrots out of the ground to sell and that was the end of it.

I was your typical younger brother, always looking for a rise out of my elder siblings. I'd end up on the losing side as Liam, Kieran and Marcus would all set about me, especially if we were playing football in the garden. We used to hold nothing back and they didn't miss too often when we were rolling around, arguing about whether they had scored or not or whose turn it was to go in goal.

Dad nicknamed me 'The Crab' as a kid because if I didn't get my own way, I let most people know about it. Liam is quite educated and he would call me the Latin name for a Crab, which used to just wind me up even more.

White Strand was the name of the team that Dad played for. We'd all pile in the car to watch him on a Saturday afternoon, sometimes having a kick-about as he played. Afterwards, Dad would drive us home, we'd be coming down the back roads and I'd say, "Dad, didn't you used to be a rally driver?" "What makes you say that son?' he'd answer, before dropping down through the gears like some Formula One wannabe. I'd be in the back getting battered by my brothers for egging Dad on, crying laughing as they screamed and shouted for their lives in the back of this crammed Toyota. They were different times.

Dad smoked 60 a day at least back then. One day he was having a fag out of the car and he went to sling the cigarette butt out of the window but it blew back in to the car and landed, still lit, all over Sinead's Communion dress. This was a First Holy Communion. A big event. The dress, which was made of a really light fabric was smouldering and looked like it would go up at any second. Sinead can smile about it now – sometimes.

We get together now and roar laughing at the times we had and the upbringing Dad and Margaret gave us. It's hysterical looking back. We are all so close as a family because of that. It was hard work but there was a lot of love and camaraderie in that house which lasts to this day.

We were all very competitive which probably comes from Dad as well. Winning was the only thing that mattered. Nobody cared that I was the youngest, smallest and weakest – I'd get smashed every day.

Kieran was the captain of the school team, he also played Gaelic football and was very good at athletics too, getting an All Ireland silver medal for high jump when he was 13 or 14, so he would love to fly in and nail me. Marcus and Liam were never far behind. I was always put in goal as the youngest. They'd punch me, kick me, tackle hard and do all they could to push my buttons. I lost my temper but I loved it all really.

Neville Southall was my hero growing up and that's who I'd be when my brothers were lashing the ball at me. I even used to commentate and dive at the same time – "Oh what a save by Neville that was" – I'd only be Packie Bonner when Ireland played. Southall was just unreal, he was the best goalkeeper in the world in the 1980s without question, and I just loved him.

I've never really asked him but secretly I think Dad was thrilled that he had four sons who were just as sports mad as he was. He's played Gaelic football and soccer all his life and was still an in-demand goalkeeper well into his 40s.

About a month or six weeks after Mum died, a team from near Rathmullen came in and asked Dad to play for them. I'd stand behind the goals, studying what Dad was doing. Maybe those early days, stood in the wind and rain, watching Dad perform, set me up for what was to come? Who knows how early you start learning stuff in life…

As I grew up, I still played football with my brothers but, naturally, I also made mates from school. With County Donegal being so big and open, we had plenty of opportunities to get into mischief – though we had to be careful, too.

Living where we did, the Troubles were on our doorstep and the fields were often full of British squaddies in camouflage, faces painted, doing training drills. Apparently sound travels across water easier than over land and as we were right next to the river, you could hear explosions taking place. The windows of our house used to rattle when a bomb had gone off in Strabane and life for the local glazier was busy and good.

It's only now, looking back, that you realise it's not your average upbringing. We'd go swimming in Strabane and you'd be walking past these young lads with full kit, machine-guns, everything – young British soldiers who were probably more scared of us than we were of them.

If you wanted to go over the border into Northern Ireland you'd be pulled up and get questioned by the soldiers. The car would be checked for bombs underneath and if anything didn't fit right with them, they'd drag you into this shed and you'd be grilled about where you'd been and what you'd been up to.

Dad never, ever tolerated any anti-British sentiment though. It wasn't 'BRITS OUT' in our household, not for one second. "They're just doing their job," he'd say to us, before saying hello to them and going about his business.

Looking back on it all, Dad set the example of how we should view the world. Dad also made us dream and he showed us, through his words and his actions, that anything we wanted was possible if you put the hard work in.

The question was, did you want to pay that price?

\*\*\*\*\*

If you played soccer rather than Gaelic football in Lifford then you played for Lifford Celtic. I played both but soccer was the sport I preferred and it felt like more of a natural fit. I'd say that my goalkeeping definitely improved over the years because of my background in catching and kicking during Gaelic games as a kid.

I've always loved how honest and hard-working Gaelic is. It is a truly wonderful sport. In 1992, when Donegal won their very first All-Ireland championship, I was through the fences at Croke Park and on the pitch with my brothers, screaming, going absolutely crazy. There was a Given car-load down for the match from Lifford and to beat Dublin – who were the red-hot favourites – was unbelievable, one of my happiest memories. Lads like Martin McHugh and Anthony Molloy were heroes to me and to have been there to celebrate was special.

I'm good friends with Pat Shovelin, the Donegal goalkeeping coach. He visited me at Aston Villa and watched how we trained. In 2014, when I was home, the then Donegal coach Jim McGuinness and Pat invited me to train with the team in Convoy. It was fantastic, such a huge honour. The fitness levels, work-rate and professionalism were outstanding.

I have such massive respect for the sport and all the players in the GAA. We had a huddle before training and Jim was very inspirational. The lads were really revved up. I was ready to fight myself by the end of it because the passion Jim showed was unreal!

Lifford Celtic was the strongest football team in the area. I played through all Lifford's youth sides until I was 14, when I started playing for their men's team, the first XI. Fourteen is young obviously to be in goals for the men's side, especially because I wasn't particularly big or tall. I'm still not that tall now for a goalkeeper, but I'd inherited Dad's talents and I was also used to playing on the edge, thanks to my endless battles with my brothers in the back garden.

The Given boys were always in scrapes, no matter what code of football we were playing. Every year in Lifford, there would be a Married Men v Single Men Gaelic game. It was the roughest, hardest game of the year. One day, me, Liam and Kieran played for Lifford club Naomh Padraig Leifear against Glenswilly and it wasn't much different.

A few of their guys were trying to knock lumps out of me. I was in midfield that day rather than in goal for some reason and it was all going off while Liam was having an almighty battle with their defenders. Next thing, someone is sparko'd and Liam's marker is on the floor, seeing birdies.

The pair of them ended up brawling and both were sent off. The word got out that there was trouble down at the match and before we knew it, all these Massey Ferguson tractors turned up. The locals were getting restless. Cars started pouring into the car park. Suddenly there were fights everywhere and people were throwing punches in every direction.

A bloke called John Tourish used to drive the minibus and he wasn't messing about. The minute the ref blew the final whistle we all legged it to the bus, chased by the locals. He was revving it in the car park shouting "C'mon lads, hurry!" It was proper mad, pitchfork stuff. He squealed this bus out of the car park as men, women and children followed, braying at us.

When we got to the safety of the main road, we lined up on the back seat, dropped our shorts and said our own unique farewell to the good people of Glenswilly – a row of white arses pressed against the window! That kind of madness set me in good stead for what was to come when I played for the men's team.

Robbie White, Lifford's manager, spoke to my dad about picking me for the first XI. Robbie had a bit of a short leg, and quite a bad limp, but he was an older fella that everybody respected. He absolutely loves Lifford Celtic and has been involved there all his life. You know how every club – whether amateur or professional – has that diehard few who would do anything for it? Well, in Lifford, Robbie White's your man.

One day, the phone rang in the house. "Seamus, is your boy ready for the full side?" Robbie asked Dad, straight to the point. "Of course he is," came the answer. "The boy is good enough and if he's good enough then who cares if he's old enough?"

Dad's belief in me was touching because I didn't always get life all my own way as a young footballer.

For my school, St Columba's College in Stranorlar, I sometimes started as a striker and I enjoyed playing outfield but in one senior All Ireland final against Greenhills College in 1991 I had an absolute nightmare in goal. The final was at Finn Park, where Finn Harps play their games, so it was a massive deal. I wanted an early touch so I would get some confidence but I had the worst possible start.

Seconds after kick-off, I made a really bad mistake, a really tame free-kick shot went through me and into the back of the net. Master Jimmy Rodgers made life worse by subbing me, dragging me straight off, about three minutes into the match. There were tears in the dug-out, that's for sure. It was a stupid mistake but to sub me that early was a really bad call. A lad called Peadar Molloy was put in goal in my place and we lost quite heavily in the end. Kieran and Dad were watching from the sidelines and Dad wasn't exactly pleased with the fact I'd been hauled off. However, Kieran always swears that Dad turned to him and said, "That'll be the making of him." I wasn't so sure at the time.

Despite Dad's faith in me, I was a bit nervous stepping up into the Lifford Celtic first XI but I knew the older players would look out for me on the pitch. If there was a high ball and the opposition surrounded me or tried to bully me, they'd be straight in. The likes of Kipper Lynch or Hugh White didn't let anybody take liberties with their goalkeeper. "What the fuck are you doing?" would be enough to let the opposition know I wasn't to be touched. I felt like they had my back.

One of my strengths back then – and something I took through my career – was my ability to let those in front of me know what I wanted, expected and demanded. Even at that young age I would be happily organising and shouting at the back four, telling them where to go on the pitch and alerting them to any dangers coming their way. I've always prided myself on those communication skills and it all started there, in goal for Lifford Celtic.

The older players would take their medicine if they deserved it. If someone messed up then I'd let them know – but I'd also get an earful back if they felt it was worth it. Don't forget it wasn't professional but everything about playing with the men was an education. There was to be no sheltering of this wee kid from the realities of life, no hiding him from the kinds of thing grown men get up to when they're in their own company.

We used to prepare for home matches in a pub, called Harte's Bar, in Lifford, on the corner of Main Street and Butcher Street. We would get changed in the back lounge and then get a lift down to the ground, Greenbrae Park. We wore a green and white Celtic-style shirt.

The older lads used to love getting changed in Harte's. There were tables and chairs dotted everywhere, ashtrays fit to burst and we'd be amongst it all, kit and boots strewn everywhere, the odd empty Guinness glass lurking around, regulars milling at the pool table in the main bar coming in now and then to wish us luck or to see how us young fellas were getting on and remind us that they themselves were a hell of a player 30 years ago, didn't you know?

After the match, the older lads would pull on a tracksuit and be straight into the bar on the other side.

They were always good times in Harte's. If we were on a good run and doing well, there would always be a buzz; the craic flying, someone singing on a table, a round of drinks here and there, sandwiches being shoved down starving mouths, footballing punch-ups described in great detail, each player becoming more mighty, more magnificent as thirsts were quenched and stories of greatness magnified by the pint.

I'd get a lift down to Greenbrae Park with Ronnie Brennan. Ronnie was a man who loved his cars and he always sped through the gates of the ground like a lunatic. There was a field between where you drive in and the start of the pitch. Ronnie would love to do wheelspins and doughnuts on the grass. I'd be flying around in the back of the car, smacking into the seats left and right, laughing my head off. Our pre-match warm-up wouldn't be stretches and a Lucozade, it'd be a sandwich in Harte's and then 15 doughnuts in Ronnie's latest set of wheels.

*****

I suppose my career really took off when Lifford got down to the semi-finals of the FAI Junior Cup in 1992, which is played by loads of junior clubs across Ireland – that's junior in the sense of amateur rather than age group. We were a tiny club in the grand scale of things but we got to the last four and that was big news across Lifford, Donegal and Ireland as a whole.

In that year's competition, we saw off Letterbarrow, Deele Harps, Ballytre and a few others before we were drawn away to Bagenalstown FC in the quarter-finals. So far, so good.

Until a few weeks before the game that is.

During a basketball match at school, I tripped awkwardly as I went to stop a shot and fell. I looked down and my wrist was no longer in the location that God had originally placed it. Before I knew it, I was in plaster and my chances of playing for Lifford in the quarter-final were gone.

The match was played in Port Laoise in Leinster and Dad went with the team and stood behind the goal instructing Paul Malaugh, my replacement, what to do. He did well enough and Lifford made it through. That gave me about a month to get my fractured wrist healed and strong again before the semi-final against Neilstown Rangers at Oriel Park in Dundalk.

# SHAY

Robbie picked as strong a team as possible for that match. There was me in goal, Hugh White, Robert Campbell, Seamus 'Kipper' Lynch, Michael French, Daniel McGavigan, Richard White, Tom Devenney, Liam Doherty, Hugh Doherty and Georgie Gethins. We had a strong bench, too, with Paul Melaugh, Ronnie Brennan, Martin Gallen, Dessie McGlynn and Thomas Hegerty. It was tough and tight and there wasn't going to be much in it. Unfortunately for us, they scored near half-time and that was it, we couldn't get back into the game. We'd never got that far before and haven't been since.

I was gutted, as you can expect, but the Junior Cup of 1992 began to unlock some doors that I didn't even know existed.

People had started to notice the scrawny wee kid in goal, the one whose mouth was bigger than he was. This kid had started to grab a reputation for bravery and a determination to keep Lifford Celtic's sheets as clean as can be

Don't forget, I was only a schoolboy playing against full-blown men. That was pretty unheard of. I was also helped massively by who my old man was. As well as being a goalkeeper who had seemingly played for nearly every club in Ireland, Dad had also been the secretary of the Ulster Senior League and knew just about everybody worth knowing in Irish football.

Ahead of the match against Neilstown, he'd worked the phones and suggested that if scouts couldn't be bothered with the long-haul trip from Dublin to Donegal to watch me in goal, then the least they could do was pop up to Dundalk for the afternoon and see if the rumours they were hearing had any truth.

Did Lifford Celtic have a goalkeeper worth keeping an eye on? Would the phone start ringing?

# 3

# PARADISE LOST

INDEED the phone would ring.

After the Junior Cup performances, I began to get offers from a few places and the very first team I went to was Bradford City would you believe.

The reason being, Frank Stapleton was the manager at the time and the Irish connection obviously played a big part in it. I flew on my own from Belfast and to say England, and Bradford, was a culture shock, would be putting it mildly.

You've got to remember where I'm from. I'm from the middle of nowhere and it was my first time in a 'big' city. I was picked up from the airport and the first place they took me to was Valley Parade to show me around. We went to a hotel for the night and then the very next day we went over to Germany and played in an under-19s tournament.

The football itself didn't bother me, nor did the fact I was playing in a tournament surrounded by older lads. I'd had plenty of this before with Lifford Celtic and if I could scream, shout and organise a back four full of men, I could certainly hold my own with lads just a few years older than me.

Frank was great with me. I think he had the sense that other clubs were interested – the scout network in Ireland never keeps any player quiet for too long – and I think he wanted to use the fact he was an Irish legend to persuade me to sign for him. It nearly worked. It was Frank Stapleton after all; an Irish hero and somebody I'd grown up watching. "You've got a better chance starting here," he said. "Work your way up, learn the game."

It was the classic kind of patter that all clubs and managers try and persuade you to sign. The closest I had to an agent was my dad, who was a streetwise guy, and he was on the other side of the Irish Sea at that moment!

I played ok while I was in Germany and Frank was first class but, by then, interest from Celtic and Manchester United had started to come through back at home and that changed everything. When I heard there was interest from those two sides, it was very difficult to still think Bradford would be the right call at that time. Absolutely no disrespect to them but when the likes of Celtic and Manchester United want to look at you, then you have to do it. It is a massive credit to Frank that he also then saw the bigger picture. "Shay, you're too good for Bradford City," he said. "You need to pursue these other chances." Frank was an ex-Manchester United man himself and that might've swayed his decision.

My head had been turned by the talk of Celtic as they were heading over to Ireland on a pre-season tour and their manager was the legendary Liam Brady. The same Liam Brady who had been told so much about me, as it happens, after the Junior Cup run.

This was absolutely unbelievable to me. Liam personally rang Dad at home and I was to be invited up to Dublin to meet the first-team and stay with them in the Burlington Hotel while they were over.

It was mad. Training with the first-team, eating with them and mingling with some of my heroes was a strange situation to be in at 15 years old. Here was me, a lad used to thinning out spuds or selling turnips in Lifford, training with Packie Bonner and Gordon Marshall. That just doesn't happen does it? I was treated like a first-team player, eating lunch with all the squad, talking to them, trying not to let on about how excited I was.

Paul McStay, Tony Cascarino, Chris Morris, Charlie Nicholas, John Collins, Tommy Coyne; you name it, all of the Celtic side were staying in the Burlington and treated me so well. It wasn't like I was a trainee or a triallist – I was shown plenty of respect by everyone and Liam was great with me. We didn't talk much, he'd just ask me if I needed anything and would check I was doing ok.

One day we went to the University College Dublin grounds to practise and I was overawed by how intense it all was.

Liam had them set up so that there were twice as many attackers as defenders and the balls were just constantly flying at the goal. It was fast, it was deadly serious and it was tiring. Gordon Marshall did seven minutes, non-stop, Packie followed and finally it was my turn to do the same. The attackers were going up the wings and crossing into two or three strikers in the box, lads like Charlie Nicholas, and we had to keep out as many as we could.

"You need to be good here," Dad told me beforehand. As if I didn't know already! It came to my turn and I did well, I kept enough out and felt like I'd impressed them.

As the week went on, I remained in good form and I felt I had done myself justice. It appeared that Celtic felt the same.

One night, we got back to the Burlington, had dinner and then later on, as Dad sat with Liam Brady out of my earshot, he told him, "Mr Given, I think we've a five million pound goalkeeper on our hands here."

We went back to Lifford, absolutely thrilled by what had happened and I took all my fresh new Celtic training kit, a brand new set of boots and some pristine gloves. We had no money at home so this was like Christmas. They were probably sweetening me up when you look back now but I was totally buzzing at the time.

*****

It was clear that Celtic wanted to sign me but, in the meantime, Dad again took a phone call that was a bit of a once-in-life-time moment. The then president of the Football Association of Ireland, Fran Fields, had given Alex Ferguson our house number and he wanted to enquire after me. "Seamus, send him over, at least for a trial," Ferguson told Dad.

We'd made a verbal commitment to Celtic at this time but nothing had been signed on paper so it was felt that I could still go over to United without jeopardising that.

Growing up I was a Celtic fan but I'd always respected Manchester United too. I think that is pretty common when you're from my part of Ireland so when I heard they were interested

I was on the next flight. Dad gave me a pep talk first. "Get over there and show them, do your best. Work hard. You will be fine." It was probably standard stuff but it all helped. Dad was a goal-keeper too so he understood the position and he also understood how close I was to being able to make sport my living.

I was at the stage where I had some belief in myself and, with total respect, it was clear I had more talent and more to offer than just playing once a week for Lifford Celtic. I knew I must have a chance. If you get to train with Manchester United then you must be doing something right and that gave me a lot of confidence.

Once I arrived in Manchester I was given a lift to The Cliff, United's old first-team training ground in Salford. I walked into the training centre and all the balls and jerseys were being laid out. Next thing, the first XI squad came in and went along the line, autographing each ball and shirt as they went by.

I remember Peter Schmeichel walking past, still muddy from training, and I was totally amazed. Shit, he did exist in real life. It was surreal because I'd only ever seen him on television. I was just in awe. He had been my big idol for the previous couple of years. I wouldn't speak to him, or any of the first XI really. I was too overawed. They were human beings. 'Oh God, I can touch Bryan Robson,' was all I could think. That sounds bizarre but that is what it was like. It was even more bizarre because of where I was from.

If you lived in Manchester, you would probably see Bryan Robson or Nicky Butt all the time but, let me tell you, Bryan Robson rarely walks down Butcher Street and nips in Harte's for a pint!

The Cliff wasn't that flash back then. I think the first-team had the main pitch near the building, then a goalkeeping section to the right, fenced off, and then behind a stand on the far side was another few pitches.

We all got changed in the same building and even that was mad. Nowadays, the kids change in a different building but back then you were all in together.

They wanted to have a good look at me but I got a bad knock in the first week and couldn't really train after that. I was disappointed because I felt I didn't have chance to show them what I could do but to be fair to Fergie, he wanted me to come to the club and he again rang Dad to put him at ease. "We'll keep him here and get the injury sorted," Ferguson said. "We'll take care of the wee man."

He really made me feel welcome. "Are you enjoying it?" he'd ask. "How are you getting on? I hope the rest of these young lads are looking after you." He went out of his way to come and speak to me in the canteen and as others have previously said, he was always great with young players, especially those a fair way from home.

I wasn't there very long but you got snippets of an idea of how good some of those United kids were going to become. We played a game with Nicky Butt and Paul Scholes and people were already pointing Scholes out as an absolute superstar of the future. Robbie Savage also stood out, but mainly for the shock of blond hair he had.

I can't recall seeing David Beckham but I remember early on, Keith Gillespie taking me to a bookies. I'd never been in a bookies in my life and even at that young age he was mad into his horses. I was walking around like a lost sheep, staring at the tellies and all the newspapers on the wall. Keith was loving it.

By the time I was fit enough to travel home, I was torn between clubs but it was felt that Celtic was the best option for me – for a number of reasons. Looking back, it was my dad who had the biggest say.

"Son, Schmeichel is not going anywhere for a long time," he said. "He's coming into his own, he is still very young and he has the next 10 years in that United goal. Do you want to sit in the reserves for six years going nowhere before realising you've made a mistake? If you go to Celtic, you could play first-team, right now." Steady on Dad, I'm only a teenager, you know! But I know what he meant. He meant I stood a better chance at Celtic of going places far quicker and at a far younger age.

It was either stupid or ambitious, but I would never change what happened because I believe your path is pretty much cut out for you beforehand, you just have to walk it. Plus, as a Celtic fan growing up, and with Liam Brady as manager and Packie Bonner at the club, there were a lot of connections. Packie is a Donegal boy and he would look out for me.

Ferguson rang Dad again a few days later.

"Seamus, we'd love to have him, we'd love to sign him," he said, but Dad was adamant that the Celtic agreement had to be followed through.

"Mr Ferguson, if you haven't your word you've nothing," Dad told him. "We have made a commitment to Celtic and that is to be honoured."

"Fair, that's very fair," Ferguson said. "We'd love to have him but let him go to Celtic and do his apprenticeship and we can chat again in a few years' time."

*****

At the time, school wanted me to finish my leaving exams before I went across to Celtic you can understand why as well. If Celtic fell through and I failed my apprenticeship, what then? They were right. Celtic would have one day of lessons a week but that wasn't much.

The problem was, I wasn't mad into learning. I wasn't bothered about school. I used to play every sport for school; basketball, volleyball, Gaelic football, soccer and I also played rugby once but smashed my nose up, so that was the end of that! In other words, my strengths lay on grass, not in a classroom.

There was one religious teacher who had it in for me. Some days I couldn't make school as I had to work for Dad on the market garden or on the pitch and putt and she would think I was just dossing off. I wasn't – Dad needed me to work and that was that. Even when I was in school, I would have to take half a day off to go and play for the school football team at an away game. "Shay, you only turn up when there's sport on," she would bark at me. "If you think you can make a career out of that then there's no chance." I know she meant well. She wanted to do her job to get me educated but I wasn't dossing. I simply had no choice.

I was always happy to work in the fields, even if it was tough. If the football had failed, I would've been happy to carry on with Dad. I never wanted to go to university, that just wasn't in me. Then Celtic came along and it snowballed. Before I knew it, I was on the move to Scotland.

When the time came to go, Dad drove us to Belfast then we took the ferry to Stranraer and across the Irish Sea we went. I had my suitcase, my Sunday best on and my kit – that was it. When we got to Parkhead we were met by a member of the

Celtic youth set-up and it felt like my dad was passing me over. Like his job was kind of done. I was a man now, or nearly one anyhow, and it was up to me from now on in.

Dad got really emotional and it didn't really hit me that he was going home. I could tell he wanted to hug me but he also didn't want me to see how upset he was. I'll never forget watching him drive off in his Toyota, his poor shoulders heaving up and down in the driving seat. He was very, very upset. I'm a dad now too, so I can understand it all. My son is 12 so in four years' time he could be leaving home. But he's so young! That brings it home, the fact that I was such a young fella when I went to Glasgow.

From Lifford, Celtic is not just up the road. Back then there was no internet or easy means of communicating with my family. Nowadays we are on the WhatsApp all the time, keeping in touch and staying close but back in the early '90s it was one phone call a week if you were lucky.

I just couldn't get my head around it all. Every day, the routine was the same. At the end of training I'd return to digs and I knew nobody. I had no friends, no family, no cousins, no one. I missed home and my own bed so much. I think I went home once every three months or so. There weren't regular daily flights between Scotland and Ireland like there are now.

Packie Bonner knew my dad from Donegal football circles, going way back and when I was really struggling with home-sickness, Packie used to ring Dad and say, "Seamus, you need to get over, you need to keep an eye on him."

Packie rang the house one day and my sister Sinead answered the phone. "Hello, can I speak to Shay please?" he said. "Who's speaking?" Sinead said. "It's Packie Bonner," he replied. "Yeah, right, course it is – stop messing around, who's speaking?!"

Dad would sometimes come over from Friday until Sundays, looking to cheer me up. Dad and Margaret would visit and we'd go for a drive, a meal, a big walk on the Sunday. My brother Liam had also moved to Belfast and I'd ring him for a chat. "Shay, if you jack it in now you will never forgive yourself," he said. "You will never know what might have been."

It was a very big culture shock. Lifford is still small now, never mind then and to go from there to Glasgow was a big ask. It might as well have been on Mars.

They put me in digs not too far from the stadium and on the very first night I was in there, a guy walked past the window. He was eating fish and chips and he must've been drinking. He threw these wrappers into the front garden and saw me looking at him out of the window.

"Fuck OFF!" he shouted. I closed the curtains and threw myself under the covers.

Eventually I went to see Liam in his office, who was happy to listen to my worries. "Look, I can't stay there," I said. "I just can't, it's impossible." They shipped me out to Bishopbriggs a bit further out from the middle of town and put me in digs with Nigel Melly, a guy from Derry, which definitely helped.

They put us in with an older family and straight away I felt a lot better even though it was still daunting. I know homesickness has happened to a lot of players, and players from Ireland especially.

Many have packed it in and gone home. At that age, it's tough when your family and friends are all miles away and like I say, in those days, when you were gone you were gone.

*****

During my time at Celtic, Packie was a huge help. Given the connection with Dad, we had a natural bond.

When it came to actually training and trying to make an impression, that was a lot easier than trying to get used to living so far from home.

Packie, Stewart Kerr and Gordon Marshall were the main goalkeepers, Paul McStay was also a big character, as was Charlie Nicholas – he was always fun, as you can imagine.

I remember one day we were doing sit-ups. I'd never done gym work before. I'd dive around all day long but working on physical strength back then wasn't a priority.

Anyway, we were doing sit-ups in the gym and I wasn't breathing out. My face was turning beetroot purple. Charlie took one look and wasn't happy.

"For fuck's sake breathe," he shouted. "Yer head is gonna explode at this rate!"

He was always really bubbly and a great personality. It all still felt like a bit of a dream to be honest. If meeting up with Celtic in the Burlington Hotel had been strange, to actually be on the club's books was even more surreal.

When I was 14, I'd done a Packie Bonner training school for the day back home. It was the usual set-up, he would turn up and show these mad young kids some moves, sign a few autographs and everybody goes home happy. Getting to meet Packie Bonner, the hero of Italia '90, this legend of Donegal, was beyond my dreams and then, just two years later, we're sharing a dressing room, getting ready for training.

Packie was an absolute hero to all Irish people but he was brilliantly humble and had all the patience in the world with this kid he was now sharing a training pitch with.

He gave me loads of tips on how to improve. "Step off and then dive," he would always say. "Don't just dive. You'll never reach the corners. You need to step and then dive, build up some momentum first."

I do remember though that he never gave me many gloves. At the time, all I wanted was a pair of his goalkeeping gloves – he gave me one pair after about a year, and they were properly battered. Cheers Packie, I won't get much wear out of these! Maybe that was his way of letting me know I had to earn them, to work for them. If you get too much, too soon – like some of the young ones now – you get spoilt.

Packie would always drum home the same lesson. "If you think this is the hard part, you know nothing yet," he would tell me. "Getting to the top is one thing – staying there is quite another. That is what takes all the effort. You've got to put the work in, every day." I've always remembered that.

We used to get changed at Parkhead for training then get the bus up to the training ground. The first-team would anyway. Us apprentices had to run up the road to Barrowfield on our studs, slipping all over the place. We'd train in the morning and then our lunch would be soup and a roll. That was it! Or maybe a second roll if you asked nicely and the dinner staff liked you.

It was a proper, old-fashioned apprenticeship. The first XI were looked up to as men who'd been through exactly the same as us, so why should we avoid some hard work? It's done away with now for whatever reason but it was a good schooling. I was used to a day's work anyhow so it never bothered me. You would clean the boots and stands and if Parkhead was covered in snow then you would get the brushes out with the other apprentices and sweep the place clean.

Most of the jobs involved mud. I was either cleaning all the old dirty kit or sweeping out the changing rooms. I cleaned Packie's boots and also Gordon Marshall's. You would be given two or three players each, they would just lob their boots at you and God forbid if you didn't do a good job. If they weren't done properly they'd be at you. "Eh, what's this? Do these again." I think it was a good thing, it was teaching us to do a job right, how to respect the first-team and it made you realise that everybody else has been through this system. Imagine that these days? The apprentices drive in now in brand new cars and throw their boots at the kitman. There's no real apprenticeships now, you know? I think that's a shame.

Liam Brady had brought Frank Connor into the Celtic set-up and he was in charge of the reserves. He was mad but in a good way. He would shout at people all the time but he knew what it meant to play for Glasgow Celtic; all that history bottled up inside him, ready to pop at any time. "Do youse know how fuckin' lucky youse are to be here?" he'd scream at us. "You're part of the best club in the world." He was right to remind us how good life was and he was trying to get the best out of us.

Looking back, I never really got a chance to make a statement in the first XI or to challenge Packie because I was so young and living in Glasgow still had its ups and downs.

When I lived with Nigel, sometimes he would have to go in earlier than me so I'd have to take the bus to training. I'd get the bus from Bishopbriggs into Hope Street in the centre of Glasgow and then another one out to Parkhead.

One day there was this scruffy guy begging. He came up to me and it was clear he was on something. "Can you borrow us?" he said. I didn't have a penny spare so I told him I didn't. The next day I saw the same fella coming towards me and I went, "Sorry mate, I've got nothing on me" and he just flipped. "I never asked you for nothing anyway," he started, before chasing me onto the bus. 'Oh fuck, this won't end well,' I thought.

At the time I was wearing a Lifford Celtic top, which has a shamrock on it. He saw this and that was it. "Fuck off you fucking Fenian c***," he started, letting me know we were not going to be penpals in the future. Luckily enough the bus driver came up the aisle and asked me if I was going to pay him on. No fucking chance! Who pays someone on to get battered by them?! I was absolutely shitting myself but the driver got him off. Anyway, the next day, the *Evening Times* carried a story about someone being stabbed in Hope Street. I had no idea if it was this guy or not, all I knew was that I was a long way from cosy, safe little Lifford. Fucking hell, get me home. Playing football isn't that important – it's not worth getting stabbed for!

On the pitch, first-team opportunities remained virtually non-existent apart from New Year's Day, 1994, when I was called up to sit on the bench for the Old Firm derby.

With it being Christmas time, I was at home in Lifford when the phone went. I was to report back to Parkhead as quickly as possible because I was going to be Packie's back-up as Gordon Marshall was on loan at Stoke City.

I'd enjoyed my time at home but I was over the moon about the chance to maybe play in an Old Firm game, the Holy Grail.

We went off and trained the day before the game and on the way to the stadium there were fans lining the roads, screaming and willing us on. You could just tell this was massive.

My stomach was turning in the dressing room and the thought kept coming to me, 'This is real, this is happening. Today. Right this minute.' I was only a kid and now this was life or death. There was no room for excuses, no room for mistakes. If I was needed, I couldn't mess it up. Also, the win bonus was £1000 – 10 weeks' wage in one – and I was already dreaming and already spending it in my head!

We walked down the tunnel and the noise just hit you. It blew me away, I couldn't hear a thing. Parkhead was a wall of green and white with just a tiny section of blue in the corner. Madness.

I hate watching football. I wanted to be on the pitch, having a say in things and putting my own mind at rest. Watching is tough but, being honest, I was glad I didn't get on that day. I've played in the north-east derby and the Manchester derby but there's no doubting the Old Firm match is up another level. Three Celtic fans ran onto the pitch that day to confront Rangers players and some supporters even threw Mars Bars into the directors' box as we lost easily, 4-2. That was as close as I was going to get to ever representing Celtic's first-team.

Before I knew it, I would be leaving the club.

*****

People ask me why I left Celtic and the reason I left Celtic was Lou Macari. Macari had replaced Liam Brady in October 1993, just a few months before that New Year's Day defeat, and, for whatever reason, I just didn't feature in his plans.

It's been suggested he thought I was too small to make it as a keeper and that I was not good enough for Celtic; I don't know how true that is but I'd like to think I've proved him wrong.

This is what happened.

When I'd joined Celtic, I was put on £100 a week which is an incredible figure for an apprentice and way more than the other lads who were on £27.50 or £30 a week. I don't really know how or why I was on more but I do know it felt like a fortune! And just for playing football!

When I'd worked for Dad, we never got paid, we just had to do it. You might get the odd fiver here or there but our wages were a roof over our heads and food. That was life, that was my background, a background I was happy with too. And now, here I was, watching my bank account fill up by the week. On top of my wage, Celtic also paid for my digs, which was another £70 a week. Although I didn't know what heaven looked like, the chances were it was painted green and white.

I saved up hard and bought a one litre Vauxhall Nova, it had two doors and four gears. Step aside Hugh Hefner – I've made it. I paid £2800 for it and went home to Lifford, thinking I was driving a Ferrari. I remember I had to pay extra to have the wing mirrors painted the same white as the rest of the car. £20 it cost me. That Nova was my pride and joy. I'd give all my mates back home a lift everywhere whenever they needed one.

Anyhow, after playing well for Frank Connor and sitting on the first XI bench, we reached the point where you find out whether they want you or they don't. You get stuck in a waiting room and your dreams are either made or shattered. I thought I'd be ok. I'd been playing well enough, I was clearly committed and the *Celtic View* newspaper was giving me some good reviews.

Eventually, I was ushered into Lou Macari's office and a contract offer was there in writing – on the back of an envelope. Dad still has it at home.

"We want you to sign professional terms," he said. "We're

going to offer you £130 a week." On top of that, I'd now also have to pay half my digs, which was £35 a week so, all in, it meant I would actually be on less money as a professional than I'd been on as an apprentice.

It felt like a kick in the teeth. This was Celtic, one of the biggest clubs in the world we were talking about, and their offer was just not good enough, especially for somebody who had given his all for the last two years.

"There's no way you're signing," Dad said, when I told him what the offer was. "You've spent two long years away from home, you've done everything asked of you and they want to offer you just that?" He wasn't happy and neither was I. "You might as well come back here and play in the League of Ireland if that is all they think you're worth. You might as well stay as an apprentice." He had a point. Maybe Lou and Celtic were surprised I would leave, maybe they thought they were such a big club that I'd automatically want to stay. I don't know. I do know I'd not put a foot wrong in my two years and the reward for that was just not there.

So then, I was packing my bags, catching the ferry back across from Stranraer and going back to Ireland. Even then, I didn't think my dreams were shattered. It was just a case of starting again and waiting for everything to fall back into place.

I'd learned so much at Celtic, I'd enjoyed the very briefest taste of what playing in big games was all about and I wanted more. It was just a case of seeing who was out there – and who would come knocking.

Just before I left Celtic, I was asked to go and play in a tournament in Holland, one last academy competition. It was more football and more game-time and I didn't mind.

Along with the coach Ashley Grimes and lads like Kevin Docherty, Tommy Wilson and Michael Craig, we went across to Terborg in Holland to play Ajax, Wisch, Twente Enschede and De Graafshap in this under-19 tournament and we made it to the final before losing to Ajax on penalties.

Losing on penalties would be something I'd get to know all about in the coming years. Yet it was what was happening in the stands, not on the pitch, that mattered most.

I didn't know at the time but there was a fella watching me called Terry Gennoe, somebody who would come to have a massive influence on the direction of my career.

Terry, who was the Blackburn Rovers goalkeeping coach, had been sent to Holland by Kenny Dalglish, the Blackburn manager who had, in turn, been tipped off by an Irish scout called Pat Devlin. Pat knew everybody in Irish football, he was a manager at Bray Wanderers for years, and he, Kenny and my Dad all went way back. He also knew my Celtic offer was not up to scratch.

When Kenny heard I might be available, he was straight on the phone to Terry and told him to get to Holland at once. "Give him a look over," Kenny said. "Let me know what you think."

Terry headed to Holland but was sent on a wild goose chase to the completely wrong stadium a day before we were even meant to play! He finally spoke to Pat and asked him what had gone wrong and was told he was 100 miles from the action and that he had to head to Terborg, quick-smart, instead.

Over the next few days, Terry saw enough during those performances to think I was worth following up. He recommended me. "He's very raw but he wants to succeed," Terry told Kenny. "He's definitely worth it."

Meanwhile, Lou Macari had now been shown the door at Celtic. Tommy Burns was in charge and it was felt that this might see Celtic offer me a better long-term deal.

After the tournament I returned to Lifford with Dad and settled back into life at home. I wasn't back very long when Blackburn followed up Terry's recommendation and got in touch with me and Dad and said they wanted to meet us in Dublin. The same week, Packie Bonner and Tommy Burns said the same thing. Also in Dublin. We thought Celtic might have come to their senses on their first offer and that a new manager in Tommy would mean a fresh start.

Packie rang Dad and asked for a lift to Dublin so he met us at home and we all set off. At the time, Packie didn't know we were meeting with Blackburn as well as Celtic, he thought we were just heading straight to the Burlington for the Celtic talks. He wasn't aware two gentleman by the name of Kenny Dalglish and Jack Walker were heading over from England at that very moment.

We dropped Packie off at the Burlington and headed over to Stillorgan to meet Kenny and Jack for dinner and to listen to what they were proposing.

Kenny was great with me and made it clear that he wanted to take me to Blackburn and that it was the best move for me. They offered me a four-year deal on a lot more money, £500 a week, based on international appearances.

I couldn't believe the sums they were talking about. I couldn't believe they had that kind of money spare for a goalkeeper. We all shook hands and I was on cloud nine.

I was on the verge of becoming a Premier League player but out of respect for Celtic and Packie, we didn't commit to anything. We just shook hands with Kenny –"I hope to see you soon, Shay" – and Jack Walker and headed back to the Burlington to meet Tommy and Packie.

After meeting them in the grand foyer of the hotel, we were invited up into Tommy's bedroom to discuss whether Celtic wanted to match what Blackburn had offered me. I left that to Dad, who followed Tommy and Packie into the bedroom while I stayed downstairs.

They discussed various offers for a while but it was clear nothing would be agreed. They could not come up with a deal and I was on my way to Blackburn.

That was a shame in one sense because I'd genuinely been happy at Celtic. I knew I was learning and developing there and I'd always supported them as a boy.

Leaving Celtic back then hasn't stopped me following their fortunes closely over the years. It's a unique club with a special set of fans. I've been back to watch games on a number of occasions. I'll always count myself as one of them.

# 4

# IN THE SHADOW OF GIANTS

WHEN I moved to Blackburn I was far more prepared for life away from home than I had been when I'd left for Celtic but I still walked into a fair few scrapes.

I lived with Tommy Morgan and Chris Malone, two other Irish lads embarking on a football career in England. That was my first mistake! It made sense to find a house together so we went and had a look at this new-build property in Blackburn. To us, three lads fresh off the boat, it looked lovely. We couldn't sign a 12-month contract quick enough.

About a week after we'd moved in, we started to have second thoughts when we were told that someone around the corner had been stabbed. It turned out we had decided to set up home in one of the roughest estates in the town. Our attempts at playing grown-ups was backfiring badly. And we were stuck there for a year – there was no escape from the Blackburn Bronx!

Bobby Mimms and Tim Flowers were in front of me in the pecking order at Ewood Park and it was pretty clear early on that getting ahead of those two was going to be pretty impossible. Bobby's time as a No.1 in the Premier League was being restricted by Flowers in front of him and I was behind Bobby – so what chance did I have?

Still, it was a great opportunity to work with some top players and learn the ropes, especially with somebody like Terry Gennoe. Terry has been a big influence to me both personally and as a coach. When I was at Celtic, Joe Corrigan used to only train the goalkeepers one day a week, on a Thursday, but at Blackburn Terry was there all the time and that made a big difference. He was brilliant. He put on so many different sessions that really tested you and improved you. Corner drills, match scenarios, free-kick drills, penalty sessions.

I was like a sponge, I just couldn't get enough from Terry and Tim. If I could've been out on the Brockhall pitches for 12 hours a day I would've been. I would have set a tent up in the car park! I wanted to train and train and train.

My footwork was always very, very quick – it was one of my biggest strengths – we worked some more on that and we focused on the size of my vertical leap and spring; something that has stayed with me.

Tim was so established. He'd been a goalkeeping record £2m signing for the club and he was in full flight in the 1994/95 season. He was England's No. 1 and as good as anybody else in the country. I was still a teenage boy, still learning the game and what it takes to make it and Tim showed me.

In one game at Ewood Park against Newcastle towards the end of that season he was unreal.

# IN THE SHADOW OF GIANTS

Alan Shearer had joined Rovers in 1992, also for a record transfer fee, and when Chris Sutton arrived from Norwich City in the summer of '94, the now famous SAS double act was formed. It was a partnership that propelled Blackburn to the top of the table. As the season was drawing to a close, we were still top but had Fergie's Manchester United breathing down our necks. The Newcastle match was the final home game before a trip to Anfield on the last day of the season. We had just lost 2-0 at West Ham in our previous game so we were desperate for a win at Ewood Park.

Shearer put us 1-0 up but then it was a backs-to-the-wall job as Newcastle piled on the pressure. We held on for dear life and only won because Tim was incredible. He made amazing stops from Peter Beardsley, Rob Lee and especially one from John Beresford. Tim was fist pumping like he'd scored. I told him the next day in training how good he'd been and, like always, he just played it down. "It was only one game Shay, it was nothing special," he said, which was Tim all over. He set the bar for me.

Tim was always very encouraging. He would take me to one side and suggest little tips. His work-rate was phenomenal. He just didn't have an off switch. For a night game, he'd be in on the morning of the game doing an hour and a half of work before the match itself. For a young goalkeeper wondering how the world worked, it was amazing to watch and he showed me how committed I needed to be if I was to make it.

I think Tim is way underrated. You don't hear much from him these days and he never seems to make many 'Premier League Greatest XIs' but let me tell you, having seen him close up, Tim Flowers was as big a part of Blackburn's success.

After that Newcastle game, Blackburn went to Anfield and

ended up lifting the Premier League title, as everyone knows. I didn't travel to Liverpool on the day they won the title. I wasn't on the bench and I didn't want to go and sit in the stands. I probably should have done. I could've gone but it was my first year and I didn't put myself forward.

I didn't play any games and I felt at the time that I would be hijacking the party, but I regret that now. What are the chances of winning the Premier League? It doesn't happen every day and, looking back, I missed out on being a part of that, even if I hadn't played.

People say Jack Walker bought the Premier League trophy that season and although I know what they mean, I think that's harsh. I don't think what Blackburn did was bad for football because the money they paid for players stayed in the English game back then. It was an English club buying British or Irish players.

The money we paid went down the leagues, down to other clubs, down to helping other sides strengthen. It didn't go abroad or into the pockets of agents in the middle of nowhere.

My concern now is that there are so many foreign players in the league and so many foreign teams are being paid a fortune for players and that money doesn't get filtered into the English game, you know what I mean?

The year Blackburn won the Premier League, they signed Robbie Slater, me, Tony Gale, Tony Carss and Jeff Kenna. Apart from me and Robbie, all those lads had come in from clubs in England for a fee and that fee propped up smaller clubs. It's all different now and by no means better, in my opinion.

*****

# IN THE SHADOW OF GIANTS

A lot of the strength of the Blackburn team that season lay in the dressing room spirit. I hadn't spent too much time in and around the first-team but I knew the players were all so motivated to win the title for Kenny and also Jack Walker.

Colin Hendry was one of those rocks the team was based on and although he was as tough as nails, he was obsessed with sorting his dyed hair out. You couldn't move him out of the way after training, he'd be there hogging the mirror, drying his peroxide blond mop, as shameless as anything. Colin was one of those players who put himself on the line every game. He lived for defending. Tony Gale, Jason Wilcox, Tim Sherwood, Ian Pearce, Paul Warhurst, David Batty, Stuart Ripley; they were all good lads and players who left it all on the pitch, which is exactly what it takes.

There were a lot of leaders in that changing room and the team spirit was amazing. Chris Sutton and Billy McKinlay were always messing around, doing mad things to each other and cutting everyone's socks off – all the old school stuff.

Immediately after Blackburn won the Premier League, Kenny stood down and became Director of Football. Ray Harford took control. It was a sad day for me because Kenny had done so much to help me.

Every professional footballer will have certain people – whether they be parents, mentors, coaches or managers – who they look back on with huge respect; with the knowledge that they were massively instrumental in the way their careers have panned out. I've obviously mentioned my dad a fair few times and he is undoubtedly an enormous presence in how I got to this place in life but within the game itself, Kenny Dalglish stands out as probably the most influential and important manager I ever had.

As a young Celtic fan, I needed no introduction to who Kenny was. He might be the King at Anfield but he's not too much further behind at Parkhead. I won't be the first footballer to say how impressed they are with Kenny as a person and I think the one outstanding quality he has is how much he deeply cares for his players and how much he wants to look after them.

After signing my Blackburn contract, I went straight into a reserve match the same night and had a complete shocker. I couldn't catch a cold and cost us a few goals. I was immediately aware that this was hardly the dream start to life at Ewood Park.

Yet Kenny had done it all and knew how to deal with it. He came into training at Brockhall the next day – my first full day as a Blackburn player – looked me in the eye and with a big grin on his face said, "It's a good job you signed that contract before the match and not after it!" He was right. He totally diffused my nerves, he'd clearly guessed that I was the kind of player who liked to relax and joke and he was very dry and witty. That kind of knowledge comes from being a special sort of man-manager. A shrewd operator.

Kenny always had an aura about him. He would walk into a room and you almost knew he was there before you'd seen him. He just had this presence and character that made you notice and respect him. He used to join in the five-a-sides and, even then, some of his finishes were unbelievable. He was always joking and laughing with the players.

When he came to Newcastle, Kenny still joined in the odd training session and I always used to give him a bit of stick if we saw him getting changed afterwards.

Over time, his towel would get higher and higher as he put on a bit of weight. I wasn't letting that pass by.

"That towel's gonna be under your armpits soon," I'd tell him with a smile on my face. Kenny would just laugh and give plenty back, because he always does. He has a great sense of humour and loves the banter.

Kenny also gave me one of the best pieces of advice I've ever been given and one that I stick to even now.

"Shay," he told me one day. "Never get carried away when you're playing well, never get down when you're playing badly. You need to just try and be as consistent and level-headed as possible, whatever happens. There'll be good days, there'll be not-so-good days and you have to find a way of controlling both."

He's spot-on with that.

In your career you will have all sorts of experiences. You will go mad if you put yourself on a rollercoaster ride from one extreme to the other.

I've got some self-confidence but, even now, I don't think I have proved everything to everyone. If anything, I still adopt Kenny's mantra of trying to never get too up or down. Now, tell me, how many pieces of advice have you been given in your life that you're still using 20 years later? Exactly. They're rarities and Kenny is a rare man because he knows what is best for his players before even they do.

Kenny knew what made players tick and got the best out of our most important players, such as Al. He and Kenny had massive respect for each other – they still do – because Kenny of course had him at both Blackburn and Newcastle.

I think Al looked at Kenny as a bit of a father figure, as I did too.

*****

It was a shame when Kenny stepped down. I don't know whether Ray becoming changed his relationship with the squad – he was now the boss after all – but he was a very well respected coach and a big part of the Premier League winning season. However, it did feel strange and by the time the 1995/96 season came along, it was still clear that Tim was going nowhere and I knew the time had come for me to go out on loan.

At the time, Kenny's old Anfield pal Steve McMahon was in charge of Swindon Town and I'd actually gone to them for a month in January 1995 without actually playing. This time though, after a few phone calls were made, I was on my way back with the promise that I'd be playing for them.

Terry Gennoe and his wife Susan took me to Swindon for a friendly against Hereford United and I slept most of the way down there! I met the players at Edgar Street and I was thrown straight into the team for the match, something I loved.

I was a bit nervous but it was only a friendly. I played really well but we lost and Steve wasn't happy afterwards. "He's come all this way," he said, pointing at me. "And that's the way you fucking defend in front of him? He's the only one who can take credit for today." I think he was buttering me up to sign on loan for longer to be honest!

The season before, Swindon had been relegated and regular goalkeeper Fraser Digby was now injured so this was a chance to actually get some minutes under my belt and learn about the game. A lot of young players now will sit at the big clubs and not develop at all and I don't agree with that. You don't know someone's mentality until they are playing first-team football, wherever that is. I went to Swindon and there was real pressure to perform. There were jobs at stake and livelihoods on the line. It was a big learning curve and one that Kenny believed I needed as well.

The first league game was a six-hour drive in a bus to Hull City which seemed to last forever. We won and the bus was great on the way back, a few beers were opened and although people might say that's ridiculous these days, blah-di-blah, it's all part of a good team spirit.

I was a young bloke in a dressing room full of seasoned pros. We had to call Wayne Allison 'The Chief', he wouldn't answer to anything else. The dressing rooms were small, the laundry room was right next door to the home dressing room and you'd hear the washing machine going all day long. I went back there in 2012 with Aston Villa in the League Cup and there's a picture of me in the tunnel on the wall, which is nice, apart from the shorts – which are far too high to be legal.

I'm always happy to tell people that my league debut came in a Swindon shirt – it only happens once so you should always be proud of that. Once I got out there and played, I wanted more. I wanted to show I could do it. I played five matches in that spell under Steve McMahon and conceded just one goal as we went to the top of the league before I was recalled by Blackburn to Ewood Park in September 1995.

I wasn't there too long. In January 1996, Peter Reid, who had been given the Sunderland job full-time, contacted Kenny and Ray Harford and asked if I was available. To be honest, I couldn't wait to go. I felt a club like Sunderland would do me the world of good. "You can have him," Kenny told Reidy on the phone. "But on one condition. He plays." Kenny knew I was reaching the stage of my career where I needed minutes on the pitch.

When I first spoke to Peter on the phone and then went up to meet him and the players, he was as you would expect – loud, funny, upbeat. "Oi Shay," he had said on the phone. "Bring your hair gel." What the fuck was he on about? He said it again: "Bring your hair gel." "Why boss?" I asked him. "Cos we're on the telly at the weekend and you're starting."

My debut was at Filbert Street in a goalless draw and I felt at home straight away. I had a decent game, tipping one decent Steve Walsh effort over the bar and keeping the likes of Julian Joachim out. Iwan Roberts hit the bar at one stage but that was as close as they got. We might not have won but I loved every second; the tension before the match, the dressing room, the tactics, the noise of the crowd, the adrenaline; the works.

That clean sheet was the first of 12 I'd keep for Sunderland out of just 17 matches. Never once did I feel that I couldn't hold my own at this level or that I had to win over the Sunderland fans or players.

That team was the same as the Lifford Celtic side in that there was a lot of older players. I was still a young keeper and I felt they had my back.

Kevin Ball was Sunderland through and through. Back then you could really smash someone and the ref would just say, "Keep it down lads!" Kev would just take people out. He would lead a team-talk and wouldn't hold back. He would stand there and go, "Let's get into these fuckers. They're all getting it today. And if you don't fucking give it to them, I fucking will. This is Roker Park and nobody comes here and shows us up." You know, technical stuff…

It's hard to overstate just how positive Reidy was and although this was the verge of the 'modern' era – where pasta and early nights began to replace parties and having a good time – at Sunderland, Reidy was all about the craic and he believed, rightly, that a strong team off the pitch makes a better team on it.

Don't forget, he'd played at Everton in the mid-'80s, which was a side renowned for its thirsty approach to life under Howard Kendall. Going out for a few beers didn't exactly do that side any harm did it? It was an approach to the game I understood and completely agreed with – I still do actually.

Reidy wanted us to go out together and build up a sense of camaraderie. He wanted us to be like brothers who wanted to fight for each other. He would say, "Right lads, we are all meeting in the Chinese at two o'clock on Monday." You didn't have any say in the matter. You were at the Chinese at 2 o'clock on Monday. A lot of the clubs I've been at recently have been very regimented and you don't get to know people.

I felt at home during my time at Sunderland. I'd even had my name sung at Roker Park. Playing for them had helped me catch Mick McCarthy's eye for Ireland and I'd helped them get back into the Premier League. I have a lot to thank them for.

I returned to Ewood Park when that loan spell ended and, by the start of the 1996/97 season, I knew I had to move on. I wanted to be somebody, I wanted to be a first-teamer for a big club. Blackburn sensed this and they offered me a new and improved contract to stay beyond the end of the 1996/97 season. But I knew I wanted to let my contract run down. It was clear Tim was still going to be the No.1, he was the top keeper in the Premier League and so my options were pretty clear: I had to move. I had done my apprenticeship. It felt like I'd ticked all the boxes. I was also desperate to stay in the Ireland team and that meant regular first-team football was a must.

# SHAY

Before I left, I did finally get an opportunity to play for Black-burn when I came off the bench in a League Cup match against Brentford and then I finally made my Premier League debut against Wimbledon.

When you imagine your first Premier League start, you imagine the noise, the excitement, the pressure, the expectation, your first save and the 90 minutes you've got ahead of you. What you don't imagine is Wimbledon. We played them at Selhurst Park and the thing I remember the most is the sound of their stereo blasting out. The wall of our dressing room was literally vibrating, the noise was that loud. It was like getting changed in a dungeon. The walls were peeling and it reeked – everything felt like it was designed to intimidate the opposition.

We walked out and lined up in the tunnel. They all looked massive. They were well aware I was a new boy. And they let me know it. "LET'S TEST THIS FUCKING NEW KEEPER BOYS. COME ON!" they were all shouting.

Tim Sherwood turned around to me as we were about to go out and sorted it. "Ignore those," he said. "They're just trying to unsettle you. You'll be absolutely fine."

It was an education for me but I did alright and we held on until Wimbledon finally got a slice of luck to allow Dean Holdsworth to tap in from close range after we'd been battered for 85 minutes. I made one decent save towards the end from Marcus Gayle and, generally speaking, I did ok. Wimbledon were on fire that season and were actually front-runners for the title when we went there.

What it had shown me was what I already believed inside; that I was good enough to be a No.1 somewhere.

# 5

# BOY IN GREEN

*In we squeeze, the wheels on Dad's car springing up and down as we fly into the back seat.*

*I am with Dad, Marcus, Liam and Kieran. There are the usual arguments about who is sitting where, how much legroom I have and what should go on the radio.*

*Excuses with school have been made, because there's no chance we'll be home from Dublin in time to get to class tomorrow.*

*Dad fires up the car and off we're headed, mid-afternoon, to Lansdowne Road for tonight's Ireland match.*

*I'm the youngest, barely scraping into my teens, but my older brothers are just as thrilled, just as excited to be heading to the city to see the Boys in Green again.*

GROWING up, we barely missed a match at Lansdowne Road and travelling to Dublin for matches was all part of the excitement.

For every home international, Dad made it his job to cram all his boys into the Toyota for the four-hour drive and he probably remembers every mile of every journey. I mean, would you want to spend that much time in a confined space with that many excited schoolboys?

Watching Ireland and being Irish is incredibly important to me. I was brought up as a patriotic Irishman and I remain that today. Whatever else has happened in my sporting career, good and bad, the one true constant is the love of playing for my country, for the Irish fans and a nation that, although small, wants to take on and beat the best.

Before my Ireland career started I was the biggest fan you can imagine and now it is all over, I've proudly and happily returned to that status. In fact, it sounds strange to say it, but my only regret about being a footballer is that when Ireland have made it to major tournaments, I've been on the pitch rather than in the stands with my mates and brothers. Don't get me wrong for a second. I'm not saying I didn't want to play for Ireland because I did, but I often used to think, 'Well there'll be some almighty craic tonight in them stands' when we were doing well.

I'll always remember those journeys with Kieran, Marcus and Liam, the three of us punching each other for pretty much the entire journey. I also remember Dad taking us pre-match to the airport hotel once to meet the players. He'd sorted it through Packie Bonner. We got there, me starstruck, and I got Packie's autograph while Paul McGrath hovered in the foyer. They were all there – these players I worshipped as my Irish heroes and my autograph book soon filled up, these giant men only too happy to stop and chat with the Given boys.

We thought we'd died and gone to footballing heaven.

I always try and give anybody time because even now, at 41, I remember the thrill of that day when they gave me their autographs and what that meant to me.

When Ireland qualified for Euro '88 and Italia '90, Lifford came to a complete standstill. Anybody who had a car was in it, bumper to bumper in the high street, kids and mates hanging out of every window, sitting on the roof, horns blaring, pub doors full of dads toasting Ireland's success and toasting the future of the national team under the mighty Jack Charlton, the most Irish Englishman to ever manage the national side.

Dad got these tickets to the presidential suite at Lansdowne Road for me and him one night. We went in, the tickets were on the halfway line, and then after the game, at pitchside, Big Jack was being interviewed by *RTE*.

I can't remember which match but if you went through the archives, you'll find a young Shay John James Given in the background, waving like mad, trying to get on the telly! I was about 15 at the time, made up that I might be famous in the morning.

Little did I know, in the space of four years, I would go from all that – from basically being Big Jack's stalker – to playing in goal for my country. Dad always said I'd play for Ireland before my 20th birthday and I never really believed it would happen but it turns out Dad was spot on.

The date of my debut was March 27, 1996. We were playing Russia at home.

Getting changed next to some of those same players I'd worshipped as a kid felt surreal. Paul McGrath was on one side, Roy Keane on the other. The dressing room had plenty of my heroes in and plenty of guys I respected. Andy Townsend, John Aldridge, Niall Quinn – they were all in there. It didn't seem two minutes since Dad's epic journeys from Lifford, paying on the gate at Lansdowne Road and going crazy in the stands when Ireland did well.

I suppose one of the most amazing things about my debut for my country that evening was the faith put in me by Mick McCarthy. The match was Mick's first in charge of the national team and to roll the dice like that on a youngster like me was pretty unique. I'd played a few junior internationals for Ireland and done well and I was fortunate that it was only a friendly so nothing was riding on it but, still, how many teenage goalkeepers do you see in international football these days? I was also lucky because Alan Kelly had suffered a prolapsed disc injury at Sheffield United. He came over for the game but it went again the day before the match. He had to literally crawl off the training pitch the day before the game and that gave me my chance.

There's a lot on your shoulders as a young goalkeeper but I thought I was ready. It felt like a World Cup final for me. It's ok looking back now at a long international career but at the time, you have no crystal ball – you have to make the most of it and try and enjoy it. For all I knew, that was my going to be my one and only cap. In the years to come, I would always try and make other debutants feel comfortable and tell them to savour it, because it does go so quick. "Try and take it in, enjoy it, remember as much as you can," I'd say.

If you think I was pleased to get picked for the starting XI, you should have seen how the Givens reacted as a family. Put it this way, there were 40,000 in Lansdowne Road that night and I reckon I was related to half of them. All my aunties and uncles, cousins; Lifford Celtic mates and pretty much the rest of Lifford had jumped on a bus from home to be there.

Dad was especially proud, as goes without saying. Just before I left for the dressing room we had a word with each other and I could see how happy he was. All the effort of getting me to Celtic and then to Blackburn and Sunderland and everything else was paying off.

"Now Shay," he said. "Don't look up at the crowd during the anthems, just focus on your football – focus on your job." It was good advice. He was trying to make me feel at ease with the situation and the fact I was on a vertical learning curve.

It was part-thrilling, part 'fuck me!' But it was only natural that I'd be nervous.

I knew I was on the ladder and climbing it to be where I wanted to be but, as Packie Bonner had drilled in to me time and time again at Celtic, "Getting there is one thing, staying there is something else. Everybody wants your jersey, everybody wants your position, everybody wants to knock you down."

As we sat under the stands at Lansdowne, getting changed, I couldn't help but think about where I'd come from and who I was representing. It wasn't just for me, this match. It was for my family and it was for Lifford and Donegal and for my mates and everybody else who knew me.

Also, it was for Mum.

I used to carry a glovebag that always had a little vial of holy water in it. Dad had given it to me as I left Ireland. I blessed myself, sat there in my seat, and thought about everyone and everything that had helped get me to this point in my life.

I carried that holy water for a long part of my career. I suppose it gave me comfort and a reassurance. It was holy water from St Patrick's Church where Mum was buried so there was a real link to her and it was special because Dad had given it to me.

I'm not overly holy but I'd say my prayers before a game. It was a comfort thing to get myself ready. I was just hoping that she'd be proud of me. I'll admit that part of me was thinking how great it would've been to have had Mum there but I couldn't afford to think too much about that. I didn't want it to become too big, too much, I needed to use my thoughts about Mum as a strength rather than get too emotional.

Eventually, it was time to go out and warm up. That was the best thing for my nerves. All goalkeepers will tell you the same thing; it's the waiting that kills you. Pre-match jitters soon wane when you start diving around and feeling the ball.

We went back into the dressing room and I finally reached for the shirt that had been hanging on a peg above my seat.

Me, Ireland's No.1. Jesus.

As I pulled it on, I remember thinking, 'Nobody can ever take this moment off me' and I loved it apart from one thing – it was the most horrendous, multi-coloured purple number you've ever seen! It looked like some kids had been let loose with a set of crayons. It also felt far too big for me. Back in the day, everyone wore XXL – that was your lot. All our goalkeepers were XXL because Packie was a big lad and it was one-size-fits-all. Typical Ireland.

By this stage, I was used to the 'Roker Roar' and noisy games but that night, Lansdowne Road sounded like it had 100,000 in there. It's always been a brilliant, wonderful ground for atmosphere and it was probably because it was my first time but, to me, I thought my eardrums would cave in.

We lined up and the anthems began. The national anthem means a lot to Irish people, in the sense that it makes you want to run through a brick wall for your country. I remember it dawning on me that this is it, this was where my international career began. It was a very special moment.

As we broke off to get ready, I repeated to myself that I had to remove all emotion from the game. This wasn't the Shay Given Show – this was about Ireland winning. Unlike an outfielder, when you go into a game revved up, a goalkeeper can't just go bang, nail somebody and get rid of the tension. You have to keep a level head and a calm mentality. You can't get too carried away.

One thing that didn't change, even on my debut, was me roaring at everyone in front of me. When the ref blew his whistle, that was it – game on. I made my presence known from the first minute by using my mouth more than any other part of my body, shouting at the lads loud and clear about what I expected from the back four in front of me. I wasn't dishing it out when it wasn't needed but just organising, keeping things tight and letting the lads in defence know what I wanted and what we had to do.

I was only a kid but I was telling the likes of Paul McGrath and Terry Phelan to shift left and right – just as I'd shouted at the boys back at Lifford Celtic to do the same. I'm probably kidding myself but I think they listened! It's important to organise. All you're doing is trying to help your mates and team-mates out. I suppose, looking back, shouting, "Left shoulder, pick up" at an Irish legend like McGrath all night might have looked strange but Mick had picked me to do a job so I was sure as hell going to do it.

We lost the game 2-0. I didn't really have any chance with the goals so I took some positives from the night. We could easily have finished the game with a draw because we had some decent chances and we missed a penalty. It was only a friendly so we'd lost no points and Roy Keane getting sent off for cleaning someone out towards the end meant the headlines were about that rather than some wee scruff in goal!

Afterwards, I met my family again and we all had a big picture taken. You couldn't move for Givens. They were all there, from all four corners of Ireland – if Ireland had a fifth corner there'd have been some from there as well.

A bit like the Sunderland squad, the Ireland team loved to get together for some bonding and for the craic. Jack Charlton had been a massive believer in letting his players roam free and do what they wanted – including a couple of pints – as long as they didn't let themselves down. It was all about treating his men as adults and Mick, having been one of Jack's favourite players, followed that tradition and always allowed us some time to let our hair down and bond.

You learn more about a team-mate in a bar than you do on a treadmill and the spirit in the Irish team was always fantastic because we never missed a chance to have a get together, a few beers and a laugh.

After my debut, I played against Portugal and the Netherlands and it immediately felt like I was part of the group. For one match, I got the flight across to Dublin with John Aldridge from Liverpool.

I was still working everything out and wondering how it all worked and John was keen to show me. John was an unbelievable player and a strong character in the dressing room. He couldn't wait for the plane to land. "We're out tonight lad," he was telling me on the flight, a few beers in. "We're all out tonight, that's for sure."

Niall Quinn was the same. Quinny had been around forever and was – and is – an Irish legend. Time and time again, people mistook him and thought all he could do was head the ball when, in fact, he had a superb all-round game. He was brilliant with me when I first broke into the side. "Shay, you'll be doing just fine," he'd say, big grin on his face.

One night we were in the airport hotel in the build-up to a game and he was itching to go for a beer. "We need to get out lads, we need to get out," he was saying over dinner.

The windows in the hotel were barred and didn't open all the way, like a prison. We all had a few drinks at the bar and were enjoying the craic. Then the alcohol wanderlust kicked in. We wanted to get out onto O'Connell Street in the heart of Dublin city centre to see what was happening.

A few managed to sneak through the front entrance but that was soon shut off so we were all stuck, a few quid burning a hole in our back pockets and the desire for *Just One More* growing by the second. The next thing, Quinny has a solution. From nowhere, he produces a screwdriver, begins unscrewing these window bars and we all ease ourselves out to taste freedom and meet up with the rest of the escapees. *Where to now, lads?*

It was the funniest thing I've ever seen. The next morning over breakfast, Quinny was recounting the story to everyone. "Fucking hell," he started. "I'm in my 30s, I'm married with two kids and I'm unscrewing the window so I can go out for a few extra pints!" He was such a funny bloke.

Gary Kelly would also turn out to be one of the funniest people in the Irish set-up. He is bananas. Ian Harte is his nephew and it was madness when they were out together. Hartey would do whatever Gary did, he was like his shadow. It was hilarious to watch.

# SHAY

In Dublin one night, Gary jumped on one of the horse and carts that takes tourists round the city. He had this dirty looking blanket on his head, whipping the horse as he whizzed around Temple Bar with passengers on board.

He also had this thing about running into hedges for no reason, just for the craic, just to get a laugh. He'd get out of a taxi, spot a hedge and he'd be off, full pelt into it. He'd wrestle himself out of it, about 20 minutes later, bruised and bloodied, his shirt all ripped, with this stupid smile on his face.

When he got married, I'd had a knee operation about three days before. At the reception he had everybody up, shirts off, trousers rolled up, doing this mad Riverdance-style jig around the reception area. I didn't fancy any of that, I was on crutches but he still dragged me up. I had no choice! He's such an outgoing character who is great to have around.

Ireland players had always enjoyed a pint together, even with the fans and the media. That's just the way we were. It was never a non-stop jolly-up. We'd have a night out when we all got back together and then that was it, game heads were on until we played.

Those nights out meant we got to know each other really well and who knows what advantage that gives you on the pitch? What I do know is this: no team ever got *worse* by getting to know each other better. Sports science and all that stuff is great, to a point, but a lot of it is theory and in practice, a few pints and a good laugh works just as well.

I think the reason Ireland had been successful in the past was because we were such a tight, tight unit. We would be in each other's room, telling jokes and stories, sitting in on Quinny's card school, relaxing and enjoying the environment. Sitting in the room watching DVDs all day would have sent us crazy. With Ireland, the lads were like family in a way, we all became best mates and that came across on the pitch. The bottom line was, we all loved playing for Ireland. We adored it, it was everything to us. And we'd never have done one single thing to hurt our country or hurt our chances.

*****

I had performed well in my early matches for Ireland but, quite rightly, I wasn't a guaranteed name on the teamsheet for every match. I was competing hard then with Alan Kelly for the main spot and my lack of regular first-team football back at Blackburn did me no favours either.

At one stage, Mick dropped me for a match against Macedonia and explained that it was a lack of game-time at Blackburn that was costing me. I couldn't really have any complaints with the logic of that. I know some people would probably like to hear that me and Alan were always at each other's throats or that we hated each other but the fact was Alan was always really helpful and supportive to me and we got on really well. It was the same with Dean Kiely too. We all wanted to be No.1, of course we did, but our relationship – at least as far as I'm concerned! – was excellent. Later in my career Alan would be the Ireland goalkeeper coach and he was very talented. It was good that there was a lot of competition for the jersey – it should never just be handed to anyone without them having to sweat for it.

Getting on with Alan and Dean wasn't difficult and I don't know if it's my personality or theirs but, touch wood, I like to get on with most people. I like a laugh and a joke and I like to make training enjoyable and lighten the mood. You can be too uptight and tense before big games and it's important to get the balance right with a bit of humour sometimes. Most goalkeepers I've worked with have shared that approach and shared the idea that the manager picks the team, not us, so let's get on and help each other as best we can. We just had to train and let the boss deal with everybody else and that was the attitude I took into the 1998 World Cup qualifying games.

When I look back at that entire Group 8 qualifying scenario I still cannot believe we didn't make it to France. It still breaks my heart.

We were in a group with Romania, Lithuania, Macedonia, Iceland and Liechtenstein. Yes, I know Ireland is a small football nation but we'd been at the last two World Cups, we'd shown we were a good side and we had some class in every department. Andy Townsend, Niall, Tony Cascarino, Denis Irwin, David Connolly, Ray Houghton – these were no mugs these guys and yet, somehow, we ended up failing to qualify. That baffles me and breaks me.

In the campaign itself, the goalkeeping duties were split between me and Alan and maybe that was half the problem. Only Tony Cascarino played every game in the qualifying stages and we just couldn't get the same 11 onto the field together every time we played. Don't get me wrong, every player picked for Ireland was good enough but Mick just couldn't quite get the consistency he wanted. Tony Cascarino was an interesting character. He would wake up early if we had an afternoon nap and would walk around in a towel all day. He'd pop in, say hello and help himself to half a Snickers. Not a full one, as he was 'on a diet'. Little did we know he was going into every room and doing the same!

We got off to a flier, beating Liechtenstein 5-0 in Eschen and then Macedonia 3-0 at home before a draw with Iceland at Lansdowne Road gave us seven points from three matches.

It was then that it started to go wrong until, eventually, we ended up needing a late Cascarino goal against Romania – his seventh of the campaign – to secure us a play-off place.

Anybody who says they like play-off games is lying to you. Yes, they hold the key to moments of great joy but someone also has to lose and have their hearts broken. And I don't ever fancy my odds, even in a two-horse race.

We were picked out to play Belgium at Lansdowne Road. Again, the place was absolutely heaving; you couldn't hear yourself in there. It felt like no opposition side would stand a chance.

On the way to the game, as always, we had a tape of songs we used to sing together on the bus. They were Irish rebel songs by *The Wolfe Tones, Paddy Reilly and The Dubliners* and U2 would always be played in the dressing room. It was often the start of the *Joshua Tree* album that would blare out. We always loved a sing-song. The old Irish battle songs would get the blood running and it would hit home that we were going out there for Ireland. There was a real togetherness and as we all sang *'We're On The One Road',* I felt we were ready for this.

Some of the lads in that team were not born in Ireland but had qualified through their parents or grandparents or whatever and they'd be as passionate as the rest of us. We got off the bus and we were flying, ready to go, feeling great.

Back in the dressing room, I looked around and felt so confident. Steve Staunton, or 'Stan' was sat in one corner, tying his boots, Denis Irwin sat nearby slowly taking it all in, preparing himself for what was ahead. We had class all over the pitch, a manager in Mick that we all respected and trusted and we felt great. The only slight downside for us was Roy Keane was missing.

Our confidence increased early on when Irwin smashed home a trademark free-kick but, fuck me, did the Belgians come at us then. Luc Nilis scored a fine equaliser after 30 minutes and it turned into a really tough night, 1-1 the result. Yet when the final whistle went, I still believed we could go to Belgium and do what we had to do in the second leg. Their away goal meant we had to score and I had all the faith in the world that we would and could do it. Again, look at that starting XI teamsheet from that night; Shay Given; Jeff Kenna, Kenny Cunningham, Steve Staunton, Ian Harte; Gary Kelly, Lee Carsley, Alan McLoughlin, Andy Townsend, Mark Kennedy; Tony Cascarino – you can't tell me it wasn't good enough to represent Ireland at a World Cup.

We travelled to the Heysel Stadium in Brussels for the second leg and I was still convinced we were good enough. After about 25 minutes, Luis Oliveira raced on goal after a fantastic through ball cut us in half at the back. I had no choice. It was pouring down and very greasy but I had to come out and try and play the ball – and if not the ball then the man – I couldn't just let him score, could I? Anyhow, Oliveira skipped by me and slotted into an empty net.

We weren't done yet. Andy Townsend and Ray Houghton combined for Ray to head home an equaliser. After goals against England in Euro '88 and Italy in USA '94, Ray had a knack of scoring important goals and this was right up there.

With 20 minutes to go it was anyone's game until, not for the last time, the referee decided to get in on the act.

Gunter Benko overruled his own assistants to give Belgium a throw-in when it was clearly our ball and that threw us all out of position. Nilis got played in with a great ball over the top and he slammed it past me for what proved to be the winner.

It's a goal I often think about but never really want to watch again. Was I slow off my line? Did he catch me flat-footed? Do I hate Gunter Benko? All these questions still need an answer. Ok, apart from the last one.

Maybe I should've stayed on my line and beat him standing up, maybe I should've come out further and faster. We will never know. But as a goalkeeper, when you have made a decision you have to stick to it. You have to stick to your guns otherwise you're in no man's land and that's the worst place for any keeper to be. In the end, he nipped in front of me and that was that.

The rain continued to pour, the Belgian fans continued to sing and before we knew it, we were out. I was so young and the loss hurt that much that the emotion started to get to me. We weren't going to the World Cup. How do you start describing how *that* feels?

It all got too much, I'd watched Ireland at Italia '90 and USA '94 and now I wouldn't be going to France '98. I could smell Paris from Heysel, I could walk it in a long afternoon — and now I'd be at home, watching it on the telly. Soon enough, the tears came. As we walked down to where the Ireland fans were, I couldn't hold on any more.

Mick Byrne, the legendary Irish physio, tried to console me as I thanked the fans. "Shay, be proud, be proud, you couldn't have given more," he told me, but at that moment my heart was too broken to really take it on board.

You just feel like you've let the whole country down and nothing that anyone says can pull you out of it. It was my chance to help get Ireland there as a player myself, after growing up watching my heroes, and we'd missed out by nothing at all. The dressing room looked like every dressing room after a tough loss. Boots and shinpads lying everywhere, lads lying on the floor, some just staring into space. We could hear the stadium rocking from inside as well, which hardly helped the mood.

And the silence, my God the silence. You'd think there would be at least some noise in a dressing room but there was none whatsoever. A dream, gone.

I was so low but I remember Packie speaking to me, trying to sort me out. "Shay, don't worry about it," he said. "That is football. You will get another try at this, this is just the start."

Those words were kind and what I probably needed to hear but nothing much was going to dig me out of the gloom. He also had a few tips on how to deal with the reaction to the game too. "Don't go to the press and say much," he said. "Don't say 'I should've done better for the second goal' or anything. Don't hang yourself out to dry, there's enough who'll do that for you."

That was the kind of solid advice Packie was full of. Getting his guidance on how to deal with international heartbreak was just what the doctor ordered.

Unfortunately, I'd be needing plenty more of it in the years to come.

*****

After the World Cup qualifier disappointment, I remained in the side but would, again, have to compete with Alan Kelly for the No. 1 jersey when it came to trying to get us to Euro 2000.

This qualifying campaign would be the type that would leave me scratching my head in years to come.

I played in the first three qualifiers, as we beat Croatia – who had come third in the World Cup just a few months before – thrashed Malta 5-0 before then getting beaten in Belgrade by Yugoslavia 1-0.

As always in a qualifying group, it's always just a result here or there that hurts you and that Yugoslavia result would turn out to be one of the more crucial results.

Alan then came in for me as I'd not long had cartilage surgery but we beat Macedonia and Yugoslavia at home which put us in a brilliant position. A loss to Croatia then knocked our chances but we could still go through as long as we beat Macedonia and Yugoslavia didn't beat Croatia in the last round of matches.

Macedonia – it's always Macedonia isn't it?

We'd lost 3-2 in a crucial France '98 qualifier and they were gunning for us again in Skopje. I wasn't playing but we went 1-0 up and with Yugoslavia only drawing against Croatia, our tickets to Euro 2000 were booked. All we had to do was defend one last corner and we were there but, unfortunately, Keith O'Neill let his man slip away, they equalised and we were back in the play offs.

I'm told that before the match, Keith had been going mad in the dressing room, screaming at everybody and asking the likes of Tony Cascarino and Denis Irwin if they were up for it. That didn't go down too well. Denis Irwin had just won the Champions League with Manchester United so he knew a thing or two about winning big games. Keith's nickname was 'BSE' because he was like a mad cow, he was nuts.

I was still injured for the Turkey play-off matches so went to the Tyneside Irish Centre with my brother Marcus to watch the second leg after we'd drawn 1-1 at Lansdowne Road.

It was good to watch the match as a fan, have a few drinks and cheer the lads on but unfortunately for us, Turkey held us to a goalless draw, Tony Cascarino got punched during a few nasty scenes after the final whistle and it all ended on a bit of a downer.

We were all gutted to be missing out on another tournament because we'd done well under Mick and it was just the odd result that kept slipping at exactly the wrong time that meant we were finishing second in qualifying groups and not first.

I'd had my struggles to get into the side because of injury and the form of Alan but I believed in myself and wanted to keep succeeding. After all, I was now at Newcastle United and I wanted as many adventures for Ireland as I was enjoying at St James' Park.

**HOLDING ON:**
Me with Mum...

**EARLY DAYS:**
(*Below left*) aged
18 months and
(*below right*) lined
up against the wall
with Donal Burns
and Gareth Friel
before my First
Holy Communion!

**ALWAYS MISSED:** (*Above left*) with Mum, Dad, Uncle Buddy and my brothers and sisters in July 1980. Mum must have known she was ill. (*Above right*) With my family at Mum's graveside. It was the right decision for us to be at the forefront of the day. You can see her grave from our home in the background

**THE LADS:** (*Left*) My brothers and cousins have always been a big part of my life. (*Above*) The home-made pitch where I learned to hold my own

**CROSSING THE CODES:** Me posing before an All-Ireland U-14 final at McGinn Park and lining up for Gaelic club Naomh Padraig Leifear in 1986 (*centre, with the ball*)

**ALL TOGETHER:** (*Left*) a family photo. Pictured (*back row, from left*) Liam, me, Marcus, Kieran. (*Front row, from left*) Michelle, Jacqueline, Margaret (*with Paul*), Dad and Sinead. Above: At the golf driving range where I worked for Dad

**LEARNING:** At Blackburn Rovers, Swindon Town and Sunderland. I was desperate to prove myself

**NEW ERA:** I was grateful to Mick McCarthy for giving me my chance. Training with Packie Bonner (*right*) after being called up in March 1996

**ALWAYS THERE:** With Dad in 1998 – he has been such a big influence on my career. (*Right*) I couldn't stop the tears flowing when we failed to qualify for France '98

**BIG TIME:** As soon as I joined Newcastle I was up against European opponents. (*From left to right*) Barking instructions against PSV, organising things against Juventus and celebrating against Barcelona

**RAISING THE BAR:** Lining up for a team photograph on September 17, 1997 – the night we beat the mighty Barcelona at St James' Park 3-2

**OVER AND OUT:** Arsenal's Marc Overmars slips the ball past me to score in the 1998 FA Cup final. We had our chances and losing was hard to take

**GOING IN WHERE IT HURTS:** Diving to deny Manchester United's Andy Cole in March, 1999

**SHUT-OUT:** Diving to make a save in the FA Cup semi-final against Spurs at Old Trafford in 1999. We kept a clean sheet and were going back to Wembley

**SAVING THE BEST:** Turning a David Beckham free-kick around the post in August, 2000

**HOME ARE THE HEROES:** Mobbed by the fans at Dublin airport after qualifying for the 2002 World Cup

**THE HEAT IS ON:** Cooling down during a training session in Saipan. (*Below*) Packie puts me through my paces

**BREAKING POINT:** With Roy Keane during training in Saipan. The storm is brewing...

**SAFE HANDS:** Climbing high to collect a corner as we take a point against Cameroon

**MEN IN GREEN:** The team that would go on to take a point against Germany with a 1-1 draw, Robbie Keane scoring a last-gasp penalty

**MARCHING ON:** Snuffing out the danger against Saudi Arabia. A clean sheet helped us qualify from the group stages. (*Right*) Celebrating with Stan – Steve Staunton

**SO NEAR AND YET SO FAR...** I came so close but Spain's Gaizka Mendieta scores from the spot and the World Cup dream is over

**THE POPEMOBILE:** I couldn't believe the reception I got when I came home. The streets of Lifford were rammed as we went round in an amazing car!

**TAKING THE MIC:** On stage in Dublin during the homecoming. It was Jason McAteer's birthday so I thought I'd lead everybody in a little sing-song

# 6

# HITTING THE BIG TYNE

KENNY Dalglish sat opposite me in a tiny Italian restaurant just around the corner from St James' Park and as the main courses began to arrive, his plans for Newcastle United were served up to me.

At the end of the 1996/97 season, I'd been offered a contract extension by Blackburn but the Sunderland experience meant I knew it was time to move on, so I followed Kenny to the north-east and I could not have been more excited.

As I was stabbing my pasta with a fork, Kenny was straight onto it. "You're coming up to do something memorable, we can do something special up here," he said. "And you're coming to play – you're not coming to miss more games." To hear that at 21 was massive. 21 year-olds don't play regular Premier League football in goal. It just doesn't happen. I can't remember the last time a team had a regular goalkeeper aged 21. Joe Hart and David De Gea maybe – but there's not many.

# SHAY

Back then, Newcastle were challenging for the title, year in and year out. I wasn't going to a team heading for a relegation fight, a scrap to survive. I was going to a top club, with an amazing stadium, a fanbase as mad about football as any on earth, I was being promised regular first-team football and I'd be playing for Kenny Dalglish.

Life didn't get much better than this.

Pavel Srnicek, Shaka Hislop and Steve Harper were at St James' Park so to get the nod from Kenny, and to be picked for the first game of the season against Sheffield Wednesday, was massive. I was nervous – nothing wrong with being nervous by the way, I was nervous on my Manchester City debut aged 32 – I just wanted it to go well.

Benito Carbone scored for Wednesday, a brilliant overhead kick, up and to the left of my dive. There was nothing at all I could do about it. In the end, we won 2-1 – Faustino Asprilla scoring both for us – and so the day could not have gone much better. Some players go under at St James' Park – they don't want the ball, they go hiding, they go into themselves, but you can't be scared and I wasn't. I've always had strength of mind, it's something I pride myself on. I was more than ready to walk out of that tunnel and onto that pitch. I felt at home immediately.

Football is a religion in Newcastle and the fans worship their players. It doesn't stop on game day. If you went out for a coffee up there, the fans would be around you, asking for an autograph or photograph or even just wanting to chat. I didn't know any different really so I enjoyed it. To me it was just life.

Going into that dressing room, full of some big characters was a test for me, as was the job of trying to stay in front of Pavel, Shaka and Steve.

The summer I joined, Kenny had also dipped into his contacts book and brought some real legends of the game to the club. I joined at the end of May and by the beginning of August he had signed Ian Rush and John Barnes.

As the season went on, Rushie didn't score that many goals but, to be fair, we also struggled to create chances for him. Growing up in Ireland, he'd been one of the biggest names, a complete legend, but you would never have known he was this footballing star, he was just quiet and came in every day and worked his socks off.

John, or Digger, was a right character. He used to have this big Lexus car and he was one of the first guys to have the TV screens in the back of the headrest. Sounds dated now but they were cutting edge at the time. We were well impressed. He'd blast up to training and half the squad would be in the back of this Lexus, watching X-rated movies. There were regular screenings.

We'd be in the changing rooms, changed and focused for a hard day's training and Digger would come in waving the DVD in the air, and that would be that. Out we'd race, elbowing each other out of the way to get a good spec. We'd be crammed in his car, studs on his leather, watching away. He always had to remember to switch the DVDs back so that something else was showing when he got home!

The one thing I remember most about Digger was how much time he had on the ball. All the best players are the same. He just looked so relaxed and somehow had extra time to do what he wanted with it. He never warmed up before games. I don't know if it was just with us or something he'd done throughout his career but on matchday, we'd be out there doing our warm ups and he'd be back in the changing room, having a soak in the hot tub. I was only just starting out and at 21 you try and absorb the best pre-match knowledge from the older pros. I was like a sponge taking it all in while Digger would be using one – he'd be covered in foam, slowly stretching in the bath, happy as anything! That was just his way of preparing and loosening off his muscles – the first time he touched a ball was when the match kicked off. I bet the sports scientists these days would be pulling their hair out!

Kenny brought Rushie and Digger in because of their experience. He knew them inside out and they all got on very well. Kenny trusted them. They didn't always start but they were great players to have in the squad and around the place.

*****

If I wanted an idea of exactly what I'd let myself in for at Newcastle, it came as early as my second game. No messing about, I was straight into Champions League qualifying action in front of an absolutely rammed St James' Park.

Against Dinamo Zagreb, I was one of five new signings to start the game and that goes to show you the trust Kenny put in his players.

"Go out and play, go out and express yourselves," he said before the kick-off. This was all completely new for me. From Swindon to the Champions League in very little time at all.

There was plenty of solidity and style about that team. David Batty could run all day and Philippe Albert was a total class act at the back. We had the madman Tino Asprilla running the game for us up front with help from Rob Lee and everywhere you looked you saw players who were favourites with the fans. I immediately felt completely ready.

Don't forget, I'd played for Ireland by now, so I was used to big occasions and big crowds. I'd got the taste for it and couldn't get enough.

We won the first leg thanks to a collector's item – two John Beresford goals – and then we scraped through at their place to get into the Champions League proper.

Temuri Ketsbaia scored the aggregate winner in Zagreb to get us a 2-2 draw and put us through 4-3 over the two legs. I'll never forget that game. It was mayhem on the pitch, mayhem on the sidelines and mayhem in the crowd. You could say it was the perfect introduction to life at Newcastle United Football Club.

Before you knew what was happening, we were on the verge of playing Barcelona in the Champions League and in all my time at Newcastle, the night of September 17, 1997 is right up there amongst the best.

It was only my sixth start for the club and I was getting ready to play one of the greatest sides on earth. Again, Kenny had certainly shown his complete and utter faith in me by sticking me in goal. I couldn't or wouldn't have had any complaints if he'd gone with Pav, Shaka or Harps – they had been around the club and the Premier League longer than I had – but, no, Kenny was keeping to his word in the restaurant: *"You're coming up to do something memorable, we can do something special up here."*

It doesn't get more special than beating Barcelona in Europe. It was one of the greatest games of my career. Looking back, that night still feels surreal. Before kick-off, I remember taking a look around St James' Park. It was just completely black and white; scarves and shirts and flags as far as the eye could see and I swear I've never heard a noise in a football stadium like that night. You didn't so much hear the crowd as feel them. The noise had a life and a force of its own, 'To See The Blaydon Races' was whipping around the stadium, getting louder and louder and louder. I didn't even know human beings could make that much noise. I literally could not hear what someone was saying two metres away. No idea at all. The fans had done us proud and were really up for it as only those fans can be.

I felt a little shiver down my spine. I could feel the television camera getting closer and closer to me for the headshot they do. And then that Champions League music fired up and all the advertising boards changed to show the famous Champions League logo and branding.

As the classic theme tune filtered around the stadium, I glanced around their side. I picked out Luis Figo and Rivaldo and Miguel-Angel Nadal and I realised this was as big as club football gets. Before this night, Figo and Rivaldo only existed to me on the PlayStation.

The build-up to the game in the press was incredible. Barcelona's manager Louis van Gaal had used the media the day before to basically say, "We're Barcelona, we are going to go there and win and everybody is expecting us to win." We showed him what it meant to play for Newcastle and Kenny. They were 3-0 down before they knew what had hit them.

Tino scored a hat-trick and Keith Gillespie down the wing was sensational. He's said himself that it was the best match he ever played and they couldn't get near him, he was giving their full-back the working over of his life. Every cross he sent in seemed to be inch perfect.

They put on a late charge as Luis Enrique and Luis Figo both scored in the last 20 minutes but I always thought we'd hold on. To beat Barcelona in the Champions League in front of the Geordie Nation was the stuff of dreams and it felt like we'd almost won the Champions League, it was that much of a special night.

Looking back, I think we were riled by Van Gaal's words. We were an experienced team and there was a lot of pride at stake. We were professionals, there was no way they were going to come to our patch and overrun us. Yes, we knew it would be one of the toughest matches of the entire season but it was also going to be one of the toughest for them too. That was our attitude and it was an attitude the supporters took on board as well.

That night, I was roaring stuff at the back four – I mean at the very top of my voice – and they never even turned and looked at me. They couldn't hear a thing. Unreal. When the final whistle went it was just a huge, huge sense of relief because we were not experienced in Europe, so it was a massive moment for the club.

That famous victory and the general atmosphere around the club under Kenny was great. We were all so desperate to win, we all wanted to be the best performer in training every day and we were all so competitive.

It was, of course, Tino's finest hour in a Newcastle shirt. What a player and what an enigma he was. People might wonder if he was as crazy off the pitch as he seemed on it. Well, the answer is yes! His English was obviously really poor so he'd just walk past me in the corridor or in the training room and go, "Eh Given, bastardo!" That was it! That was all he ever used to say.

When he joined Newcastle, he'd seen snow for the first time

in his life and it totally freaked him out. What's this white stuff falling from the sky?!

But in training, my God, he was unbelievable. Talk about all the tricks and flicks. He was so laid-back it was incredible. He just didn't care about anything, nothing rattled him at all. He didn't have a care in the world. It was hard to communicate with him as he'd just wink and smile.

He was a total one-off with an unusual playing style to match his unusual character off the pitch. Even when he was sprinting he looked like he was taking it easy because his stride was so long. Against Barcelona he scored some amazing goals but you never knew what was going to happen with him. Some days he was just unplayable and he loved the spotlight.

Kenny and Terry McDermott, Kenny's assistant, would do their best to get their point across to him on the training ground and to be fair to him, I think he understood more English than he spoke. They would show him flip-charts and diagrams and he would nod his head in the right moments but I'm sure there were times Kenny would look at him and think, 'He's not listening to a bloody word of this!'

Tino absolutely loved Newcastle and going out and about in nightclubs. He was out – a lot! He had lots of house parties. He would just rent houses, enjoy himself then lock up and move somewhere else when the mess inside became too bad to handle.

I just felt like I fitted in straight away to life in Newcastle and there were plenty of personalities about too which helped. Steve Watson took me under his wing when I first moved there and told me where to get a flat and the best places to go out and about.

After we beat Everton in September 1997, he took me down

to the quayside for my first big night out and then we also had a boozy lunch on the Sunday before staggering into training the next day. "Thank God it's Monday," I told him. "I'm glad of the rest and a night in."

"What are you on about?" he said. "Monday's the best night of the week – it's student night!"

We went back out on the town and it was absolute carnage – 'I'm never going to last up here,' I thought to myself! It was like Freshers Week for me; the early chaos before I settled down.

Going out was just the done thing back then and we'd all socialise together, something that I think Kenny and Terry Mac knew about and didn't mind. I mean, after all, they'd played football together in the 1980s and that Liverpool team didn't exactly stick to tonic water did it?

Terry is one of the best guys I've ever known in football and he and Kenny knew each other backwards from when they were both tearing teams apart at Anfield. Kenny trusted him with his life.

Terry didn't do much coaching but he did a great job of working as a link between the players and the manager. He didn't put on training sessions or deliver team-talks but he would keep everyone happy, report back to the gaffer how the squad was and that helped a lot. Terry worked so hard on keeping the group together and unified.

He could always have a laugh at himself too. He jumped onto the team bus one day after the game and needed all our addresses for some reason, I think it was matchday tickets or something. Now Terry has a lisp and can't really pronounce 'S' but he went around the bus and got everyone's address until he got to Steve Howey – "Sssteve, what's yours mate?" "It's 66

Seaview Terrace, Sunderland, South Shiel…" Terry jumped in. "Oi, you taking the pith out of me?" He wasn't! That was genuinely where Steve lived. The rest of the bus was bent over.

On another occasion, after a pre-season trip, Terry jumped on the coach without realising that people wanted his autograph. "Eh, Poodlehead, come here" one of the fans shouted at Terry. Well, you can imagine the players' reaction. We were falling over laughing. As always, Terry took it with a smile.

Kenny called Terry 'Ledge'. Before training you'd hear Kenny going 'Ledge this, Ledge that' and you'd be getting ready thinking, 'Fucking hell, he must be some player if King Kenny is calling him a legend.' I asked Kenny about it once, wondering just how good Terry had been. "It's nothing to do with his football career," Kenny said. "It's because he's the only one who could drink 10 pints at night, train the next day and then be man of the match on the Saturday." He could drink what he wanted and was never affected. Even now Terry is really fit for his age, there's no weight on him at all.

Terry just totally 'got' it. He didn't try and be one of the lads, he would give us our own space. He would have a quiet word about personal things and let you know you were valued.

With me he would never get too technical because I was obviously in goal but he would crack jokes, keep it light and take my mind off the game coming up. He helped us relax. "You've been here before," he said. "Yeah, it's a big game but nothing you haven't seen a thousand times. Relax and enjoy yourself. Do your stuff, stop thinking and this will be a stroll in the park."

Unfortunately despite Kenny and Terry's advice, that first year at Newcastle didn't always click into gear and the Barcelona win would be the absolute highlight.

In the Champions League we ended up losing twice against PSV Eindhoven and away from home at a half-full Camp Nou, while only managing a draw and a win against Dynamo Kyiv.

When we travelled to Kiev I was shocked by how poor an area it looked. We had to take our own chef to cook for us because there were rumours that meals could be poisoned over there.

I remember the special feeling of walking out onto the pitch to the Champions League music again before the game but I suppose that trip was probably more special for the Toon army than us. The fans were getting the chance to follow their team around Europe. Call it a piss-up if you want but they loved it. The attendance at that match was enormous, probably more than I'd ever played in front of before and Kiev were a team full of quality stars like Andrei Shevchenko and Sergei Rebrov.

As my first season went on, it was becoming clear we were lacking sharpness and missing some bite up front. Alan Shearer had wrecked his ankle in a pre-season friendly with Everton and goals were in short supply. Although he came back for the FA Cup match against Stevenage in late January, he couldn't do it all on his own.

Our lack of goals was our own fault in one sense because before the season started, we'd allowed Les Ferdinand to go to Tottenham and also sold David Ginola too which, looking back, didn't help us or Kenny.

The Geordie Nation had warned that selling Les and Ginola would cost us a lot of goals and then, as Les was packing his bags, Shearer got injured – it was actually the same day – but by then Les was on his way. That infuriated a lot of fans, especially those who wanted to see Newcastle playing the mad kind of football they'd played under Kevin Keegan. In January, we also sold Tino to Parma which dulled our attack even more and new signings like Alessandro Pistone and Jon Dahl Tomasson were just not cutting it for us.

Maybe a mini-break in Dublin would boost team spirit…

*****

After drawing against Everton in February 1998, Kenny gave us the thumbs up for a few days off.

The trip back home was just meant to be a bit of a bonding session for the lads, a bit of a chance to re-energise after what was already a tough, long season. We'd already played 42 games by then and it was felt that a few beers away from the pressure of the Premier League would do us all some good.

For one reason or another, Kenny wasn't on the trip so he'd put Terry Mac – the entertainment manager – in charge, and that was the first mistake right there! The usual kind of activities were planned – a few beers, a game of golf here and there, a couple of nights out on the streets of Dublin.

You know what's coming next…the infamous tale of the Keith Gillespie punch-up.

I was there when it happened. We'd been out all day but it was still early, it was still light outside and we'd all fallen into a bar called Cafe En Seine on Dawson Street. Now this bar is very long and narrow and all the lads were in there, having a good time, there was no commotion, we were not being hassled by anyone, it couldn't have been going better. Loads of drinks were flying down and there was a table next to where I was sat that had plenty more drinks on it. We were well on by this stage and Keith, for whatever reason, just swiped the table clean.

There were pints flying everywhere and everyone was covered in booze. "Fucking hell Keith, what are you doing?" Al asked him. "That's out of order, you need to apologise." If memory serves me right, I think he did apologise, through gritted teeth, and that was it, peace and goodwill restored to all men.

About 10 minutes later, Keith went and did the same thing again. Pints were flying here and there and tempers were starting to fray. Al started going mad at Keith, he was fuming by this point, and the verbals started between the two of them. "Right, outside," Keith told Al – the stupidest thing he ever did do – and that was it, they were heading out onto the streets of Dublin for a bust-up.

Just as Al was going through the door back out onto Dawson Street for their tear-up, Keith rabbit-punched him in the back. Keith had a swing and it hit Al flush on the back of the head and then that really was it. Al turned around in a flash and buried him, bang, right hand.

I didn't know if it was Al's punch that did it or the fall but Keith was knocked out cold. On the way down he hit this plant pot and he was properly sparked out. There were loads of people around – Dawson Street is slap-bang in the centre of Dublin – and we knew it wouldn't stay quiet for long.

The ambulance was called and we were all wondering what we were going to say to keep it all quiet. We started trying to cover each other's backs and that seemed to be going well until Steve Howey decided he was sober enough to get involved.

"Tell you what lads, I'll go in the ambulance," he started. "I'll just tell them he tripped over, hit a plant pot and we'll be grand." Steve got to the hospital and was asked by the doctors what happened, panicked and said, "Fucking hell doctor it was a hit and run wasn't it?" A hit and run! Nice one Steve, now there were Gardai out there looking for a car that didn't exist.

"I know, I know," Steve said later when he was telling us back at the hotel. "I just panicked. That was the first thing that came into my head and I just said it. Then by the time it was out there I couldn't take it back!" We were giving him so much stick. The Gardai were now on a manhunt for no reason. Talk about digging ourselves a bigger hole!

The next morning, the phone started ringing and the press were on to it in no time at all. We went and played golf and the place was heaving with paparazzi, hanging out of trees and all sorts. People were asking for autographs and at one stage a couple of blokes came over. "Sign this please Alan," the usual stuff. We didn't know at the time but they were reporters and they wanted to get up close to Alan's hands to see if he had any bruised knuckles or swelling. When you think about the lengths they go to!

The story was bubbling away but Al was more worried about Keith than anything else. They didn't want to kill each other, it was just a stupid drink row. Neither person holds a grudge. Keith has a hard head and he was discharged the next day. The first two people up to his room were Al and Rob Lee – maybe as a referee – but the three of them were pissing themselves before the door was even fully open.

*****

When we returned to England, we beat Barnsley in the FA Cup quarter-final – Keith missed the match because he still had stitches in his head – but our league form remained scratchy as we fell well below what we expected of ourselves and also well below halfway in the table.

The club was also back in the headlines after Freddy Shepherd and Douglas Hall, two directors, were stung by *The News of the World*. While sitting in the Marbella Club Hotel in Spain on the night we beat Barnsley, they were caught on tape criticising Newcastle women, the fans for paying too much for replica shirts and they also labelled Al as 'Mary Poppins' for being boring.

To be fair, there was probably a few drinks involved and they were just half-joking but they got proper stitched up by the newspaper. It was the talk of the dressing room but only because it was the talk of the bloody country when the story broke. None of us cared what had been said. I didn't have much to do with Douglas Hall, he wasn't around the club much at all when I was there but I actually had a lot of time for Freddy Shepherd. He wasn't overly chatty but he demanded respect from you and we certainly knew where we stood with him.

The thing about Freddy was that he was a Newcastle fan and he just wanted the best for the club. He spent £15m on Alan Shearer for example, and look how that turned out. I don't know what £15m buys you now but it wouldn't buy you too many Alan Shearers.

Everything that happened at Newcastle seemed to be a huge story but I didn't mind that. It was a reminder that we were at a big club, that you had to be professional and do the right things. The Mary Poppins dig didn't concern Al one bit – if you think Shearer is somebody bothered by what people think of him then you've never met him. Alan has since unveiled a statue of himself that Freddy paid for, so I think they soon made up. As for us, his mates, Freddy's comment gave us a chance to give Al some stick and we weren't going to pass that up.

If we were out in a restaurant or on the golf course, somebody would run past him with an open umbrella, dancing up and down. He always just laughed it off and told us where the umbrella could easily be shoved if we carried on!

By the time April arrived, it was clear that the FA Cup was all we had left to play for. I'd really settled in by now, I was loving the club, the fans and the city but our Premier League form remained poor. That was disappointing but I was still happy because I'd left Blackburn to try and win trophies and that was a real possibility when we played Sheffield United at Old Trafford in the FA Cup semi-final.

I know Wembley gets the nod for semi-finals now but I think they're missing the point. Growing up, semi-finals always seemed to be at places like Old Trafford, Villa Park, or other similar grounds. Big stadiums for big matches with plenty of their own history. Playing at Wembley was still an achievement in itself and was part of the whole package and joy of even getting there in the first place and I think that's gone now, which is a shame.

Old Trafford for our semi-final against Sheffield United was incredible. The thing that sticks out the most, 20 years on, is the amount of Newcastle fans in the ground. I didn't know Newcastle had that many people in the city. Our fans had the massive stand right across from the dug-out and one of the ends. There was a sea of black and white, it was phenomenal.

The atmosphere was absolutely unreal and the volume as we walked out of the tunnel just seemed to crank up. The match itself was scratchy but Shearer won it for us, 1-0, with about as ugly a goal as you can get. My Ireland mate Alan Kelly brilliantly stopped his header but the ball bounced on the line and Al absolutely smashed it into the net as we held on.

When the final whistle went, the sense of excitement and relief was so strong I could almost taste it. Growing up, in the garden with my brothers, playing at Wembley was the ultimate dream and now, here I am, about to play there for real.

The six-week gap between the FA Cup semi-final and the final was the slowest six weeks of my life, especially as the city of Newcastle got increasingly impatient for the big day.

Everything about the final dominated the place and the excitement seemed to grow by the hour. As a kid in Ireland, FA Cup final day was something special. Back then you'd watch the television for the whole day, from the players in the hotels, the buses, all the build-up, the match, the celebrations and then we'd be back out there in the back garden, trying to recreate what we'd just watched. To be one of those players wandering around the pitch beforehand, in my new suit, was just magical.

Before the match there was a lot of nervous tension in the dressing room because it had been so long since Newcastle had won a trophy. It was a case of wondering if we were the group of lads who were going to do it, going to end the club's long wait.

I managed to control my nerves and I wasn't too bad at all considering the millions watching around the globe. You know it's a big game because it's the final of one of the greatest competitions in the world. In recent years it might have lost a bit of shine because teams play their second string – which I think is ridiculous – but everybody would still love to win it.

In the dressing room I slowly slipped on my boots and gloves, swigging a bottle of water, keeping calm and focused. Kenny tried to keep it relaxed beforehand, there was no ranting and raving. He didn't want to build the match up too much – we already knew how big it was, why make it worse? Kenny won two FA Cups at Liverpool so if anybody knows what it takes on the day to prepare for the 90 minutes ahead, it was certainly him.

After all the build-up, all the excitement in the city, in the media and everywhere else, what hurts the most about that final is the fact we never really turned up. We just never got going, even if we did have a couple of chances to win it.

Dennis Bergkamp was missing for our opponents Arsenal with a hamstring problem and that gave us a boost but, saying that, the Gunners were on fire that season. They had class all over the pitch. They'd already won the title and we'd lost to them twice in the league. Nicolas Anelka missed a sitter early on, a close header that he should have buried but we couldn't capitalise. It was a boiling hot day and it just seemed to me that they were a touch quicker to everything, especially their first goal.

When Marc Overmars held off Alessandro Pistone, I tried to spread myself and make myself nice and big and he just toe-poked it through my legs. There's not much you can do about those. We kept running and running and although we didn't have many chances, Nikos Dabizas hit the post early in the second half – it was the kind header we needed to go in if we were to test Arsenal's mentality.

After Nikos went close, Al also hit the post. It was one of those shots that sometimes bounces out and sometimes goes in off the woodwork. We just couldn't catch a break, we could've been 2-1 up in no time and then who knows what might've happened?

Before we knew it, Ray Parlour had put the world's most boring, standard ball over the top and yet our defence had split. Anelka took a couple of touches and lashed it low past me. That was the difference, those are the margins. We had 20 minutes left but the game died, there and then.

Arsenal were a really fine side that year and we didn't play that well but at the same time, goals change games and we were unfortunate not to at least get back into it. We knew they were strong but you also need a bit of luck that we just didn't get.

When the whistle went, I slumped on the Wembley turf. When you're on the wrong side of a result like that, it's tough to take. The game is all you've thought about for weeks and now... nothing. Nobody really remembers the losers. If you went to the pub tonight and were asked who Arsenal beat to do the Double in 1997/98, not many people would remember.

David Seaman always had a lot of time for me and we'd always chat a lot before and after games. "Keep your head up," he said when I got up to start shaking some hands. "There's plenty of time in your career yet."

I respected him so much because he was at the top level for so long but I didn't think anything about what he had said. In the moment you don't think about the future or what is to come, the sense of disappointment is just too much.

When we had to go and get our medals, the Newcastle fans were still there. That was unbelievable. Most fans are halfway up the motorway if you're 2-0 down with five minutes to go but give them their credit, they were unreal that day, staying in the ground long after it was all over. I felt so bad for them.

# SHAY

Going up the steps to get a loser's medal is the worst idea in the world. It's all part of the history of the day but it is horrendous. You just want to leave the winners to get on with it, get back to the dressing room and get as far away from Wembley as you can.

Afterwards, we went back to the hotel and had drinks and food. The first few hours were like a wake, obviously, as we played the match through in our minds. It was also the end of the season as well so we started to relax as the evening wore on. We vowed to come back stronger next season and tried to enjoy ourselves as best as we could.

Sat around a table in the hotel, nursing a beer, there were so many emotions going through my head and I all I kept thinking was, 'I wonder what the Arsenal players are up to now?' That played tricks on me all night. I imagined parties, laughing, a big gang of team-mates staying together and taking in the fact that no matter what else happened in their lives, they would always be able to say they were FA Cup winners. For us, it just wasn't meant to be. Still, as David Seaman had said, I was only young. I still had plenty of time to be stood on that Wembley pitch at the final whistle, victorious. I was only just getting started.

*****

Unfortunately, my hopes of continuing to learn and develop under Kenny Dalglish were dashed pretty much the moment the 1998/99 season had begun as we began with two draws and the Newcastle board decided we needed a change.

How did a man who had won more League titles, FA Cups and European Cups than I can ever dream of get the sack?

I think one of the most difficult elements of Kenny's time at Newcastle was the fact he was following Kevin Keegan. Few things are bigger than being a 'King' but a 'Messiah' is one of them and to follow Keegan was pretty much the impossible job, a bit like when David Moyes followed Fergie at Old Trafford.

The Newcastle fans all wanted, expected and demanded Keegan's entertaining but gung-ho style of football but Kenny was always trying to get the balance right and wanted to tighten us up at the back a bit more. I think Kenny was also unlucky because we had some bad injuries with Al doing his ankle.

We were still challenging in the Champions League, even with a different style of play, and the Barcelona win also showed that we could still play attacking football. People will say, "You defend him because he brought you to Blackburn and New-castle" and that may be true but I also think he should've been given more time. It's not like he lost the dressing room, you know? It was just a few results here and there that weren't going our way. When he went, we were all disappointed to see him go. It just didn't add up.

I was still very young and I've although I've now seen a lot of managers sacked across my career, he was one of the first. I was impressionable and I remember it being tough.

After the sacking he came in and spoke to the players. He tried to put a positive spin on the situation. Even then, right at the end, when he had just lost his job, Kenny Dalglish was trying to do the best for the team and thinking about others before himself.

That is Kenny all over.

## 7

# RUUD AWAKENING

DESPITE being gutted for Kenny, when Ruud Gullit joined Newcastle United, you couldn't help but be excited. One of the absolute kings of European football was coming to manage us and he was going to take us forward.

What can I say: I even believed this myself back then.

In football, and in life itself, some people are just tone deaf to what's happening around them. It's as if they sort of get it but they don't quite understand or plug into a place or a people or a purpose.

I soon found out that Ruud Gullit was one such person.

Right from the moment he arrived in Newcastle, he seemed arrogant. Is that a Dutch thing? I don't know. What I do know is that it was always more about Ruud Gullit than it was Newcastle. Like he was doing us a massive favour to leave London for the north-east. That kind of attitude would hardly help him win fans over.

# SHAY

Like me, most supporters welcomed Ruud. They felt he would bring a bit of Kevin Keegan back, a bit more flair and a return to the days where Newcastle scored three, conceded two and charmed the pants off the rest of the country. Wrong. Gullit brought nothing but division and we went nowhere but backwards under him.

When a new manager comes in, there's always a clean slate for everybody. This is good and fair in one sense – and a complete pain in the arse in another. When you are already established in the starting line-up, it can make you think that you've got to earn that right all over again. There's nothing wrong with that. Being made to stay on your toes is a good thing. But when you've had as many managers as I have, the novelty starts to wear off after the first decade or so…

From the start, it felt like Ruud didn't like the goalkeeper group one bit. Terry Gennoe had joined Newcastle from Blackburn Rovers by this point and I was thrilled about that. Ruud, it was safe to say, wasn't quite as enthralled by the closeness of me, Harps and Terry. We always trained together and Ruud was constantly on at Terry to make us do more, or involve us in games more often. It was as if he wanted to break us up for some reason even though every goalkeeping group around the world trains together. He certainly didn't seem to rate me, either, for whatever reason.

It wasn't exactly a good start then and it got worse on August 30, 1998 when Michael Owen smashed a hat-trick past me in no time at all as Liverpool won 4-1 at St James' Park in Gullit's first match. The ground was full that day of fans in dreadlocks celebrating the start of the Gullit era. They were soon pulling their hair out at what was going on at the club.

# RUUD AWAKENING

We soon won four games on the trot against Southampton, Partizan Belgrade in the UEFA Cup Winners' Cup, Coventry and Nottingham Forest but already relationships were feeling strained. For a start, Gullit had an issue with Rob Lee for some reason. He barely acknowledged him on the training ground or before matches and we just couldn't work that out. Rob Lee was a great player, somebody who gave it his all and who demanded the best from everybody around him. Gullit would just ignore him, maybe because he was so close to Al.

We would call Rob 'Al's shadow' because wherever Al went, Rob followed, wagging his tail! He loved a beer and the craic although if I let a goal in he used to throw me the 'Rob Lee look'. I would want to rip his head off. Most players don't have much time for goalkeepers anyway and when I conceded he'd just stare right at me. The look meant he thought I should've saved it. If the goalkeeper is at fault, what does that say about the 10 in front of him? They must have all failed too! It really wound me up. I'd be fuming at him. He'd then turn away and know he'd got me. It was all forgotten straight away, we always got on really well off the pitch.

Rob had a lovely house in Durham that I think he bought off Kenny Dalglish. After Gullit joined, we all went round for a BBQ and his children were there.

That day, we were in and out of the pool and while everyone is on the beers and enjoying the BBQ, I found this quadbike. I jumped on, no helmet, and set off. As I was speeding across Rob's garden, I went over this little bump and the next thing, this quadbike has flipped backwards. All I could see was the sky. I was upside down, somehow, and fearing the worst. Then the bike flipped back round and I miraculously managed to land it back down in one piece. Rob's kids were buzzing. "Wow, Shay that was amazing! Do that again, do it again, please, please."

"Nah kids," I said, shaking. "Let's leave it at the once." My heart was racing out of my chest. Rob was laughing his head off. "DO it again Shay, the kids loved that," he grinned, knowing full well I had shit myself.

There were precious few other laughs to enjoy for Rob at the time and it wasn't much better for me, Harps and Terry. This was still early on in my Newcastle career but me and Harps had really bonded and we pushed each other as much as we could.

As always happens with a new manager, there were plenty of changes in personnel. Gullit didn't help us or himself much by getting rid of Steve Watson, a local lad and a footballer who could slot in pretty much anywhere on the field. He was off to Aston Villa which didn't make sense to me. He was just the kind of club heartbeat we needed.

Despite that, we did recruit some top players, lads like Dietmar Hamann from Bayern Munich and Nobby Solano from Boca Juniors. They were quality performers who brought loads of bounce and personality to the squad.

Hamann was an exciting signing for us because it's not every day you nab a Bayern Munich player. For me that showed a lot of intent from the board.

For the first few weeks he'd been in to training, you could see he was a super professional and clearly a seriously good player. We had a night out in Newcastle as a team-bonding exercise and I didn't know if he was going to come or not. He was German, from a European super-club and he was surely going to be a bit straight, a bit too professional and serious to enjoy a mad night out with us lot? I got that one wrong.

We went to a place on the quayside for dinner and I was weighing him up. I reckoned he'd be on the water and salads all night while we tucked into steaks and glugged Guinness. All of a sudden, he grabbed hold of his beer, necked it in one, turned to Derek Wright, the physio, and said, "Get that down your fat head." That'll do for me! He fitted straight in. So much for salad and water. He was all about chips and beer.

There was a nightclub called Julie's down by the quayside. When I first got to Newcastle I don't think I realised just how big a party city it was but I'd soon learnt that it was mad as fuck for a night out. Hamann loved the craic but he always turned up the next day, ready to go. Nobby Solano was in the same mould – mad as anything yet also completely dedicated to his job.

Nobby was – and still is – a great character. He was such a funny lad. He'd bring this trumpet with him everywhere. You'd be at training and you'd hear him before you'd see him. We shared training facilities with Durham County Cricket Club at Chester-le-Street. You'd be getting changed in the morning and suddenly you'd hear this trumpet bellowing down a narrow corridor, ripping our eardrums out. I know some footballers like to blow their own trumpet but he did it literally! He'd sneak up on people too and let them have it – *The Last Post* blaring out at full volume.

Nobby was that nuts I think he even joined a samba band in Newcastle. He absolutely loved the place. He was more or less a Geordie within about 10 days. He learned the language quickly and had a brilliant personality to go with his skills. What a wand of a right foot. He would whip it in with his instep, outstep, whatever; he could do the lot. In training he'd always tell all the

British lads to relax when they had possession. "Hey, hey, it's a ball, not a bomb, calm down." Every dressing room needs a lunatic, it's about getting the mixture right and he was the right kind of person we needed.

I invited him round to my house one day for a BBQ. He turned up with a couple of cases of this Casa Modelo beer. "Nobby, what are you eating mate?" I asked him, all ready to cook something up. "Shay, nothing, nothing," he said. "I'll do it." He'd brought these big bags of meat with him, full with slabs of steak and chops. "You just keep bringing me the Modelos," he said. "I've got this." He spent all day on the BBQ, cooking away, making people laugh – and drinking these beers. He'd still be there now if I kept him supplied with Modelos.

*****

On the pitch in 1998/99, the losses kept coming and we just couldn't get a foothold in the table or really start making any progress anywhere, including the League Cup where we lost in a penalty shootout to one of my old teams, Blackburn.

The good news was that great players kept signing for the club. Dunc Ferguson announced his arrival in style, scoring two in a 3-1 win against Wimbledon in November. It's since been revealed that Dunc didn't fancy Newcastle – well, Newcastle certainly fancied him.

My first thought when I met him was that he was fucking huge! You didn't mess with Dunc. Some of the stuff he would do in the gym would scare me. He was a machine on the punch bag. I wouldn't like to fight him. I'd throw a punch, run and hope he didn't catch me. Duncan was also a really good lad to have around the club and would always get stuck in to the piss-taking that went on constantly.

After a great start, he had a few issues with injuries but a fully fit Duncan Ferguson and Alan Shearer up front would scare any team. You can imagine the teamsheet dropping in the away team's dressing room. They knew if one didn't get them then the other would. Al and Dunc didn't play together enough to be honest but they could've struck up a really lethal combination. It was like having two bouncers up front.

During training sessions, Terry Gennoe would push us hard and we enjoyed it but there was always an edge to training. We would have a drill where you had to step and drive into the corner, to make sure you had shots on goal covered. Pavel Srnicek had originally taught that to Harps and he developed that with me. Lionel Perez also came in around this time and used to train in a cricket box because of the way he dived around like a big starfish and left himself exposed somewhere very tender indeed.

We left everything out there, every day – and that is the part of the game the public doesn't see. In the cold, in the pouring rain and snow we would be out there, pushing ourselves and each other.

One morning, in the absolute depths of winter – and winter in Newcastle really is winter by the way – we were doing a training drill at Chester-le-Street and Terry had been out early to find some part of the training pitch that wasn't frozen over. The only bit he could find was next to this hedge with the River Wear running behind it. The grass was a bit longer which pro-tected us from the hard ground.

Halfway through this drill, I made a mistake and kicked the

ball away in frustration. I hated making mistakes and it was just an instinctive reaction. It sailed over the hedge and into the river. "Fuck's sake Shay!" Terry shouted. "That's that gone then isn't it?" It was absolutely freezing and we all trudged beyond the hedge to see this ball bobbing on the water. The next thing, Harps gets one of those rubber ring lifebelts that are stationed next to rivers and is trying to lasso the ball. Can you imagine that now? Can you imagine Premier League goalkeepers bothering to rescue a training ball from a river?!

All of a sudden, this rubber ring slips through Harps' fingers so now there's a football and a rubber ring, heading off to the North Sea. Terry looked around and saw a million pound goalkeeper here, another one there and came to the conclusion that Newcastle United Football Club could afford to lose its goalkeeper coach but not any of its actual goalkeepers. "Off you go then," I told him, not believing he would even do it.

Fair play, he stripped down to his boxers and jumped in. As he hit the water, you could hear all the breath leave his lungs, it was that cold, but good on him, he got the ball and the rubber ring. He staggered out, his skin going a nice shade of purplish blue, his teeth chattering at a hundred miles per hour. "Fffor fffffuck's sssssake Sssshayy," he said. "Nooo mo-mo-morrre missstakes todayyy please."

We all had this desire to never make an error, even on the training ground and nobody wanted mistakes less than Terry, especially that day.

It didn't end there either. Paul Winsper, the fitness coach, was doing a warm-down with the team and Big Dunc had clocked Terry's little swimming lesson. "I bet you couldn't do that," Dunc said to Paul. "Go on, I dare you." Before you knew it, money's been discussed, bets have been made and Paul's jumped in too, just to prove that he could! Paul was as fit as a fiddle and breezed it. The pair of them got quickly changed, teeth chattering, and while Terry got the flu, Paul got a fortune!

On a day-to-day level, Gullit kept himself to himself – he was often to be found checking out his own reflection in the little training room he and the other coaches used – and despite that, the atmosphere around the dressing room and amongst the players was actually really good at the time.

At Christmas, we did a Secret Santa. It was the usual; names came out of a hat and you had to buy someone a stupid present. Now Alessandro Pistone was always injured, he always had tight hamstrings and if he didn't feel one hundred per cent he wouldn't play. A few of us questioned his heart and that gave me the perfect idea for a tongue-in-cheek Christmas present.

After pulling his name out, the next thing I know, I'm in the butcher's. "One heart please," I said. "The full works." It was a proper lamb's heart, full of veins and bits hanging off, the lot. I wrapped it in Christmas paper and gave it to him. He was not happy, but the rest of us fell about laughing.

Dietmar Hamann was bought a copy of 'Mein Kampf' by some thoughtful individual while Big Dunc rang every safari and zoo in the north-east as he tried to get a llama for Nobby Solano. It's a good job he didn't actually, Nobby would only have ended up riding it around the training ground while blasting out his trumpet.

I was falling about at the presents – Temuri Ketsbaia got a hairbrush – but soon enough, the laughs were on me. A couple of weeks before the Christmas do, Alan had come up to me quietly for a word. "I need a favour, can I have a couple of signed gloves for charity," he asked. I quickly found a pair, signed them and handed them over, happy to help. I never thought anything of it until I got my Christmas present.

Alan, God bless him, had bought a shop mannequin and stuck my signed gloves on him. That was his subtle way of letting me know how agile he thought I was. "He moves far better than you do," he laughed. To make matters worse, the mannequin's head had a massive cardboard box stuck on it, in tribute to my nickname as 'Boxhead'. Everyone was falling about again, just as they were when Paul Dalglish was given a football on a string – the joke being that he might then be able to control the ball for a change!

Life around the training ground was always light-hearted although Georgios Georgiadis, the Greek winger who'd joined from Panathinaikos, definitely disagreed one day.

When we trained at the Chester-le-Street, there was one pitch in the middle of the athletic track. The rest of the place was pretty open and members of the public would walk around or walk their dogs in the wide open space.

George was doing some warm-up laps one day, stumbled and fell over – right into Tyneside's biggest pile of dogshit. He was covered in it, all over his legs and hands. Somebody must've walked a lion across the training ground, never mind a dog. We were as sympathetic as ever to our team-mate's terrible plight.

*****

Christmas came and went with our form remaining patchy in the Premier League. The one bonus was how well we were doing in the FA Cup again. We beat Crystal Palace, Bradford

City, Blackburn Rovers (after a replay), thrashed Everton and then it was time for a second consecutive semi-final, this time against Tottenham Hotspur.

I'd actually been sent off against Crystal Palace in the third round. A ball came over the top, it hit my knee then my arm and the referee waved play on. It was totally accidental. I didn't try and handball it and that should have been that. The linesman thought otherwise and started waving his flag. Next thing, I'm sent off – for the only time in my career. I was raging, and to make matters worse, as I was walking down the tunnel, Lee Bradbury put them 1-0 in front. Thankfully we turned it around but it wasn't a nice feeling. And the linesman who was convinced I had handballed it? A bloke called Howard Webb. What happened to him?

The semi-final was another special atmosphere. It went to extra-time and was tense but Al converted a penalty and then scored a brilliant goal, driving it in off the underside of the bar to send the fans crazy and leave Gullit dancing on the sideline. Ruud was telling us we could be heroes in the final against Manchester United and I had everything to look forward to, or at least I thought I did.

In the six weeks leading up to the game, me and Steve were both in and out of the team, as if Gullit couldn't really decide what he wanted to do. I played in a 3-1 home loss to Everton, Steve came in for a draw with Sheffield Wednesday, then I was back for another draw with Wimbledon before Steve played three Premier League matches on the trot: a draw with Middlesbrough, a loss to Leicester and another draw with Blackburn. Harps had the gloves but I'd played in all the FA Cup matches and expected to come back in for the final.

Meanwhile, in the coaches' training room at Chester-le-Street, which was just a smaller changing room where the coaches got changed, Ruud had decided to drop me but didn't have the character to come and tell me to my face. "Go and tell 'your mate' he's not playing next week," he told Terry Gennoe, whose job it was to break the bad news to me. "I will go and tell him" Terry told him. "You should be doing it – but you're not big enough." That's how life was at the club at the time – everybody was at each other's throats.

"They're going with Harps," he said. "I wish he'd told you himself but there you go."

"What the fuck?" I asked. "What's the reason?" This was not Terry's doing and it shouldn't have been his job to tell me. He explained Ruud's thinking.

"Your kicking is putting too much pressure on the team," he said. That was a lame excuse. Maybe my kicking was a bit weak at the time but I was still doing everything else really well.

Ruud should've had the balls to tell me, to look me in the eye. He was the manager and this was the FA Cup final. I'd played in every round, I'd not been a passenger – I'd made some good saves and helped get us there. It was the wrong decision and it made it worse that Terry had to do his dirty work. Terry himself left the club shortly afterwards to join Kenny up at Celtic. Another good man with a lot of experience and football knowledge going through the St James' exit door for no real reason.

That was it for me and Ruud. When a man does that to you, how are you going to respect him?

I suppose, looking back, it was an early crossroads in my career and it made me a stronger person. I could've crumbled at being dropped, I could've disappeared forever but I would not let it beat me. It wasn't the first real setback I'd faced, it certainly wouldn't be the last, and I had to try and find the positives and come through it.

It was a tricky situation because me and Harps had a really good relationship so I couldn't get too downhearted because I knew what a massive moment it was in his life.

We got on great together and he would know I was devastated but, equally, I had to keep spirits up for his sake. He was a local lad, the FA Cup final was only his eighth start so it was the stuff of dreams for him. The year before I think he'd been cup-tied so watched the match from the stands with his family and mates. Now he was playing in the final 12 months later. That takes some doing.

In the dressing room before the game, Ruud was still banging on about us becoming heroes to anybody who would listen but for me, the day itself is a bit of a daze. You're on the floor but you can't show it for the sake of the team, for Harps and for the entire club. It felt like I was there but I wasn't there at the same time, you know? It felt surreal.

We lost 2-0, the same as we had when I'd been in goal the year before and, again, it was the dressing room was completely shattered afterwards.

For the second time, we got on the bus to go back home and again the fans were everywhere, still supporting us. I felt for Harps, told him there had been nothing he could do for the goals and did my best to lift him.

We had a dinner that night, which we needed about as much as Ketsbaia needed that hairbrush, and Ruud made a speech about how losing was new to him and it wasn't what he had come to Newcastle for. You see what I mean about being tone deaf, about missing the point? He was all me, me, me, I, I, I.

*****

The obsession with control and being the top dog at the club was, for me, the undoing of Gullit in the end. After the summer, we began the 1999/2000 season with three straight losses and then a draw before we were due to play Sunderland at St James' Park.

I was actually injured for that game. I remember the big main stand was being done. Oh yes, I also remember the single stupidest decision ever made by a Newcastle manager.

Life for Al under Gullit had got progressively worse to the stage where they were just ignoring each other completely. Al had been given a big new contract by Freddy Shepherd that made his life easier but Rob Lee was still getting the cold shoulder, especially when new signing Kieron Dyer was given his shirt. It was just ridiculous, the petty antics of a man who wanted to be seen to be the biggest and best in the club.

I don't know if he couldn't deal with Rob's status in the club or Al being the hometown hero – who knows? – but when he dropped Alan and also Duncan Ferguson for that match, and rubbed it in by picking Sunderland fan Paul Robinson instead, Gullit had just packed his own bags and didn't even realise.

We lost that night as Niall Quinn and Kevin Phillips scored for Sunderland after Dyer's opener and although Alan and Duncan came on, we couldn't pull it back.

Al was in first thing the next morning – about 8am – to see Ruud and ask him what the hell was going on. He got to his office door and Duncan was already there, ready to do the same thing! Both of them, ready to have it out.

It was so tense around the place, something had to give and, in the end, Gullit was out of the door.

His recent behaviour had not really had any affect on me because I had zero relationship with him by this point. He was very aloof and stand-offish and I was still very young and inexperienced. I was not going to barge his door down like Al and Duncan were ready to do.

Maybe it was the way I was brought up to respect my elders, I don't know, but I was never going to cause trouble at the time. Sure enough, I soon didn't have to worry about him at all.

There was zero disappointment in the dressing room when he left. I certainly didn't care one bit and me, Rob Lee and Al all had a wry smile or two.

Personally speaking, I think the decision to drop Al and Duncan and therefore speed up his exit was because he was resigned to the fact he was going anyhow. I don't know if he wanted a pay-out or to be sacked or what because it was a decision that was always going to cause trouble.

I genuinely think he wanted to move Alan on too. I think he wanted to show that Newcastle could win a derby without him and that would've given him the chance to say we could cope without Shearer. It was all madness. He'd even come out and said the Tyne-Wear derby wasn't that big a deal and that he'd played in bigger. Again, tone deaf.

Again, me, me, me.

On top of all that, the results were simply not good enough either. We were now a lower mid-table side, at best, and that was a long way away from where we'd been under Kevin and then Kenny and that means, in the black and white world of football – and the black and white world of Newcastle – that you lose your job.

It was time for Newcastle to get back to being a club that had a smile on its face. Fortunately enough, the man to do that was right around the corner.

# 8

# WHERE'S MY FUTURE?

THERE are right fits and wrong fits at all football clubs.

Football clubs aren't normal businesses or companies. The chief executive of one company could probably walk straight across the road and through the front door of another and be just as comfortable in the job.

No, football clubs have a heartbeat and a pace and a rhythm about them and it is crucial that the manager – the most important person at the club – understands what makes it tick. Bobby Robson certainly knew what made Newcastle United tick.

By the time he replaced Gullit, both he and the squad were as thrilled as can be.

Bobby wanted to get to know you and wanted to work out how to get the best from you. He had us all in early on for a little meeting, asking us about our families and the club and whether or not we could cope with the pressures of playing for Newcastle United.

The buzz he gave the place was massive, especially for local lads like John Carver, Alan and Harps.

The change in our approach under Bobby came almost immediately although, for me personally, I was injured with a knee cartilage so Harps stayed in goal until I returned to fitness in October 1999. Then I went back into the first-team.

After taking over a side at the bottom of the Premier League, that first season under Bobby was little more than a rebuilding job as we got to know him and he got to know us. We hauled the club back on to its feet and although we lost to Roma in the UEFA Cup (we'd qualified for the competition because we'd been runners-up in the FA Cup final), it felt like we were slowly going places.

The fans' highlight that year was a trip to Wembley. Were we going back there for a third consecutive FA Cup final? No. The decision had been made to stage semi-finals at Wembley – not something I agreed with, as I've already said. It didn't seem fair, either. We were facing Chelsea, whose fans could crawl there in half an hour whereas the Geordie Nation would have to travel the length of the country. Still, I couldn't moan too much because I was delighted to be Bobby's first choice for the game.

Neither me or Harps were what you'd call settled in the goal-keeping position under Bobby when he first arrived. I played a few, he played a few, I played a few, he played a few. My knee problem didn't help and Harps was in good form as well. Apart from getting dropped by Gullit the year before, I'd been brought to the club to be the No. 1 so this new shaky ground wasn't what I was after at all.

On the day of the semi-final against Chelsea, Bobby was in his absolute element. Returning to the north-east and taking over at St James' Park had been done for days like this. The spotlight was on Bobby and his players and he loved that.

Before any match he was always keen to make the foreign lads realise exactly what the club meant to the people of Newcastle. "These people have paid a lot of money to come down here and watch you," he said. "They believe in you and I believe in you, so go and win the match and then we can come down here again and really give them something to cheer."

When I look back on the match, the fact it was two goals from Gus Poyet that did for us still leaves me chewing. He always seemed to score against me. Poyet was well known, famous even, for those late runs into the box and no one went with him. For the first goal, he lobbed me early on after getting in behind. We then lost Duncan Ferguson to injury which didn't help but Rob Lee absolutely smashed a header in after a superb cross from Al and we were back in it. Then Poyet's header late on beat me. We were all going home from Wembley with nothing to show for it. Again.

When we beat Arsenal at home on the last day of the season, we had done enough to eventually finish 11th. In the space of 10 or so months, Bobby had taken us from bottom but, more importantly, he'd brought some spark and life and self-belief back to the club.

The squad were back to their old ways, laughing and socialising together a fair bit and me, Harps, Al, Warren Barton, Speedo and Rob Lee would often be found out and about together.

Warren – who used to get stick for trying to look like a hairdresser – and his wife Candy used to sort out a lot of trips and meals. If we were travelling, he would always organise the bus and there'd be champagne on the journey for everyone. Sometimes he'd have a Murder Mystery night at his house. We had a big off-the-field togetherness and we took that onto the pitch which definitely helped the team. That kind of thing has changed over the years. These days you don't really socialise any more with your team-mates. You don't get to know people's personalities or what makes them tick. At Newcastle, we would always welcome a new player, go for a night out and get to know each other.

One night we went to a restaurant in Durham called Cathedrals. It started out as a civilised evening but then it descended into chaos as usual. After filling up with lager I decided to mix it with red wine and as we started the bus trip back to Newcastle, the lethal combination of drinks decided to pop up and say hello. I sat there with a bucket on my lap all the way back. Trust me, Durham is a long way from Newcastle when you're holding a bucket of spew in your hands. The lads were typically sympathetic though, especially Dr Shearer, who was checking I was ok by sitting next to me, pissing himself laughing while he whacked me around the head every two minutes.

There was a little restaurant called Louis on Osborne Road in Jesmond and we would head down there a fair bit as well. You could pop in during the week and there'd always be some of the squad in there having dinner and letting their hair down. The New Rendezvous Chinese was also a popular spot.

If we were heading out into town, a great guy called Steve Burns would look after all the lads and we'd start in his pub, The Black Bull, which is close to St James' Park.

It was nothing to look at but it was a great place to begin and then it would be Julie's, The Apartment, Jimmyz, The Quilted

# WHERE'S MY FUTURE?

Camel and a load of other places. There was never any trouble, it was always just a good night out and that was probably down to Steve, who always made sure we got in and out of places in one piece together. He used to sometimes organise away days for the fans and was a big bloke who you wouldn't want to mess with either.

I was a happy man then inside a happy squad at Newcastle at the end of Bobby's first season. We were heading in the right direction, the whole feel of the place was positive and I was doing well for club and country.

Why then, you might ask, was I looking to get out of the place just six months later?

*****

In the run-up to Christmas during the 2000/01 season, I picked up an injury in a 2-0 loss to Derby County and I was replaced by Harps at half-time. Until that point in the season, I'd been the first-choice keeper. I'd played about 20 matches and signed a new four-year deal in September 2000 so until that thigh problem I had little to really worry about.

The problem with my thigh had been a niggle for a while but I was soon ok and I expected to go back into the side immediately, only to be told that Harps would be kept in for a Boxing Day match with Leeds United that we won. He then kept his place for the next few games over the New Year period.

At the training ground and around the team I was doing an Oscar-worthy impression of somebody comfortable with Bobby's choice but inside I was raging.

From the age of 16, I always wanted to play. Every match I

was missing was a match I couldn't get back; that was gone, forever.

All this was building up in my head. I knew I was good enough to play in the Premier League and I wanted to be on the team-sheet. You only have one career and it's short enough (though maybe mine is longer than others!) and I just thought, 'I need to get out of here, I need to be playing football.'

Because of Bobby's decision to stick with Harps, I suddenly came to the idea that I wanted to leave Newcastle.

Looking back, I might have been a bit young and hot-headed but at that time it felt like the right thing to do. I talked it through with Dad and Michael Kennedy, my solicitor, because I wanted to get a wider opinion. "Well if that's how you feel, you have to go," Dad said. "You can't waste your life sat on a bench. If you need to go, you go."

That was all the advice I needed to hear.

After an FA Cup draw against Aston Villa, with Harps still in goal, I handed in a written request to Bobby and Freddy Shepherd. I think it shocked Bobby more than Freddy because I'd been to see him in his office the previous week. "Boss, I should be playing," I'd told him. "I'm fit again and I didn't sign a new deal to sit on the bench."

"Leave it with me son," he said. I think he thought those words would be enough to calm me down. Instead, another match slipped by and my head exploded. I think Bobby was frustrated that I hadn't spoken to him in more depth before I put in the request but by that point I was committed and would genuinely have left.

I released a statement to the press that I think still represents both my feelings about it then and my feelings about it all now.

# WHERE'S MY FUTURE?

It read as follows…

*The board have told me that they will give me a decision later in the week and in the meantime I will train with enthusiasm. I thought that my consistency in the 20 or so early-season games would have meant an early recall. When this did not happen and I was given no explanation, I felt I had no other way of making my feelings known. There are many players who would not have reacted in this way, but I am a passionate and committed player, desperate for Newcastle to do well.*

Harps knew I wasn't happy but I can honestly say it wasn't awkward between us. We were really great friends and, in all honesty, I think it's good I was in that mood.

As a manager, you don't want players happy to sit around. You want them to be frustrated and eager to get out there. Surely, you want footballers who want to play football? I was hungry to play and to perform for Newcastle.

Harps was exactly the same. He would go and see Bobby all the time when I was No.1 and ask him if he could go out on loan. Bobby wouldn't let him – he wanted two top-class goalkeepers at the club at all times. Harps was certainly that.

After my statement was released, the papers in Newcastle had a field day. Alan Oliver on the *Evening Chronicle* could be brutal. The paper is massive in the city – people buy that before a national newspaper – and it carried so much sway and influence. Alan would back you if you'd done something good but he'd let you have it if he wanted to. Laurent Robert once tried to swing for him in the press room at Newcastle after he'd been given a four out of 10 in the paper. The press was full of 'who does he think he is?' stuff but I wasn't being arrogant or after a move: I just wanted to play football. It was a difficult time but Harps totally showed his class. You'd never have guessed we were competing for the same spot.

For example, I had this mad habit of always tapping my hands hard into my gloves when getting set and it would be Harps who would spot if I was off a bit, because I wouldn't be doing it.

"Shay, get forward, get forward, tap your hands," he'd shout at me, knowing that something wasn't right. It's the little things like that, the body language, that we'd recognise in each other. Steve could've downed tools and done nothing to help me. He could've taken a step back and just let me struggle but that's not the kind of man and friend he is.

I can't speak highly enough of him.

I always knew he was there and that he could've played instead of me at any time. He should've played for England, he was that good. That also scared me. I knew that if I let my game slip by even one per cent then Harps was capable enough and big enough to end my Newcastle career for good.

My transfer request also didn't affect my relationship with any of the other players. At the time, I was so in the zone I wouldn't have noticed anyway. As I say, I was at a level where I felt I should've been playing in the Premier League week in and week out. I was fighting for my career.

We were on the bus on the way to Villa for the FA Cup replay and I was handed a letter to say the club were refusing my transfer request. It was a relief in a way because I hadn't really wanted to leave in the first place. No part of me had any desire to go but, even still, I had to register my disappointment somehow and a formal transfer request back then was the best way of doing it.

Eventually, with me not budging and the club not budging, it all came to a head. I met with Bobby one day in his office. "Shay, you need to withdraw this request son," he said. "You need to get your head down, focus on playing and focus on Newcastle."

I'd been recalled by this point for a 3-1 away win at Elland Road – where the fans gave me a massive ovation, which meant an awful lot – so I was playing again and it was a natural step to officially retract the request. "Boss, all I'd wanted to do was show how much I wanted to play for Newcastle and how frustrated I was," I told him, honestly. "I know son, I know," he said. "Let's get this business finished." I quickly wrote a letter to the board to withdraw my request and that resolved everything. It was good to be back in the team and back on solid ground. I hadn't been tapped up, I hadn't asked for more money, I hadn't wanted anything other than the No.1 spot back and now I had it, everything was fine. Bobby, being Bobby, ensured it was water under the bridge straight away.

That year, 2000/01, was another season of consolidation. It won't go down as a record breaker by any stretch of the imagination. We again finished 11th. Al was playing with pain-killing injections which didn't help and signings like Lomanu LuaLua, Carl Cort and Diego Gavilan had not produced.

From the start it was clear to me that LuaLua was off his head. We were in training one day and he came and sat down next to me afterwards, looking all serious and devout. Just as we were getting changed, he piped up.

"Shay, I have something to tell you," he said. "I once saw a man turn into a snake." What the fuck?! I was like, "Lua, seriously. That's enough now."

"Shay, SHAY, I promise you, promise you, it's true. A man became a snake." Lua was blessing himself, everything. "He was stood in front of me, and the next thing – he was a snake." "Shut up, no chance, no chance," I was telling him. He was deadly serious. "I know you won't believe me but I would never lie to you Shay." I never did get to the bottom of it.

Another one was Temuri Ketsbaia. He is best known for the night he lashed his shirt into the crowd while he was kicking the hell out of the sponsor board after scoring against Bolton in January 1998.

That wasn't the half of it. We went paintballing on a team-bonding day in the middle of nowhere once and we got split into two teams. Straight away, Rob Lee shot Harps straight on the hamstring. No problem with that I suppose, apart from the fact they were on the same team. We were all crying with laughter from the off, taking the piss, but Temuri, being the Mad Monk, just legged it straight for the opposition base and was so pumped up he kept firing at everything and everyone he could see, screaming his head off. "TAKE THAT MOTHER-FUCKERS" he was shouting, completely lost in the red mist.

After training one day, Temuri was not happy about getting overlooked and he was having a go at Bobby outside. Don't mistake Bobby's softly-spoken Geordie tones for a gentle person; he was hard as nails and was giving Temuri as good as he was getting. The next thing, Temuri dug around in his pocket and launched a mobile phone at Bobby. It somehow missed him before he stormed off. Bobby knew it was best to leave it – some Mad Monk battles could not be won.

# WHERE'S MY FUTURE?

Another player who Bobby didn't have much time for was Marcelino Elena. He was someone who just didn't live up to his pre-transfer billing. He was a big strong centre-half. Or at least he should have been. I think he missed about four months of one season with a finger tendon problem after getting injured against Manchester United and I just couldn't work him out. As a centre-half, wasn't he was meant to be the toughest on the pitch? Maybe I'm doing him a disservice, I don't know, but if you break your little finger you'd like to think you could strap it up and get on with it. He came in to training after an operation and he was covered in plaster. He looked like someone off *Naked Gun*. His elbow was out here, his arm was over there… he looked ridiculous.

Aiming to improve on our mid-table finish, we bought Craig Bellamy and Laurent Robert over the summer of 2001 and Craig, at £6m, was a real steal.

He was the kind of player who needed a kind word from the manager every now and then if we were going to get the best from him. Fortunately, Bobby was the best in the world at making you feel important. He rang Craig when the deal was done to tell him how much he admired him and said he wanted to help him squeeze the most out of his talent.

Craig was a great trainer, a hard worker and he left it all on the pitch. He was young at a big club but that didn't faze him at all. He had incredibly high standards and he was the perfect foil for Alan, who was playing more with his back to goal. Bellers could run in behind him and open some holes up in the defence.

The public persona of Craig and the real person are probably two different people.

Bellamy was Marmite for his entire career – probably still is –

but even his biggest enemies would never say that he didn't try his very best every day and, when it comes down to it, what else can you ask of a man?

"For fuck's sake that was shite," he'd happily shout in training if a pass went astray or he felt somebody was chucking it in. He didn't mind who he said it to, either, whether it was a senior player like Rob or Al or one of the young lads. I'd give him plenty back if he needed taking down a peg or two but I was privately delighted he was like that. Some people needed a rocket up their arse and he'd be happy to stand there with a box of matches.

Craig's mentality meant that he could be a world beater on his day but unfortunately for him, he struggled badly with injuries and he had some really bad knee trouble at Newcastle. That got him down and he withdrew from the main group a bit as he hammered the rehab. Even when he was injured, his professionalism couldn't be knocked – he was always in the gym, always eating right and trying his best. He would do a ton of stretches, pre-activation work and whatever else it took.

The way he and Bobby used to fall out was hilarious for the rest of us. I wouldn't describe their relationship as father and son, it was probably closer to frustrated headteacher and naughty pupil.

We got to St James' Park one day before a game and matchday rules were that you wore your club suit. Craig turned up in his, as per the club's instructions. Then you looked down at his feet and saw he was wearing trainers. Bobby went crazy. "Fucking hell son, what you wearing, get them off son, get them off," his face was becoming redder by the second. Craig wasn't having any of it. "Boss, I was watching the Serie A on telly last night and Christian Vieri turned up at the San Siro in trainers," he said. "Why can't I?" "Because…BECAUSE, SON, this is Newcastle United Football Club and you will not wear fucking trainers with a fucking suit here." The rest of us just sat there shaking our heads, trying not to giggle.

Another time, Craig got stitched up by a mate of mine called Mark Devlin. Mark was the son of Pat Devlin, the scout who had tipped Kenny Dalglish off about me after the Celtic talks had broken down. Me and Mark met just before I'd come across to England and we hit it straight off.

Fortunately for him, he got a job working for Adidas as a kit representative so he ended up working and living within a couple of miles of me in Newcastle and that was great. It was a friendly face and a mate in the area and it turned out Newcastle were the only club in the Premier League at the time with an Adidas kit so I got to see plenty of him.

Under Bobby he came into the training ground one day to show us next season's kit and that was the kind of thing Craig would love to wind Mark up about. Sure enough, during this meeting, as Mark revealed the kits, Craig started piping up about how bad they looked. "Shit Mark, these are shit," he was saying but Mark was ready. "Well Craig, you'll have no bother," he said. "The reserves won't be wearing these ones anyway." The training ground erupted and even Bobby just had a wee little grin on his face, only a small one, but enough to let Mark know he'd impressed him!

Before the 2001/02 Premier League season started, we'd done really well in the Intertoto Cup, a European competition I never really understood the point – or format – of. We'd been offered a late spot after Malaga pulled out which meant our season began in mid-July. It all ended when we drew 4-4 with Troyes in a mad match at St James' Park in the second leg of the final. We were 4-1 down at one point but got back to 4-4, only to lose on away goals.

Back in the Premier League, we drew with Chelsea and Sunderland in our first two games and then hit a winning groove. Bellamy, Robert and Shearer just clicked. All of a sudden we had speed and direction down both sides, crosses were landed where we wanted them and we were inching victories out of games we would once have lost.

We beat Middlesbrough 4-1 at their place and then edged out Manchester United 4-3 at St James' Park. Robert was absolutely on fire, helping to give Bobby a famous win in his 100th match in charge. Roy Keane wasn't such a happy man – seeing red in the 90th minute.

By the time we visited Arsenal in December we'd won nine out of 16 matches and were on the hunt to end a record we didn't like. The Highbury match was the 30th game since our last win in London, going back to 1997. We were desperate to change that statistic, not least because it meant we would go top of the Premier League.

The build-up for the match was disastrous. The old Highbury was a nightmare to get to, the traffic was carnage and the coach couldn't get there. "Quick, hurry lads!" Bobby was shouting. We were virtually changing on the bus.

Bobby absolutely despised being late, he was a real stickler for punctuality. He had this mad saying about trains. "Son, if you get to the train station at 1pm and your train is at 1pm, you've missed it. Get there 10 minutes early son, 10 minutes early. It's the same with my meetings or the team bus. Get there early.

Don't miss my train son." Bobby was going crazy at the coach driver as we crept closer to the stadium.

"What's happening, what's going on? Who organised this, this is a fucking scandal!"

We eventually got to Highbury, spilled out, dashed to the dressing rooms, had a quick warm-up – and won 3-1! That Arsenal side had Patrick Vieira, Thierry Henry, Sol Campbell, Ashley Cole and so on – they were a class act. Not having too much time to think about who we were playing probably helped. Sometimes, maybe you should just go out and play on instinct.

We headed for Leeds next and we were losing 3-1 until Robbie Elliot gave us some hope. Al then equalised with a penalty before Kieron Dyer put Nobby Solano through in the dying seconds and he won it for us by slotting past Nigel Martyn. I can just remember hearing the Newcastle fans in Elland Road making enough noise for 50,000. They'd picked up St James' Park, put the place in their pocket and moved it to West Yorkshire. We were on fire, Bobby was going crazy on the touchlines afterwards and Kieron Dyer was superb, really offering a glimpse of what he could have been if he'd stayed fit.

Kieron's story was a sad one because he just had so many injuries – mainly problems with his hamstrings and lower back. That kind of issue is common when you have so much pace. Physio and sports science has obviously come on a lot since then – he'd probably get sorted pretty quickly these days. Back then, it was a game changer. Bobby treated Kieron like his son, because of the Ipswich Town connection. His man-management probably got the best out of him.

The Leeds win kept us top. We were becoming a bit like Leicester City when they won it or when Liverpool went so close under Brendan Rodgers. The country was starting to genuinely wake up and think, 'They can't…can they?'

After the Elland Road win on December 22, Bobby's message to us was that we were on the verge of becoming a really good side – but we were not quite there yet. He was right, I suppose, but we genuinely thought we had a chance of winning the title.

Over the New Year we lost to Chelsea and United which hurt our chances and although January and February was great for us with five league wins in six, Craig's knee trouble flared up after we beat Sunderland and when we then lost 2-0 at home against Arsenal we had reached a turning point for the season. And not in a good way.

The likes of Manchester United and Arsenal will inch away from you over the course of a season if they do have that extra slice of luck with injuries or that extra show of class from time to time. Losing Craig was massive for us and Arsenal showed they had more talent to call upon during that win at St James' Park.

You'll remember the goal Dennis Bergkamp scored that day.

Did he mean it or not? That's the big question 20 years on.

First things first: where's 20 years gone? I put on Twitter a while back that he'd had a bad first touch and it was a fluke, which brought me plenty of abuse!

What I remember of it is that Nikos Dabizas got too close to Bergkamp. That was the biggest mistake in the world against a player as amazing as Dennis. Dabizas was brilliant in the air but his positional error that day was the green light for Bergkamp to try something different.

And, for the record, I DO believe he meant it. A player like him is three seconds ahead of everyone else, he chanced his arm and you have to applaud that. Eventually. It only takes 20 years…

# WHERE'S MY FUTURE?

Nikos was a decent player but he wasn't shy of passing back to me when he was in trouble which usually led to me being in even more bother than he was. He'd just lash it in my direction and go, "Thanks Shay" as I dealt with the problem of an awkward bouncing ball. I'd see 'Dabizas 34' running in the opposite direction and with no other options available, I'd sometimes have to shank it into the crowd – cheers 'mate'!

The loss to Arsenal was followed by one to Liverpool and then a draw against Ipswich Town. In the space of a fortnight any hopes of winning the title looked to be over. At the same time, Arsenal also beat us in the FA Cup in a Highbury replay and the season then looked completely different.

Arsenal won their last 13 matches that season to win the league while we only won six during the same period. We had given it everything, Al was still scoring goals by the second but we ran out of steam, finally finishing the 2001/02 season in fourth spot.

From 11th to fourth was a brilliant turnaround for us and says more about Bobby's man-management skills than any other statistic. We'd earned 71 points, we'd given ourselves a Champions League chance, we had a boss we all loved, a stadium that was as good as any in the country, the best fans you could ask for and we were back as a force in the Premier League.

I joined up with Ireland's 2002 World Cup in a confident mood, raring to go and ready to show the planet that not only was I one of the best goalkeepers in the world but I was playing for a country that would do everything in its power to cause a shock or two and be one of the World Cup's biggest talking points.

Oh yes, we certainly managed that...

# 9

# MICK AND ROY

"*C'mon get in here!*"

*It's 7.30pm on Thursday, May 23, 2002.*

*In the ballroom of the Hyatt Regency on the tiny island of Saipan, Gary Kelly, being insane, is up for the craic.*

*Most of the squad are sat around in shorts and flip-flops, sweat still running off us despite the air con whirring.*

*Around three big round tables sits Ireland's 2002 World Cup squad. Two of the tables are full but on the third there's only Kevin Kilbane, Niall Quinn and Steve Finnan.*

*Kev and Quinny were late down from the room they were sharing – the two of them are big mates – so sat on the remaining empty table before helping themselves to some pasta from the buffet.*

*Next thing, Roy Keane comes in and sits with them.*

*This is strange – Roy is never late for anything. He turns to Kev and says, "It's going to go off tonight."*

*Gary Kelly doesn't know what's going on, though.*

"*C'mon get in here!*"

# SHAY

*The Hyatt Regency has an in-house band playing in the next room and Gary wants to have a bit of fun.*

*"C'mon, get in here!" he shouts again at the band, inviting them into the plush surroundings that have become our make-shift canteen. They march in with their grass skirts and ukuleles and start performing. Next thing, we're all up on the tables, taking the piss, having a dance to this band who were loving it.*

*A moment of so later, Mick walks through the door, stands very respectfully while the band finishes 'Stand By Me' and then politely asks them to leave.*

*They shuffle out of the door.*

*Mick asks for a bit of quiet, takes out a copy of The Irish Times, looks Roy Keane in the eye and says, "Roy, care to explain this?"*

\*\*\*\*\*

I'M not really sure where to begin with Saipan – it's a story that has been told a thousand times and has become a huge part of Irish World Cup folklore.

Looking back now, it seems clear to me that the meeting Mick called that evening was the result of a problem that had been bubbling for some time. There had always been friction between Roy and Mick. Roy got sent off on my debut against Russia, which was also Mick's first match, and I don't honestly think the two of them ever really saw eye to eye.

There was a bust-up on a tour of the United States in 1992, which I can imagine happening. Ireland were playing in Boston and Roy was late getting on a team bus. Mick gave him a mouthful, Roy gave plenty back and from that point forward there was always aggro under the surface.

# MICK AND ROY

Roy is one of the best players to ever come out of Ireland but, as everyone knows, he also had the kind of temperament that could flip. He could really lose it at times. Some said that he was a complex character and that if you took that spark out of him, he wouldn't be the same player. That may or may not be true but what is certain is that aggression was a part of Roy's make-up while Mick has never backed down from anybody or anything in his life. The ingredients for a clash of personalities were in the pot from the start.

*****

*Mick doesn't get another word out.*

*Roy is up for this, he's out of his seat and he's into Mick.*

*A minute ago I was laughing, singing along to the band. I'm now slunk in my chair, in complete and utter shock. Roy is going personal, Roy is going heavy and it feels like Roy is going too far.*

*"Why the fuck are you asking me a question? Who the fuck are you? You were a shit player and you're a worse manager. You're a wanker as a man, you're a wanker as a manager and you shouldn't be managing my country. Fuck you, and you can fucking stick your World Cup."*

*Mick edges in a word here and there, asking why Roy had not played in the second play-off leg with Iran, and that makes it worse. He implies that Roy was fit to play and he has let his country down, which would make anyone angry, let alone someone like Roy.*

*For about eight or nine minutes Roy keeps it up, slating every last thing he doesn't like about Mick, the Ireland set-up, our preparations for the tournament, the delay in the delivery of our training gear, the state of the practice pitch, our professionalism as a squad, everything he can think of. By the end he's not even raging any more, it's just a total destruction of Mick, personally and professionally.*

*Roy is hemmed in because of the way the seats have been arranged around these tables for dinner. The only thing between him and Mick is Kev Kilbane, who just so happens to have sat in the worst place in the entire room at that moment. He's like a tennis umpire, looking left and right, left and right, wondering where the next volley is coming from.*

*The boss stands there, absorbing Roy's abuse. He's clearly taken the approach that it's best to let Roy get it all out, in front of everybody. Finally, after 10 minutes – or several lifetimes, depending on how you feel about it – Roy sits down. He's said his piece.*

*****

To me, Roy had seemed a bit 'off', a bit distracted for the entirety of the build-up to the World Cup, even from the moment we left Ireland. He complained about how chaotic our preparations were and, to be fair, he had a point. If you believe in omens there were plenty to choose from. When we got to Dublin airport for our flight, it was bedlam, full of fans, the Taoiseach, Bertie Ahern, was there for some reason – was it election time? – and there were people dressed as leprechauns with Guinness hats on, you name it.

I've never minded being with the fans, signing autographs and posing for photographs but Roy was never as comfortable with the public as most of us. He has an edgy personality and I think he was shielded from having to do too much of it at Manchester United. He just felt uncomfortable with the circus at the airport that morning, which was fair enough and totally understandable. People want a lot of Roy and sometimes he doesn't want to give a lot back.

The atmosphere wasn't helped by the fact reporters were also mingling with the squad, including some who had criticised Roy for missing Niall Quinn's recent testimonial. Neither Roy or Quinny had any issue with that because Roy needed treatment for an injury at the time so it had all been paper talk but, nevertheless, it was an unwelcome hiccup in the build-up to the tournament.

After leaving Dublin, we had to stop at Amsterdam en route to Tokyo which, again, wasn't ideal. Roy was looking tense when we eventually landed in Tokyo and awaited another plane journey to Saipan. Yet it would be unfair to say he was being completely unapproachable or argumentative with Mick or anyone in the squad at this point. It was a 23-hour trip from Dublin to Tokyo and that's enough to put anyone in a quiet mood. Roy was just keeping himself to himself.

There's a radio station in Ireland called *Today FM* that does a show called *Gift Grub* which is a mickey-take of famous Irish people.

One of their recordings was a spoof impersonation of Roy and Alex Ferguson having an argument about wages and not being paid on time. Roy was going mad at Fergie down the phone on this radio clip and I had a copy of it so to lift the mood as we waited at Tokyo airport, I played it in the lounge as we waited for the remaining connection. Although the Roy on the radio was fuming, the real Roy was fine, he was laughing about it with the rest of us.

Some people are nervous around Roy because he can be unapproachable at times but I just treated him like anyone else and enjoyed the craic. The *Gift Grub* spoof was only a laugh, and Roy was more than happy to go along with it. He was a bit distant from the lads but that was just Roy sometimes, I never gave it any real thought.

*****

*"Well," Mick says, still as calm as anything. "I don't know what happens now. Because either you go or I go. And I'm going nowhere."*

*Roy gets up again, takes one look at us all and goes, "Good luck lads, all the best" and walks out.*

*We sit around, staring at the tablecloth, staring at the ceiling, staring at our flip-flops. Nobody wants to say a word, nobody can say a word. I've never felt collective shock like it. Twenty five blokes, mute, stunned, tongues cut out, heads scrambled, minds blown.*

*****

When we got to the Regency Hyatt in Saipan it was at the end of nearly an entire day's travelling and we were all knackered but the hotel itself was beautiful, a big old place that stretched right down to the beach. We couldn't have asked for a better place to put our heads down. But Roy wasn't happy. He was content enough with the hotel but everything else about our set-up was second rate, not good enough for a team about to play in a World Cup.

The next morning we jumped on a bus for the drive to the training ground and it all started to fall to pieces from there on in. The pitch we were meant to train on was full of potholes, stones and sand; it was bone dry, and to make matters worse, we had no footballs to work with, no bibs, no cones, no energy drinks, no nothing.

Something had happened between Ireland and Saipan that meant the delivery of all our sports equipment was stuck some-where – God knows where – and so for the first day we just had to do some light runs and light training with no balls.

We all wore our own stuff and just got on with it as best we could. "Who cares?" I told Quinny. "It's not the end of the world. We'll be fine, let's just get on with it."

I'll tell you who cared. Roy did.

Mick was up front about the problems and how unhappy he was that our preparations were being messed around because of the missing kit but Roy in particular was still really pissed off, going to see him that night in his hotel room to make his feelings clear.

That night we had a bit of a party with the media pack who were following us around. It was a bit of a throwback night to the Jack Charlton days, a few beers, a bit of a BBQ and an opportunity for the squad and the reporters to get together and chat to each other honestly and off the record.

I got into football right at the end of the era when journalists and players went on the drink together all the time which often meant that more stayed out of the papers than made it in. Mick was keen to get that relationship going again. After all, we were away from home for a fair old while with these lads watching our every move so we might as well embrace the situation and play the game.

Roy didn't see it that way. He wasn't happy about this BBQ. He thought the whole training base set-up was too relaxed. I didn't agree with him on that. For starters, Saipan wasn't meant to be a full-blown workout. We'd all travelled out on the back of a long season, the complete point – the whole idea – of Saipan was to recuperate from that, keep our fitness simmering and also slowly get used to the demanding conditions we would face at the World Cup. Yet Roy wouldn't have that, he wanted every-thing done at 100mph and his mood continued to get worse. Finally, in only our second training session, it all kicked off.

After we'd complained about how dry the pitch was, the groundsmen at the training area had reacted by flooding it overnight, which meant it was just as bad the day after but for completely different reasons. The result was the same, a poor playing surface and more tension bubbling. Roy was looking for somewhere to vent his frustrations and he picked out the goalkeeping group as his target.

Before we'd left the hotel, Packie Bonner, who was there as our goalkeeping coach, had asked Mick if me, Alan Kelly and Dean Kiely could start training earlier to get out of the heat. That meant we were finished before the main group. Training for keepers is always physically intense because you are constant-ly up and down, diving and recovering your position, so while you may not cover thousands of metres running, you're still tired.

This wasn't Newcastle weather or Ireland weather – I could hardly breathe it was that hot, it felt like putting your head in an oven and the three of us did a lot of work that day with Packie.

After it was finished, we were sat under this tent on the side of the pitch, out of the sun, when Roy marched over.

At the time I was pouring water down my throat as fast as I could. I was gasping for a drink. Roy wanted some goalkeepers for a seven-a-side match but, as I say, Packie and Mick had already agreed we'd do a short, sharp session and then rest up.

"They're knackered," Packie told Roy. "They're supposed to be knackered, it's a World Cup," Roy said, fuming at Packie, who isn't the kind of bloke to back down from anybody.

Alan Kelly is another one in the same mould and he told Roy that it was none of his business how or where the goalkeepers did their work. In other words, fuck off. Yet despite all the harsh words, it soon blew over. Roy and Alan get on well and they were mates again before any harm was done.

You're never going to get on with every member of a 23-man squad all the time and lads exchanging words on the training field happens every single day. And anyhow, Roy was always at people in training. In mini-games and passing drills he would make huge demands of the lads, screaming about bad passes and a poor tempo and, for me, that was brilliant. That was one of his strengths and it was just a sign that Roy was desperate for Ireland to do well.

But this was not the same. The way he was acting now felt different. He seemed to be making a big deal out of absolutely nothing and finding problems where there were none.

To me, it felt like he was deliberately cutting himself off from the group. I don't know if he was missing his kids or his family or his dogs but nothing seemed to please him. He wasn't in a happy place. I can't tell you what Roy's mentality was but to me it seemed that he just didn't want to be there. We're all human and there are players who don't like being away from home, stuck in hotels and I'm not saying Roy is like that but, for me, it was clear something wasn't right with him.

After the training ground argument with Packie and Alan, we got wind of a story that Roy was going home. For one reason or another, he'd decided enough was enough. It was only after the event I found out that Mick Byrne had convinced Roy to stick around, running around the hotel between Roy's and Mick's room to smooth everything over. At one stage, Colin Healy's bags were packed back in Ireland and he was about to leave for Tokyo but Mick – and a phone call to Alex Ferguson – eventually convinced Roy to stay. It looked like everything was calming down and sorted out.

The next day, we attempted to train on the pitch and again we made the best of it. Roy was there with the rest of us and afterwards he was chatting with two journalists, Paul Kimmage and Tom Humphries. All members of the Ireland squad had to do formal media interviews at some point so I thought nothing else of it. It was just Roy's turn, no problem.

There was a nine-hour time difference and back in 2002, don't forget, there was no hotel Wifi, there was no Whatsapp or anything like that so when we trained on the Thursday – the day the row broke out – we had no idea whatsoever what Roy had said to the papers. It just never dawned on me that Roy's interviews with those journalists would be a problem. The idea never crossed my mind once. I was too busy keeping a ball out of a net to worry about stuff like that.

Little did I know that Roy had gone for the jugular and nailed Mick and the complete Irish set-up, suggesting the entire Saipan trip was a bit of a piss-take.

# MICK AND ROY

The *Irish Times* had originally planned to hold off publishing until the weekend but they knew they had gold on their hands so sent the interview to press on Wednesday night. Eventually a copy of the paper was faxed through to the hotel and Mick told Mick Byrne that we'd be having a meeting after the main meal.

*****

*Roy Keane is one of the greatest players in the world, he's the finest player in our squad, a true Irish great. And he's just walked out on a World Cup campaign.*

*The room remains tense and silent, the mood is surreal. Somebody needs to do something or say something to make us all come back to planet earth from whatever trip we've all just been on. Dean Kiely sticks his hand up. He's a good lad Dean, a really fine goalkeeper and trainer and we've always got on. "Boss," he says. "If you need a midfielder, I can play there – I'll do you a job."*

*Perfect. The room falls about laughing, the tension and the embarrassment disappear in a split-second. Gary Kelly joins in as well. "GET THAT FUCKING BAND BACK IN HERE," he shouts one last time, before getting serious. "We're with you Mick," he says. "We have to stick together. Now are we behind Mick or not?" The room breaks out into a round of applause for Mick, who still looks pretty shocked by everything that has just happened. In the space of about 15 minutes, Ireland have just become the biggest sporting story on the planet. For all the wrong reasons.*

*****

# SHAY

I never want to be in a room with an atmosphere like that, ever again. It had always been my dream to play at a World Cup and now I was there, now I was actually there and it was all falling apart around me.

It was without doubt the biggest bust-up I witnessed in my professional life. "Did that really happen?" Quinny asked me as we walked out of the ballroom.

I just couldn't get my head around it all. On the one hand, I didn't think there was a way back for Roy after what he'd said but also, this was Roy Keane. He was a giant of a player, he was the captain and I didn't want to lose his influence on the pitch. Ireland were a better side with Roy Keane in the team, no question, so despite the chaos there was part of me that knew we'd miss him. However, the part of me that mourned Roy going was smaller than the other part of me, which was screaming that it's a team game and the team comes first.

I understand that as the captain Roy was probably trying to make a point and remain professional but the bigger picture for me was the fact Roy was our best player, our leader on the pitch and someone we all looked up to. If every other player had accepted the situation, could he not have just got on with it like the rest of us? Yes, the balls and bibs should have been there, yes the pitch should have been better. I get all that and I agree with it. But life doesn't always go to plan, does it?

My issue wasn't that Roy was raging at the shambolic set-up. What I couldn't believe was that Roy had chosen to go now – a week before our opening game against Cameroon in the biggest sporting tournament on earth. If the pitches had been bobbly at Malahide and we'd had no kit to train with before a mid-summer friendly against whoever, then I'd be next to Roy, telling both Micks, McCarthy and Byrne, and all the support staff, that it was a disgrace and we deserved better.

It's a timing thing for me. Nothing matters more than playing in a World Cup for Ireland – I'd would've jumped in a canoe on the Liffey and paddled there myself if that's what it took to get to South Korea and Japan – so surely to God we can put anything and everything to one side for the good of the job that's in front of us? Crossing that white line and representing Ireland should've outweighed every other issue.

After the meeting, everything seemed to happen at a million miles an hour. A press conference was called for 9pm to explain what had happened and why Roy was gone.

The squad was 100 per cent behind the manager and Gary's round of applause for the boss soon after Roy had stormed out said it all.

I was still angry and confused and I remember thinking that the speed at which the press conference had been arranged was a mistake. Everyone's blood was up. We should have taken a step back and all just calmed down a bit. Mick told the press that he'd "sent Roy home" which I thought was wrong because it heaped too much pressure on himself. It wasn't Mick who'd done anything wrong – this was all on Roy.

Alan Kelly, Quinny and Stan all sat next to Mick in this press conference to show that the squad backed him and, to be fair to the lads, they spoke for all of us and didn't shirk it, something that means they still have a non-existent relationship with Roy to this day. "You're the senior players and I need your help on this one, you have to stand with me on this," Mick had said to them beforehand. I could understand why.

Everything around the hotel turned to chaos. The media

jumped on us and wouldn't let us go, reporters were sprinting through reception, trying to grab quotes – any quotes – from anyone slow and stupid enough to get caught by them.

Fraser Robertson was there covering it for *Sky Sports*. For some reason, after Roy had said his piece, he wasn't around the hotel so missed the scoop of his life. I think he'd popped out for a coffee and walked back in casually to find reporters sprinting around trying to find a phone to ring Ireland and lads shouting questions here there and everywhere. "Is there something going on I should know about lads? What have I missed? What's happened?" he asked me. "Ah, nothing," I told him. "Nothing at all."

Apparently the country was split down the middle and Eamon Dunphy would eventually even wear Cameroon colours on air before our opening group match in support of Roy. It was all pure madness.

I was rooming with Al and he went up to see Roy and was with him for about 30 minutes. He got back to the room, opened his laptop and started writing down everything he'd seen that day. He wanted a live account of what had just happened while it was still fresh. He was tapping away for quite a while and was asking me what I thought too.

For me, the problems with the facilities and organisation in Saipan was just another chapter in a long running tale. It was nothing new. It was another case of shrug your shoulders, get on with it, take the piss and become stronger as a result. Ask Big Jack or Quinny or Cascarino or whoever you want, we'd always been a bit ramshackle and a bit hit-and-miss, but that had never, ever led to weakness, in fact, if anything, it had created strength.

# MICK AND ROY

Quinny and Jason McAteer went to see Roy separately to have it out but I didn't go with them. Mick Byrne also spent forever with Roy, trying to convince him to change his mind.

The two of them had always been big mates and if anyone was going to persuade Roy to apologise quickly to Mick, get it done and dusted and finished with, then Mick would be the man to do so. No such luck.

Quinny went up to speak to Roy because he was Quinny, enough said. He was at his last World Cup, he was too old for this playground bollocks and he was confident enough in himself to be happy taking on the case for the rest of the lads I know Quinny and Jason well and they don't stand for any nonsense whatsoever but it was clear nothing was doing with Roy. He was gone.

By the end of Thursday night, he was set for home and ready to get chased by a million photographers walking his dog Triggs around a footpath in Cheshire. Are you trying to tell me that's a better way to spend a summer than playing in a World Cup?

For me, I knew us being at the tournament was bringing a lot of joy back home. There are some tough places in Ireland, some places where people are struggling in life with debt and so on and we knew that, even for just 90 minutes, we could do our bit to put a smile on their faces and that counted far more than anything else.

As a squad, we'd also shown in the 18 months building up to the World Cup that we could and would fight our way out of tight corners. It was just heartbreaking for Ireland – the team and the country – that Roy would not be stood be with us, fighting harder than anyone, as he always did.

I get on with Roy. When we were reunited at Villa, Saipan

was never something we brought up. It wasn't even as if it was a big issue lurking in the background that we needed to get around to one day. It had all been and gone by then. I have no intentions of speaking to him about it either, we can't spend our lives worrying about events from 15 years ago.

Roy's obviously now back involved with the Irish set-up and you hear him talking in the media about what it means to represent your country and what he expects from those doing it. Reading between the lines when he's talking, perhaps he does have some regrets about it all.

Getting asked to captain your country at any level is an incredible honour but to be asked to do it at a World Cup is something else entirely. To then throw that away is surely going to keep you awake at some point, questioning whether you did the right thing.

With Roy being on board alongside Martin and a big part of the management team now, I think he's probably got a wider angle on the whole episode. I reckon he would go down the Mick McCarthy route himself if a player did what he'd done.

These days the Ireland team has the best travel and hotels available and everything you could ever want is provided for the players.

I think the probable turning point for that was Roy's outburst in Saipan because it made the FAI sit up and listen and it made the FAI rediscover its chequebook. I think the players of today can certainly trace the professionalism of the current squad back to Roy kicking off that day in the Hyatt Regency ballroom.

That's all well and good.

But, hell, the country paid a huge price in 2002 to make sure 2017 was different.

# 10

# HOPE AND HEARTACHE

SAIPAN was off the scale but it wasn't like it hadn't already been a dramatic build-up to the World Cup. We should have expected two play-off games against Iran to be full of incident – and they were. After the Belgium defeats that ended our 1998 World Cup hopes, I can't say I was exactly looking forward to having to go through the play-off system again. Like a trip to the dentist, it seemed like something we had to go through from time to time.

We had a famous victory over Holland to thank for finishing in the runners-up spot.

That game, on September 1, 2001, was simply one of the most tense but ultimately incredible 90 minutes I've ever played in and the win not only broke the Dutch, it gave us a lift that helped carry us all the way to the tournament. It was also one of the best atmospheres I've ever experienced in an Ireland strip.

Just over a year earlier, we had drawn 2-2 in Amsterdam in

what turned out to be an eventful week which all started with an ill-fated night out in Dublin. Phil Babb and Mark Kennedy had enjoyed a spot of early hours dancing on a parked car that happened to be owned by a police officer. Mick didn't dodge a tough decision and threw them both out of the squad, to be replaced by Richard Dunne and Jason McAteer, who both played their part in the 2-2 draw. Jason provided an assist for Robbie Keane and then scored himself to put us 2-0 up before the Dutch pulled things back. Alan Kelly was in goal that day and it was a result that gave us encouragement.

Before the return game, the media were asking me if my confidence was low because I'd made quite a high-profile mistake for Newcastle not long before. It came in the Premier League opener against Chelsea at Stamford Bridge when Boudewijn Zenden's shot had squirmed out of my grasp in the first 10 minutes. But Mick was right behind me. He was brilliant, telling the press and anybody else who'd listen that I was his first-choice goalkeeper and I'd be playing. I had to park any nerves and just go for it. I had a job to do, keeping the ball out of the net. I just told myself to keep it simple.

Right from the kick-off I knew it would be far from easy. I was called straight into action, diving to my right to save a low shot from Mark van Bommel. That was in the fourth minute. Two minutes earlier Patrick Kluivert had shot wide after finding himself in a great position. It was going to be a busy afternoon...

Fortunately, we had a man called Roy Keane on our side. For me, Roy was a standout performer that day and he loved a big occasion. That day he stepped up. After about 30 seconds, he absolutely nailed Marc Overmars – welcome to Ireland – and that set the tone for the match and paved the way for a famous 10-man victory.

It was Gary Kelly who saw red, getting sent off just before the hour for a second foul on Overmars. Mick sacrificed a forward, taking Robbie off and bringing Steve Finnan on and it was Finnan who provided a ball to the back post where Jason McAteer arrived in time to calmly slot home. It was a great finish because, arriving at pace, he could so easily have smashed it over the bar.

With 30 odd minutes left, we still had so much to do.

Before Jase's goal, Kluivert and Zenden both had glorious chances and then in the second half, we had a narrow escape at one stage when Stan attempted to head the ball back to me. We got in a mix-up, he nodded the ball past me and I got tangled up with Ruud van Nistelrooy. If it had happened outside the area I'm sure then the ref would have given a free-kick. I just tried to use a bit of know-how and I managed to get my body in the way to make it look like an innocent collision. He then stumbled on top of me and the ball just rolled wide of the post by inches. That was a big moment. It felt like the entire ground was shaking. The older stadium always had a special atmosphere but this afternoon was a one-off.

They finished the game with what felt like 11 strikers. Jimmy Floyd Hasselbaink, Van Nistelrooy, Pierre van Hooijdonk and Kluivert were all on and gunning for us. Every time I looked across at the touchline it seemed that they had another six feet four inch forward waiting to make an entrance.

To hear that final whistle was immense. The media and the fans had built this game up into this crescendo and it was all people were on about for days. Holland were the big favourites.

Louis van Gaal was the manager and they all came across as arrogant in the build-up, so for us to beat them was unreal. Knocking them out of contention guaranteed us at least a play-off spot. Holland and Portugal had been favourites to go through from our group but we showed the togetherness we had and Roy was at the heart of that.

My strongest memories are of the scenes on the pitch after the final whistle – celebrating and hugging with the crowd going bananas. Come on you boys in green! We weren't at the World Cup yet but we'd given ourselves another wonderful chance to get an invite to the biggest football party on the planet. This was what it was all about. I lived for days like these.

*****

I look back at my contribution in the Iran games with a lot of pride and satisfaction. Maybe the fans forget, but to me, the saves I made stand out in my memory. I knew how big they were. We won the first leg at Lansdowne 2-0, thanks to goals from Robbie and Ian Harte.

I made two saves against the same player, Ali Karimi. In the second half, he was put through on goal but he took a big touch and that gave me half an opportunity to dive at his feet and grab the ball. You could hear the relief in the crowd because the last thing we wanted to do was concede an away goal – that would've made Tehran an absolute nightmare place to go.

Later, Karimi caused us more trouble as he turned Gary Breen, cut in from the wing and slotted a shot low to my left. It was just one of those shots you either manage to read or you don't and I just got down to it in time.

The big thing about that save was I was well set, I wasn't moving forward or back and that is crucial as a goalkeeper. If I had been moving forward or backwards as he hit it, then he scores. You can make a million great saves in training and think, 'that was wasted' but stops like that against Iran, in such a big game, were why I never minded the hours and hours of diving around in the pissing rain and the cold. You do the training so you can perform when it matters most. The next day we all went to a hotel for a swim and Stan was talking about it. "Some save that mate," he said. It was nice that my team-mates had recognised it.

The papers were full of how we were halfway there and the second leg was revved up even further by the Iran coach Miroslav Blazevic who was keeping everything nicely in perspective by promising to hang himself if Ireland won on Iranian soil.

Our preparation for the game wasn't helped by Roy being ruled out. Roy had a long-standing knee issue which flared up after the first leg but after returning to Old Trafford, he played the following Saturday for Manchester United. His absence in Tehran was one of the slow burning bugbears that exploded so badly in Saipan. There was no doubt we would miss him in the second game but what could we do? One thing we Irish have – and pride ourselves on – is a resilience and a self-belief that we can scrap ourselves out of any corner.

Before we left for Iran, Mick warned us: "Lads, the hotel, the pitch, the food, everything will be shit. They'll be doing everything to ruin this for us. Expect the worst and be ready for it. "

There was a time difference of three and a half hours and the biggest mistake Mick made was to try and get us onto their time straight away. It just caused havoc with our body clocks. When we went to Europe with Newcastle, we always stayed on GMT so our bodies would train at their 'normal' time but Mick, for whatever reason, had a different approach.

The night before the game, I remember constantly tossing and turning. I just couldn't get away. You know what it's like, everyone has been there – you end up chasing sleep, which just makes you even more awake. I was lying in bed, the night before the most important Ireland game since God knows and the country's first choice goalkeeper was pulling an all-nighter.

In the end, it got too much so I hopped out of bed and walked down the dark corridor at the Azadi Hotel until I found Mick Byrne's room. "Mick, I need a sleeping pill, I'm going to be in trouble here," I told him. We were all meant to go for a walk in the morning but that got sacked because I was still in bed after popping the tablet.

After the usual team meal, we travelled to the Azadi Stadium. Bloody hell! There were thousands of fans in there five hours before kick-off. On the bus on the way in, we could hear the atmosphere. We looked out of the window and Iran looked bleak; concrete everywhere. The stadium was this old-looking giant bowl.

We got off the bus and had to walk underneath the stadium. Abuse was flying from all quarters. My Iranian isn't too good so I don't know what these thousands of people were shouting at us, but I'm fairly sure they weren't inviting us for dinner. Situations like that never put me off. In fact, I used to enjoy the abuse; it motivated me. The bigger the game and atmosphere, the more I wanted to shut them up.

We went out to warm up in one corner of the pitch and it felt like we were in the middle of a battle. The Iranian fans were throwing these firebombs onto the pitch – they looked like mini-grenades which were blowing up as soon as they hit the turf. Me, Alan Kelly, Dean Kiely and Packie Bonner needed camouflage, not goalkeeping gear.

I remember we were stretching near the goalmouth and one went off about 10 metres away. "Fucking hell, that was close," Dean said before, next thing, another landed about a metre away, dug into the pitch and exploded, sending dirt and soil right into my face.

"Jesus lads, it's only a game of football!" I laughed. What else could you do? Bits of the stadium were up next, concrete raining down like confetti; oranges, food, you name it but I just had to shrug that off and get on with it.

The longer the game went on, the more it played to our advantage. We had a good chance through David Connolly that slipped wide and I then remember my best moment, punching a cross away from the head of Ali Daei.

I got some solid distance on it but it fell to Karim Bagheri, who hammered it back in, low and hard to my right. I got down, strong wrist and managed to keep it out before scrambling the ball out for a corner. I saw the first save late, through someone's legs and then Daei nearly got the rebound but I was up fast to react. I knew it was a big moment in the game. If they scored then, would we have kept them out, in front of their mad fans, for another 30 minutes?

They scored in the last minute of the game and that was disappointing. There was still a minute of injury time to go after the goal. We took the kick-off, the ball ended up with Gary Breen and I remember him passing it back to me. Don't do that! I don't want the thing! Seconds to go and the ball's at my feet on a bobbly dry pitch. 'Cheers mate,' I was thinking, as I watched Breen's shirt disappear up the other end. I put my foot through it and felt my heart rate slow down as it soared into the distance.

The celebrations on the final whistle were just insane. We had about 100 fans in the stadium and we knew we had to get over to them to thank them for making the journey. The telly reporters were jumping in front of us, asking me how I felt. "It's unbelievable, it feels unbelievable," I told them, desperately wanting to get through them to the lads.

Part of me still wished I was back in Donegal. I knew it would've been absolutely rocking. We were a million miles from home, we'd run the gauntlet and survived. It just felt incredible. I'd suffered the Belgium defeat so this was our chance to really embrace winning and what it meant to be an Ireland player.

The only thing missing was a drop of the hard stuff. Iran is obviously a dry country so we couldn't pop the cork on any champagne to celebrate – spraying water bottles around the dressing room had to do instead. No bother, I would've taken that before kick-off!

The dressing room was buzzing. Kevin Kilbane had the biggest smile on his face, Ian Harte looked knackered but full of energy at the same time and Mick was just beaming and quite emotional, knowing he'd done his job. He'd savoured the euphoria of playing in a World Cup himself and now he was taking his own team there. If it meant a lot to Mick, it meant just as much to Mick Byrne. He'd been there in Belgium and comforted me when I was crying my eyes out so to see him in Iran, beaming, was just unreal.

We left Tehran that night, a plane full of players, fans and press and the minute the wheels were up, the beers could finally be opened and the free bar was put to use. The cabin crew presented Mick with a bottle of champagne that he opened straight away and Quinny had us all singing before the plane had even taken off. Anyone could get up and have a go, players singing with fans, press lads singing with players – it didn't matter, the craic was mighty with whoever fancied it.

Packie Bonner had his 'moment', saving the penalty from Daniel Timofte against Romania at Italia '90 and some people might say my biggest Ireland memory was the Thierry Henry handball, but I think it was the saves made against Iran and looking back, they're something I take a great deal of pride in.

I'll always be part of a squad of players who got their country to a World Cup and nothing will ever change that. People forget how small Ireland is and how small our pool of players is. In England, they've literally got millions of lads to look at. Of course they're going to qualify for the big tournaments. We've a lot less in Ireland and many play Gaelic football, too, which means there's even less to choose from. So we have no divine right to qualify for the World Cup. Yet we managed it, together, and it was glorious and special.

The Irish team at that time loved nothing more than a get-together and that meant we were a very close group of lads. Gary Kelly was usually the one put in charge of looking after us, which was never a good idea, and often we'd all head on to Gibney's bar in Malahide.

"Ok lads, 10.30 curfew and bed for 11 please," Mick would say in a meeting before we'd leave. "Gaz, you're looking after them tonight. If they're not back by 11, it's on your head."

"Ok boss," he'd say.

We'd go to a bar and at 10.45 just as we were finishing up,

Gary would pull us together. All in lads, all in. "Right fellas, you heard the gaffer," he'd start. "It's on my head if we're late back so…WHAT YOUSE HAVIN'?"

\*\*\*\*\*

By the time it came to kicking off our 2002 World Cup campaign, we were a tight unit – some of it forged on the pitch, some in a bar and some in Saipan and then Izumo, where we had flown to the day after Roy's outburst. We were in Group E and our first game was against Cameroon. After the 'Mick and Roy' circus had left town, we just wanted the football to begin.

*Saturday, June 1. 3.30pm:*
*Republic of Ireland v Cameroon,*
*Niigata Stadium, Niigata.*

Before the game, not for the first time, thoughts came to me of home; of Mum, of all my family and mates – some of whom were in the crowd. We had a walk-about on the pitch and I tried to spot The Bear's 'OK SHAY' banner, which was decked in Irish colours, his way of letting me know whereabouts in the ground he was sitting. Dad, Liam and Paul were all in Japan and it was nice to know they were all in there, willing us on.

Samuel Eto'o was on fire that day but it was Patrick Mboma who got the first goal, in the 39th minute. We were not overawed, and no panic set in. Robbie, Duffer and Matt Holland all played well and it was Matt who scored in the second half to level things up. Robbie also hit the post. We had held our own, that's for sure and on another day we could've won. The point meant we were up and running. We desperately needed both the match and the point. It felt like we had sweated out a lot of the tension and anxiety around Saipan. Now everything with Roy was gone, just as it had to be.

*Wednesday, June 5. 8.30pm:*
*Republic of Ireland v Germany,*
*Kashima Soccer Stadium, Ibaraki.*

Germany had beaten Saudi Arabia 8-0 in their first group game, Miroslav Klose scoring a hat-trick. My personal build-up for this game was based around me thinking I was going to be a busy man! It was always going to be tough but we didn't fear the Germans – we were excited and up for it. This was why we played. Germany, with more World Cup wins than I've had nights out in Newcastle, and now it's our turn – Ireland's turn – to show them how much the World Cup means to the players and the country as a whole.

Facing down Oliver Kahn was one part of the game I did give some proper thought to. The giant German was a hero of mine, he was a truly wonderful goalkeeper and to be on the same playing field as him was a thrill. Mick Byrne went into their dressing room afterwards and grabbed his jersey for me, which I still have hanging up at home.

We played so well against Germany. It was Klose – who else – who put them ahead in the 19th minute with a typical header. It didn't put us off playing our game and Germany threatened little – until Michael Ballack's pass found Carsten Jancker clear in the box. I rushed out to confront him and breathed a sigh of relief as I saw his shot go wide.

As the clock wound down and the goal didn't come, I allowed bad thoughts to creep in. *It doesn't look like we're getting back in the game here.* Germany were world class at closing games out. But they hadn't banked on the Irish had they? With seconds left, Kinsella smashed it long, Quinny got his trampoline out, nodded it on to Robbie who smashed it in.

Cue madness and bedlam.

Bringing Quinny on had changed the game for us. It meant we went a bit more Route One – but why wouldn't you? Why wouldn't you play to your strengths? It's a World Cup match, not a tea party. Quinny was a big ingredient in mixing it up for us. He was brilliant at knocking the ball on, out-jumping defenders and generally being a massive nuisance, dragging them here and there. He was a pain in the arse basically. A big, magnificent pain in the arse.

We couldn't believe the fans in the ground that day. A sea of green (and sunburnt red!). We'd all heard the stories about hundreds of people using credit union and bank loans and even selling their cars to get there. If it was France you'd think, 'Fair enough, pop across the Channel' but Japan and South Korea are the other side of the world and there they were, in their thousands. Everyone went bananas when the goal went in. Robbie did his classic cartwheel celebration before getting mobbed down by the corner flag; Mick was going crazy as the pitch flooded with green shirts and orange bibs and the fans, of course, were jumping out of their skins. I was all alone down the other end, losing my mind – but that is the goalkeeper's lot; you miss out on the mad celebrations. I didn't mind, it felt unreal. Even when I watch Robbie's goal back now, the hairs stand up on the back of my neck.

# HOPE AND HEARTACHE

It was Hollywood stuff and, to me, one of the greatest moments in Irish sport. A piece of history which felt like a victory, probably because the goal came in the 92nd minute. A result like that gives you so much bounce and momentum.

After the game, we went back to the hotel. Our families had arrived for the first time. Jayo Duff, Damien's brother, had a guitar in the hotel and we all had a really great night. It had been a tough few weeks, no doubt about that, so to be able to come together as a team was just what we needed to do.

*Tuesday, June 11. 8.30pm.*
*Republic of Ireland v Saudi Arabia,*
*International Stadium Yokohama, Yokohama.*

Saudi Arabia were regarded as the weakest team in our group, so we knew this was a great chance to get to the knockout stages. Robbie, Gary Breen and Duffer all scored in an easy win and the thing I remember the most is Duffer bowing after he'd scored the third goal. That was a sign of respect to the people of Japan because the way we'd been treated was incredible.

Everybody was so kind and helpful. You'd go to training and to games and all the hotel staff would be lined up, all the way from reception to the bus, bowing and wishing us luck. There'd be two rows and we'd walk between them as they clapped and smiled. It was a nice touch from Duffer for the people of Japan.

Damien was a class player and there was a period where it seemed that he would be the man of the match every single time he played for Ireland. He came over at 16 to Blackburn when I was there and I was a little bit older than him. He was fresh off the boat and even then he had so many skills and so much talent. He went into first-team training and he was skipping past older pros like they weren't even there. He was raw but brilliant. He was a left winger, out and out, no messing around; beat the full-back, put the cross in. It's an art you don't see much of these days.

Getting into the second round meant so much to us because it felt like we'd proved a lot of people wrong. After Saipan, all the media was basically saying, 'You're doomed'. That spurred us on even more and forged greater togetherness. We thought we'd show everyone that we had all got us to the World Cup, not just Roy. Getting out of the group stage showed people that we were a good team and that Spain, in the next game, would be in for one hell of a hard match.

*Sunday, June 16. 8.30pm:*
*Republic of Ireland v Spain,*
*Suwon World Cup Stadium, Suwon.*

I try not to live my life with too many regrets or grudges – what's the point? – but the loss to Spain hurts more than pretty much every other result.

Put together.

They were obviously an amazingly talented side but we gave them hell from the first moment and how we didn't win that game and make it to the quarter-finals remains a mystery to me.

After going 1-0 down to a Fernando Morientes goal in the eighth minute, we got a penalty and Ian Harte stepped up. I was already preparing myself for it to be 1-1 because as he picked the ball up, I remember thinking, 'He's got one of the best left foots I've ever played with, no way he's missing this.'

We used to call him 'Mallet-foot' because when he hit a ball, it stayed hit. If he connected as he could do, Iker Casillas could've dived a week early and not saved it because that's the venom Hartey puts through the ball.

You'll have to ask Hartey what went wrong then because for whatever reason he changed his mind late on and opened up his foot which made it an easy save for Casillas.

Shortly after half-time, Quinny came on and caused carnage again, totally mixing the game up, before Robbie equalised in the dying seconds – yeeesssss! – to take it to extra time and then, before I knew it, penalties.

*Fucking penalties.*

The longer my career has gone on, the less I've enjoyed spot-kicks. I've had nothing but misery with them and that World Cup was the biggest example of that.

You can get yourself into such a mental tangle with penalties, double-bluffing yourself, over-thinking, maybe studying videos too closely. In recent years, I've watched videos of Wayne Rooney and if the last three have gone to your right, what do you do? Do you go right, hoping he sticks to his pattern or do you think he's got to change at some time, so go to your left? And what if you do go left and he sticks it right? People will be saying, "Why didn't you go right when you know he prefers the right?" and so on. It can get too much and sometimes it's best going on instinct alone.

I also feel that luck is always involved. There are times when I just feel like it's hard to get it out of your mind that you're jinxed. Even recently at Stoke, we beat Luton 8-7 in a penalty shootout and I never saved one then either. In training, I save more than my fair share but maybe I over-think them when it comes to a match, I don't know. The advantage is obviously with the striker but, as a keeper, it's your one chance in the game to grab some glory, to know what it feels like to score a matchwinner and I don't feel I've done well enough.

"Just do me one thing," Mick said to us all as we huddled on the pitch before the shootout began. "Pick a spot and stick with it. Don't change your mind." I wouldn't have had any problem taking a penalty. A goalkeeper takes more dead-ball kicks than any player so it would never have bothered me. Mick said, "Who wants one?" and plenty of hands went up, including mine.

Robbie scored for us before Hierro made it 1-1 and then our penalties fell to pieces. Holland, Connolly and Kilbane all missed for us but because only Baraja had scored for them – Juanfran and Valeron missing for them, after Finnan scored our last – it was 2-2 with Spain to take one for the win.

*This was it. This was my moment.*

The night Packie saved the penalty in Italia '90, we went down to the main street in Lifford. People were falling out of pubs, flags were strewn across the roads and hanging from shop windows. The entire town was out, celebrating his amazing save and Jack Charlton's team's efforts. And now here I was, another man from Donegal, trying to do the same.

Gaizka Mendieta walked up and seemed to take an age to get there. I tried to eyeball him, tried to get into his head but he seemed so calm. He even had time to reposition the ball, which added even more tension to the moment. The boos and the whistles from the Irish fans behind my goal were deafening.

*What do I do?*

Do I stand up and hope he goes down the middle and then

look a fool when he rolls it into the corner and I'm stood there, filing my nails? Do I dive and hope for the best? In that situation, you have to go. You can't just stand there, can you?

Mendieta took a huge run-up, sprinted in and then almost fluffed it, a weak shot straight down the middle that dribbled over me and into the back of the net.

It missed my leg by a millimetre.

*By fuck all.*

These are the margins we talk about in sport. If my shinpad was a millimetre thicker, I've saved a penalty at a World Cup and given us a chance to go to sudden death and who knows what happens then?

This was my chance to be another Packie, to be another Donegal hero, but I just couldn't get the job done. It still stings me to this day. I stood up as long as I could but it's very, very difficult as a goalkeeper. It tortures me to think that if I had just stood there, I would've saved it with my eyes shut.

It was so close and so far away.

Losing like that in a World Cup is one of the worst feelings you can experience on a football pitch.

It's a blur what happened afterwards because I was a bit of a head in the oven job. The lads who missed the penalties were devastated but I felt the same.

I'd let the lads down by not saving one.

Me and Casillas swapped shirts – his is up in my bar, mine's probably in his bin at home – but Spain were really good with us and very respectful of the hurt we were feeling.

While we waited for Richard Dunne and Matt Holland to do the drug tests, we all sat on the bus in silence. The two team buses were parked right next to each other. All of a sudden the door opened and Santiago Cañizares, Spain's back-up goalkeeper was there, with a case of beers. "Have this," he said. "And well played." It was a nice touch and the beers didn't last long but they weren't the sweetest ones I've ever tasted, that's for sure.

*****

The 2002 World Cup was the end for some fine players like Stan and Quinny. It had always been an honour to play with them. Quinny is a great, great guy and loves the craic more than most. He had really good feet and he was superb in the air as well. It was like he could pass the ball with his head and he was able to direct balls onwards to his fellow strikers, rather than just hope it would skim off his head and land at somebody's feet. That is a massively underrated skill and Quinny was that all over; underrated by most. He was one of our leaders and was always up for some mischief.

After we had first landed in South Korea, some of us had snuck out to find a bit of local entertainment. It became like the *Great Escape*. Call signs went out, we tunnelled our way out of the back of the hotel and 12 of us found ourselves at the underground station. We were the dirty dozen. I won't mention anybody else's name but Niall Quinn was definitely there and had organised it.

After sneaking out, we had made our way to the underground station in Seoul and 11 people jumped on the tube in one piece. I was the twelfth. I nipped to the toilet, came back to the platform and it was deserted.

The biggest mission in history to find your mates then began and I searched far and wide, fuming, until I worked out that they would just have headed to the only Irish bar in town. By the time I got there, Alan Kelly – *whoops, another name just slipped* – had jumped on the drum kit, got the nod from two Korean singers and somehow they all started blasting out *Mustang Sally* until Gary Kelly – *I must stop doing this* – jumped on the microphone and murdered it so badly he should've been arrested. He definitely didn't have the X Factor.

We had a great night and, best of all, we'd had a good laugh without Mick knowing. Perfect. The next day in training, everything was great but the day after, you could see that Mick was furious. Turns out he had been to the pub we'd been in and as he was ordering food he looked behind the bar to see photos of half his World Cup squad stapled to the bar with big grins on their faces.

The fun didn't stop there either. For one reason or another we couldn't fly straight back home after the Spain loss so we were stuck in South Korea, nursing ourselves through the misery of getting knocked out on penalties.

The Westin Chosun hotel threw us a function with a big buffet and a few speeches. While we were up on the second floor we knew that in the pub on the ground floor there were hundreds of Ireland fans.

Once the speeches had finished, my brother Liam wanted to nip down for a beer but I really didn't want to go because I was so gutted. Liam strong-armed me into it and that was the start of an incredible night. We got the lift down into the lobby and it was just crazy from that moment onwards.

All the players were in there, the fans would sing a song, the players would sing a song in return and the craic was mighty. We ended up walking down the road to a nearby bar called Buck

Mulligans, Alan Kelly jumped on the drums again, Robbie and Gary Kelly were singing and it was just so touching to see so many fans having such a great time. Somebody threw me a Donegal GAA shirt, Robbie was wearing a Dublin one and it was an amazing night spent with the fans who'd spent a fortune on getting out there.

One of the lads out with us was Michael Flatley, the River-dance guy. He had a penthouse suite and a limousine and Gary Kelly, after a few beers, saw a chance he wouldn't miss. He jumped up onto the bonnet of this beautiful white limousine, started doing the Riverdance right on the roof of the car, the roof starting to dent under his weight, the lot of us – including Michael – crying laughing. We started the World Cup campaign dancing on top of a police car and ended it jigging on a limo!

Eventually we flew home and the KLM flight from Icheon International Airport to Dublin was more like a nightclub than a plane journey. At first, all the players were upstairs in Business Class but we all wanted to mingle so lads were running up and down the stairs to join in the sing-songs that were breaking out everywhere. Stan got serenaded with, *'We All Dream Of A Team of Steve Stauntons'*, some lads were dressing up as female cabin crew, serving drinks while Robbie and Al Kelly were singing Bob Dylan and Elvis songs – very, very badly.

We landed at about 5pm and then all headed to a massive reception at Phoenix Park which gave us an idea of just how football-mad the country had been during the World Cup. Apparently 100,000 were there and it was such an honour to thank the fans for their support. The cheers we got on that stage were deafening and Mick just kept looking around and shaking his head in disbelief that so many people had turned up.

# HOPE AND HEARTACHE

The flight home had been well stocked and after the civic reception we all went to Lillie's Bordello on Grafton Street until about 3am. We then jumped in a taxi to get a lift back to the hotel at the airport. We got chatting to the taxi driver and the fare was 30 euros. "Don't worry about it Shay," the driver said. "Get yourselves on in now." It was a touching gesture and one of those small things you remember most.

After our long night in Lillie's, life took an even stranger turn the next day as we headed on back up to Lifford.

Dad was driving me and Liam back home and it's fair to say we were not in the best of health. As we got closer to Donegal, Dad's phone kept ringing. It was uncle Packie, telling him which back roads to take to avoid the traffic. What traffic? There was never any traffic. This day there was as uncle Packie told us that thousands were out in Lifford to welcome me back home. It was just unreal, I can't even begin to describe how incredible it was. As we got into Lifford, there were people everywhere, trying to get in the car. I eventually managed to get home to say hello to the family and then we went out in an open-top car, like the worst Pope impersonator you can imagine.

The streets of Lifford were absolutely rammed, it was just the most surreal experience. All these people were out cheering and going mad and it was so heartfelt. All I'd done was go and play in a football tournament. I had to do a speech in the Diamond, a big square in the middle of town and I just thanked everybody for turning up. I felt a wee bit embarrassed that so many had made so much effort.

After that I went around all the pubs and popped into Harte's Bar, where it had all started. I ended up pulling pints in there with everyone cheering. We popped into Bannigan's and the

Erin Bar too and it was just unreal. I signed so many auto-graphs I could barely move my hand the next day but that was a price I was happy to pay for the kindness I'd been shown.

The same taxi driver who let us off the fare had also told me you could walk down O'Connell Street in Dublin when our matches were on and not see a soul. At the time, I hadn't really believed him but that reception in Lifford had brought it all home. The country was proud of us and that helped us all try and move on.

*****

As I look back 15 years later, it brings to the surface emotions that I've done my best to ignore or avoid. If I was to spend my life thinking about the 2002 World Cup I'd just go mad. Nobody misses penalties on purpose and that ball didn't bobble over my leg on purpose, so you have to put it behind you.

There's a lot of *what if* moments in my career and that's one of the biggest ones. A few years after, Spain are champions of Europe and World Cup winners and yet there was us, so close to knocking them out of a World Cup ourselves.

Imagine the momentum and the confidence and the belief we would've got from beating them? Who knows where we could've ended up.

It just wasn't meant to be.

# 11

# ZIP IT

AFTER all that had happened at the World Cup I could barely wait for the 2002/03 season to begin so we could just get back to playing football.

We got off to a wonderful start as Newcastle breezed past Zeljeznicar in the Champions League qualifying rounds and ended up in Group E with Dynamo Kyiv, Feyenoord and Juventus, which suited us just fine.

It was a false dawn.

Our early season form was bad in the Premier League but even worse in Europe. We were completely written off in the Champions League after we lost our first three matches and in a pretty miserable September in the league, we had little other than a derby victory over Sunderland and a win over Birmingham City to cheer us up.

I couldn't really work out what had happened to the Newcastle of old, the Newcastle of just a few months earlier when we were bouncing. We had to rediscover it quickly if the season was not to going to fall away to nothing before it had barely begun.

# SHAY

October was not exactly great either and by the time we lost to Blackburn Rovers 5-2, it was time for me to confront and beat a problem that had been festering for a while.

*****

Any Premier League goalkeeper who tells you he doesn't get haunted by his errors is lying or doesn't care enough about his job.

At Ewood Park during that 5-2 loss, I dropped an early cross from Lucas Neill that led to Nikos Dabizas having to handball a shot on the line which saw him get a red card. David Dunn scored from the spot and the afternoon just went from bad to worse.

All the way through the match, as the Blackburn supporters hammered me, my head was a total scramble. I was trying to look calm on the outside but I was just digging myself up. 'I've lost us the game, I've lost us the game, it's all my fault' was all that was raging through my head. I was all over the place.

The Blackburn error wasn't the first of my career but for some reason it bothered me more than most.

Of course, my most 'famous' mistake came when Dion Dublin scored past me for Coventry City in 1997. It was the year after they brought in the six-second rule which meant you either had to kick it out of your hands or drop it and kick it from the floor.

Obviously I should have looked behind me but I didn't. Dion sneaked up, barged me out of the way and scored. I'm the only Irishman who doesn't know where Dublin is, right? That joke was funny for the first thousand times I heard it. After the Dublin mistake, my mood was hardly much better a week later when Dad arrived from Ireland with a gift from my mates back home. I opened the packet and there was a wing mirror, painted in Irish colours, with a note telling me to keep an eye on what was behind me in the future.

After the Ewood Park mistake, I was dropped for the next match against Juventus in the Champions League, which was a killer for me but totally understandable.

My mindset just deteriorated badly. I was struggling big time.

Nobody had ever driven me along, or expected more of myself than me. I was my own worse critic and the Blackburn match kept whirring constantly in my head. Eventually, after a few nights of sleeping badly, I went to see Derek Wright, the club physio. "I need to speak to someone," I told him. "I don't know if you know anyone or if the club recommends anyone but I need to get some stuff off my chest."

It was back in the day when nobody really used coaches for psychological issues. Most clubs have them now but this was a different lifetime in footballing terms. It's a huge part of the game. If you can get people's heads right then the rest will follow. Back then, some people saw it as a weakness. The logic was: "You don't need a head doctor telling you how good you are, deal with your own mistakes and get on with it." I disagreed then and I disagree now. Any goalkeeper who thinks they've cracked the art is never more than 90 minutes away from a rude wake-up call.

Derek recommended a psychologist called Richard Mullen who was based in Cardiff. I still use him to this day. It is a huge positive to be able to talk to someone about the mental side of the game. At the level we're playing at, if you can improve a player by one per cent then you'd be crazy not to try it.

# SHAY

Richard came up to my house in Newcastle because I didn't want the club or Bobby to know. I didn't speak to Harps or anyone else; I wanted to keep it entirely to myself because of the stigma around it at the time. I see it as a sign of strength, personally, that you can admit you need help. But I know what whispers are like and I didn't want people to think I wasn't capable of performing. It suited both me and Richard to keep it under the radar.

Over the months, Richard put in place mechanisms to help me, one of which involved my glovebag. "If you make a mistake in another game," he told me. "I want you to mentally open your glovebag and stick the mistake in there, zip it back up immediately and get on with the rest of the game. At the end of the match, we'll open the glovebag, watch the video and deal with whatever we have to then. But once that zip is back locked on the glovebag, that's it – it's gone for that game. Park it."

People might read that and think it's pie in the sky stuff but it worked for me. It took me a bit of time to get used to but I worked hard at it. If I made a mistake in training I would use that trick, zip the bag up and get back on with it.

Another of Richard's big tips was to stay in the present. "You can't turn the clock back Shay," he'd say. "Stay in the moment, ignore the voice in your head, zip it up and forget it."

There are still people who might read this book and think, 'I didn't think he had a weakness like that' but I genuinely think that dealing with it in that way is something to be proud of. I worked every day on crosses, kicking, penalties, distribution, tactics and fitness. Why wouldn't I – or why wouldn't anyone come to that – not also work on their mental strength? I wanted to be the full package and using Richard helped me do that.

# ZIP IT

One bonus was that as well as being a qualified sports psychologist, he'd also played at Crystal Palace in goal as a kid so
knew the position, understood the ins and outs and knew what
kind of mad stuff goes through a goalkeeper's mind. He still
played in goal for a Sunday League team, he knew how lonely it
could be and he understood how much a mistake could hurt the
team. If you miss a tackle in midfield, you have another chance.
If you miss an easy shot, you can bury the next one. But you
can't magically rub a goal off a scoresheet after a keeper has
messed up, can you? He knew that and saw that.

Richard would always stress how he'd expect me to be eager
to play again after a mistake when sometimes, I was the exact
opposite. In fact, I'd say there were times in my early career
where I dreaded games because it felt so intense. But Richard
wouldn't have that "This is your opportunity to show everyone
again what a goalkeeper you are," he would tell me. "We've
unzipped the bag, sorted the problem and it's water under
the bridge. Now is the chance to get back out there and prove
yourself again."

The excitement about the next game was how he turned the
situation around mentally. Rather than being anxious about the
match, he wanted me on my toes, bouncing, looking forward to
showing any overnight critics that I was still a world-class goalkeeper. The next game was an opportunity.

I could ring Richard today and speak to him about anything
if I felt I needed to. I've used him all my career and I'd be on
the phone this second if I thought he could help me get through
something.

*****

After losing those three matches in the Champions League and then missing the 1-0 win over Juventus that got us our first points on the board, I was actually back in the team for the next Premier League match, still brooding about Blackburn, as we beat Charlton 2-1. "You'll be fine son," Bobby said. "Just another game."

Harps came back in for the Dynamo Kyiv win at home and that gave us a tiny chance of still qualifying for the knockout stages of the Champions League despite our miserable start in the group. No side had ever done that. We needed to win against Feyenoord and hope Juventus won or drew against Kyiv.

That was all the motivation Bobby needed to deliver one of his trademark dressing room speeches. He was buzzing when we got to Rotterdam and these were the kind of games and occasions that brought the best from him.

"You can do this lads, you can make history. There's thousands out there, thousands, in black and white. We can turn this around."

We were soon 2-0 up thanks to Craig Bellamy and Hugo Viana and the Geordie Nation on tour was going crazy but they pulled it back to 2-2 after the break. With the clock on 90 minutes, I lashed it straight up the pitch, Kieron's shot was saved and Craig kept his head long enough to sneak in a winner from a tight angle.

It was the last kick of the game, Juventus had also beaten Kyiv, we were through and Bobby was going nuts. "I told you Shay, I told you this could happen," he said, grinning like an excited schoolboy. The dressing room was like a kids' party and I was thrilled for Craig, especially considering his knee trouble.

For some reason, back then the Champions League format

dictated we went into a second group stage. We got drawn out of the hat to play against Inter Milan, Barcelona and Bayer Leverkusen – an absolute dream group that sent the whole squad and city into a frenzy. A few months earlier we were wondering where the next win was coming from and now we were going up against Europe's best.

We had a nightmare start to Group A when Craig got a very early red card against Inter Milan. We lost 4-1 and we were then outclassed 3-1 away from home against Barcelona. The Camp Nou is built down into the ground so from the roadside it looks good but because the pitch is really low, it's not until you walk onto the pitch that you see just how jaw-dropping it is.

After losing to Barca, we actually played superbly in the Premier League and went unbeaten for a long spell as I began to feel more confident about my goalkeeping again, thanks in no small part to Richard's advice.

We got the better of Bayer Leverkusen home and away in the Champions League. We might have been some way behind the heavyweights but we could cause a shock or two when everything clicked. Leverkusen had lost the Champions League final the season before to Real Madrid but we were rampant at home as Al scored a brilliant hat-trick and The Dream was back on. We went to the San Siro for the Inter game full of confidence.

If Camp Nou is unreal, the San Siro is something else You feel like the second and third tiers of the place are sat on your shoulders, it's that tight and close. The noise, the smoke, everything about it was spine-tingling, not least the fact it seemed to be like a home match for us – black and white everywhere.

There was no need for a big Bobby team-talk that night and we were so close, so, so close, to pulling off a win. Al was again almost superhuman in the way he popped up with critical goals. He twice put us in the lead but we got pegged back, drew 2-2 and a home loss to Barcelona then ended the Champions League dream.

We remained a really impressive Premier League side, losing just four games after Boxing Day and finished the season in third spot.

One of those losses was a 6-2 thrashing by Manchester United at home and I know that hurt Bobby's pride, especially as he and Alex Ferguson had such respect for each other.

All we'd done in the build-up was work on Jonathan Woodgate man-marking Ruud van Nistelrooy. Everywhere Ruud went, we wanted Jonathan on his tail. That was the big plan all week. During the game, United realised what we were up to and the next thing, van Nistelrooy is stood out on the left wing doing nothing, Jonathan is with him and Scholes scores a hat-trick, completely untouched, through the middle!

We were gutted but afterwards Bobby was going around the dressing room saying, "What did van Nistelrooy do? He did fucking nothing!" He was still trying to justify man-marking him out of the game even though Scholes had just had a field day!

That result aside, the 2002/03 season showed we weren't a fluke team, we were a galvanised group who were scared of nobody and by finishing third, we'd even improved on the season before. We had the foundations and the manager to build on this and get even better.

Hadn't we?

*****

It's ridiculous to think now that 2003/04 was to be Bobby's last full season in charge.

Our season started slipping from August 27 onwards. That was the day we lost on penalties to Partizan Belgrade in the Champions League qualifier at St James' Park. We won at their place, they won at ours and when Al, Kieron Dyer and Jonathan Woodgate missed our first three penalties there was nothing we could do to get back into it. I'd saved the first one, from Nikola Malbassa, but I could do nothing with the others. It went to sudden-death. Aaron Hughes missed for us, they scored and that was us out of the Champions League.

After enjoying it as a club and as a city so much the year before we were all devastated and it set the wheels in motion for Bobby's eventual departure.

The loss did at least put us into the UEFA Cup and we breezed through some of the early matches.

The biggest talking point that season came as we prepared to head to Majorca for a game in March. We were 4-1 up from the first leg against Real Mallorca and we were either winning or drawing in the league every week, so we were feeling good.

Until we got to Newcastle Airport, that is.

Tension between John Carver and Craig Bellamy had been building over something as stupid as a parking place at the training ground or John being late one day – you know, really important stuff.

We got to the airport and moved into this side-room, a kind of small suite for the players. We had teas and coffees, the usual, and then for one reason or another, Craig decided he wasn't going to travel. Fuck the game, fuck the club, fuck John Carver. He properly started losing it. When he called JC, "A

Geordie c***" that was it. The next thing, they were wrestling on the floor, rolling over and over and swearing at each other. I couldn't believe what I was watching. I was close to the action and Craig threw this chair that missed me by nothing – how it didn't smack me in the face I'll never know. It was a right commotion but we knew the airport was full of fans and press so we were desperately trying to keep it quiet and not let anybody, especially not Bobby, in the room. Harps and Speedo had their hands on the door handle, jamming it closed while Wrestlemania Toon finished on the blue carpet.

"Right, this goes no further," Harps said. "What's gone on in here stays in here." Speedo's response summed up the chances of that happening: "Phhhrp" – as if to say, 'No chance.'

Harps was a real leader in the group and the club. He was a local boy, he took every headline and negative press article personally and he always did his best to keep the group together.

The two of us had a night out in Liverpool after the races one year and we were staying at Formby Hall. We must have ended up in every bar in the city. All the lads were out and next thing, I've gone missing. I didn't have a clue where I was.

What happened was, we'd met these Scouse lads on this night out and we were having a good craic. All night they were singing, 'There's only one Jerzy Dudek' to me in the pub and I was giving them plenty back. And then the next thing, they abducted me!

Harps and John Harris, a mate, were ready for bed but, typical Irishman, the night had only just started for me. "Where we going lads?" I asked these Scousers and before you know it, I'm in a taxi to the roughest house party I've ever been to. A beer was shoved into my hand and we carried on. About 6am,

I sobered up and realised this was all a bit dodgy. "Lads, get me a taxi, I've got golf in two hours," I said. Somehow I got back to Formby Hall and Harris had taken my bed because I'd gone AWOL. There was nothing else for it. Two hours later, Harps woke up in the luxurious surroundings of Formby Hall to find me next to him in bed, still pissed, snoring. And stark bollock naked. I told you we were close!

Back in that airport suite, we couldn't keep anything quiet at the time because someone in the dressing room was leaking stuff all over the place to the press. As the reporters walked past us to their seats on the flight, we all tried to bluff that everything was ok but those lads aren't stupid. Eventually, as JC regained his composure we managed to leave with Craig. Bobby had done an unbelievable job of calming him and getting him on the flight. We turned our phones off and settled back for the journey, thinking that was the end of it.

When we landed, I turned my phone back on. I had about 15 text messages asking what had happened in the side-room suite at Newcastle Airport between Craig Bellamy and John Carver. The whole world already knew all about it

That was life at Newcastle, it was something you had to live with and get used to. A few years later one of the papers labelled us 'North-Eastenders' and mocked us all up as characters on Albert Square. That paper went round the dressing room with us all laughing and nodding our heads. It really was like that, the world's maddest soap opera.

On the pitch, despite everything, we were doing ok – until we finally got to face Marseille in the UEFA Cup semi-final. It was 0-0 after the first leg at home. Bobby used to love European ties because the cameras could record the first 15 minutes of training, so he'd be there with us, warming up, loving the attention. Then the second leg started and Bobby's smile disappeared.

To sum it up simply, we were blown away by Didier Drogba. We didn't do a lot wrong but he killed us single-handedly. It was a glimpse of the player he would become.

To be so close to a European final was a heartbreaker. The dressing room was so flat. Bobby was trying to put a brave face on, trying to show that we could learn a lesson from the match but you could tell he was only putting on an act; he was devastated too. "They came a long way tonight son," he said. "We couldn't get the job done but we will, we will."

The promise of a semi-final was all Newcastle had talked about for the last month and now, like a bubble bursting, the excitement and vibe in the club and the city was gone. The season finished with three draws, which in itself was a great effort and a testament to Bobby that he could get us back up after the Marseille result, but it also meant we finished fifth, so any Champions League hopes were gone.

After the final home game against Wolves, a 1-1 draw, the ground emptied pretty quickly and Bobby wasn't too happy about it. He thought our efforts, on the back of a long hard season, deserved more than about 5,000 Geordies clapping. It had left a sour taste to him because all he ever wanted to do was make the Newcastle public happy.

Within a few months he was gone as Freddy Shepherd decided that finishing fourth, third and then fifth wasn't good enough.

There are not enough words to describe that decision, just as there are not enough words to describe how much we would miss Bobby…

## 12

# SIR BOBBY

'BEST wishes, B-O-B-B-Y...'

The Newcastle United pen in Bobby Robson's hand would carefully shape each letter of his name slowly, precisely and with absolute attention.

"And where you from, son?" he'd ask the fan clutching his new shirt and scarf, their eyes lit up that they were stood there talking to a Geordie legend. "How long have you been following us? Where is your seat? Ok, son, you enjoy the season and say hi to your mam and dad from me." Bobby would be asking the fans more questions about them than they would about him.

Finally, the pen would be picked back up and R-O-B-S-O-N would carefully, slowly and precisely be added to the B-O-B-B-Y and the fan would move on. He was dotting the I's and crossing the T's – and he's not even got those in his name.

Sat in the Newcastle club shop before the season began, we'd all be required to do signing sessions and the Newcastle fans would be queueing around the block. The worst place to end up being sat was next to Bobby.

"Honest boss, you wanna hurry up a bit," we'd all chirp up. "There's only another 4,000 to get through here." Bobby wouldn't be rushed. He wanted to make sure every autograph was pristine for the fans and he wanted to hear everyone's life story. He just loved Newcastle, Newcastle United and the Newcastle people. I'd be dragging these autograph books from underneath his nose, trying to get the line moving a bit but he wouldn't have it and that was the measure of the man.

When Bobby came in we went from Gullit, which was all about him, to a man who was one of them, one of the fans, one of the Geordie Nation. He was just a fan who happened to be a great manager as well.

After spells as England manager and then time at clubs like PSV Eindhoven, Sporting Lisbon and Barcelona, he had this great pedigree and, just as importantly, he was from Durham, the north-east – and that means a hell of a lot up there. Straight away the fans took to him and rightly so.

So did the players. He had such a bubbly personality and was so passionate. Some bosses let others take the training sessions but not Bobby – he was right there, always upbeat and positive, shouting and bawling and getting his message across. He was so hands on; he'd be putting the cones out one minute and then shouting at us the next. He loved being in the mix. John Carver could have taken all that off his shoulders but he was never happier than when he was out there with us, a whistle around his neck, running and bouncing around like a 30-year-old.

As everyone probably knows, he was terrible with names. "Shay Brennan you've got to save that son," he shouted at me once! He called Shola Ameobi 'Carl Cort' and he called Harps 'Paul Cooper', a goalkeeper from back in his Ipswich Town days. Sometimes you wondered if he was doing it on purpose, just to see if he could get a reaction. The only reaction he got was us lot pissing ourselves.

When Bobby came in we were struggling but then we won our first home game under him 8-1 against Sheffield Wednesday and Al scored five, which said it all. Al was buzzing again. I think Bobby extended Al's career by getting him back to his very best. He gave him a new lease of life. Under Ruud Gullit, he struggled at times, by his standards. He wasn't scoring too many goals and was unhappy. I think he felt that Gullit didn't always really believe in him. Yet Bobby came in with his bubbly character and changed that. "You're the main man," Bobby said to Alan. "You will take us forward." They were two massive north-east figures and they worked really well together.

★★★★★

Before the 2003/04 season began, we went to Malaysia for a pre-season tour to play in the Premier League Asia Cup.

As me and Harps left the hotel, there was a sign being put up in the foyer that said, 'Tropical Warning: 3'. We were right there in the middle of the hurricane season and didn't think much of it. We went to the ground to train and the conditions were ridiculous with loads of sirens going off, telling people to stay indoors.

Me and Harps had to do these training drills in the stinking heat and the wind started blowing so heavily that the police turned up and tried to chase us off the training field. Bobby was walking around saying to them, "No, not yet – we've not finished, get off, get off." There were alarms going off and the floodlights could've been coming down at any second but all Bobby cared about was staying out there. Mind you, at that stage, we'd all seen bigger storms in the north-east.

We got back to the hotel and all of a sudden this Tropical Warning sign is reading an '8' and people were boarding up their houses left, right and centre. Yet we had been out in the middle of it – Bobby was oblivious.

Later on that same trip, we played Chelsea in the Asia Cup final and lost on penalties when Jermaine Jenas tried to chip the ball past Carlo Cudicini during the shootout – but missed by a mile. Bobby was going bananas on the sidelines. Even after the game he was fuming. "What the hell are you doing son? *What. Are. You. Doing?*"

I remember Jermaine had the same birthday as Bobby. One year, Bobby was given a cake at the training ground and the next thing, out came one for Jermaine as well. "Bloody hell boss," I said. "He's only been here 10 minutes. I've been here years and never had one. Did you buy him the candles yourself?!" We were giving him loads about it but Bobby just sat there and grinned.

Why do I mention the above stories?

Well, for me, they show you Bobby at his best. He wanted to train in a hurricane, he wanted to win every match, no matter the circumstances or what was at stake, and he also wanted one of his players to feel welcome and happy at a big club where it would have been easy to be neither.

Bobby was such a likeable man. He just had that way about him. It wasn't so much his tactical knowledge, it was his man-management. He worked out what motivated and drove each of us in our different ways. He invested in you, and we repaid him.

He knew when to bollock you, when to laugh at you, when to put his arm around you and when to ignore you.

Before the 2000/01 season, we played DC United on an American tour and Big Dunc was injured so he couldn't play. We got to the ground and were in the dressing room when, all of a sudden, he walked into the dressing room without a stitch on. He was stark bollock naked and had a big grin on his face. He'd been out in the day with Steve Howey and had a few too many. "Alright lads," he roared, before heading into the showers behind Bobby. Bobby, and this is why he was so special, just completely ignored him. It was like a ghost had gone past. Bobby just carried on like it hadn't happened. This wasn't the time for an argument so he let it go.

He'd talk to Craig Bellamy when he was up front with Shearer and say, "You're the best player in this club, fuck Shearer, you're the man to score the goals you're the man I'm relying on today." He'd then walk over to Al and go, "Bellamy is a little shit, he's getting on everyone's fucking nerves – you get out there and show him why you're the number one striker at this club." He could get the best out of anyone. He was an old fash-ioned psychologist who knew how to play us.

One day me, Al, Harps and a few others were in the darts room at the training ground and Bobby was in there with us, absolutely battering Craig. "I'm sick of him," he said. "He's trouble and I always knew he would be."

Two minutes later, who should walk into the room but Craig himself. "Craig, son, how are you? You alright?" Bobby said, turning on a sixpence. "Do you need anything, how's your hamstring? I need you at the weekend, son, score me a goal." Bellamy left. "He's still a shit!" Robson then carried on. And that's what I mean by man-management – he knew how and when to talk to everybody to try and get the best out of each of us.

I don't ever really remember falling out with Bobby apart from one match against Liverpool in December 2003. The ball had come over the top, I'd hesitated coming out and Danny Murphy snuck in and nutmegged me.

I'd just not quite been quick enough or positive enough to either come out and clear or stay on my line and save a shot. I was neither here or there really. The game ended 1-1 but the next day in training, we started doing these drills where the ball would come over the top and I'd have to clear.

I knew exactly what Bobby was doing and what he was trying to say. He was re-enacting Murphy's goal. And I lost it. "Fucking hell," I started. "I bet if Alan missed a fucking penalty on Saturday we wouldn't all be doing spot-kicks this morning." I was playing really well at the time and it was just one of those things. I was fuming. "Get on with it," Bobby said. That was it, that was his way of saying I should've done better.

Bobby just had this way, this manner, this habit of knowing exactly what had to be said to players to get the best from them. It was like he had an x-ray machine in his brain, always whirring, always working out what to say to make each player tick.

We played Barcelona pre-season at home in 2002 and there were 51,000 in St James' Park that night, an absolutely mind-blowing amount of fans for a friendly game. We had a really strong side out but they just took the piss and were 3-0 up after about an hour – nothing to do with me! Even our fans were applauding them and shouting 'ole! ole!' every time they touched the ball, which was a lot more than us.

Shortly after half-time the board went up with my number on.

# SIR BOBBY

Harps was coming on. As I ran over to shake Harps' hand, Bobby looked up and was shouting at me. "STEVIE, don't let any more goals in son, we're getting fucking murdered!" Harps just ran on laughing his head off but that was Bobby, mad.

***** 

All the players loved Bobby being our boss. There were plenty of opportunities to wind him up, which we never missed.

One day, ahead of a Champions League game, Steven Taylor bought this remote controlled fart machine into the dining room.

As we all sat having dinner before this European tie, Taylor stuck this machine under Bobby's table. We were all in on the joke and we and sat down to eat like schoolboys, sniggering, waiting for Taylor to hit the remote control button and set the fart sounds off.

Bobby came down to this big round table, sat with the staff and it was game on. Imagine, 25 grown men, club tracksuits on, ready to play in a Champions League match – and we're already crying, ready for Taylor to do his worst.

The starters come out and then it's down to business. Bobby was just passing the salt when, from nowhere, 'Prrrrrrrrrp'. He looked around, disgust etched on his face. We're all on it, trying desperately to keep a straight face. Bobby is fuming already but he lets it go.

Next thing, 'Prrrrrrrrrrrrrrrrrrp'.

And then, 'PRRRRRRRRRRRRPPPPPPPPPPP'.

Longer, louder, better.

Bobby wasn't having this one. "That's disgusting," he roared, standing up at the same time, banging the table with his fist. "Who was that? That's disgusting."

Well, you can imagine the state we were in. We let him in on it eventually and he saw the funny side straight away. "You bastards," he grinned, laughing along with the rest of us.

Bobby was big on respect around the training ground and big on rules. He believed in discipline at all times and he really wanted to build a spirit around the place that we would carry onto the field.

One of his favourite rules involved us all eating together every day at training. At 1pm we would all sit around these tables, but we couldn't touch a morsel until he was in there. And then, after we'd all eaten, we couldn't leave, we couldn't get up, until he told us we could. "Right lads, see you tomorrow," and then we'd all scarper.

The thing was, Bobby was a slow eater. In fact, he ate his lunch slower than he signed autographs. He loved his soup – "try the soup, son" – so he'd have three bowls of soup, then a corn on the cob, with bits of sweetcorn stuck to his cheek, and then he'd have a nice leisurely lunch.

We'd all be looking at him, for 40 minutes, desperate to get away. Looking back, what did we have to get away for, really? He recognised the importance of team-bonding and knew that eating together was part of building that.

Every now and then, Al or Speedo would bang on the table and shout, "Come on, hurry up boss" but that was the worst thing you could do. He'd just make you wait longer! Al was often impatient, desperate to go, but after I'd left and he became the manager, what did he do? The exact same thing as Bobby had. You could see why Bobby did it. It stopped lads from showering and just shooting off. We got to know each other personally, as men, and that means you stick together even more.

Bobby also demanded respect in any team meetings. One

time we were in the players' room, he called a meeting and Craig Bellamy was in the second row, with his feet up on the chair in front of him. Bobby wasn't having that.

"Hey, son, would you put your feet up on a chair like that in your house?" Bellamy went, "Yeah, I fuckin' would – it's my house, I bought it!" "Well this is my house," Bobby said. "And you won't do that in here!"

We had another signing session one day and this guy asked Bobby how he was and how the family was, then he said, "Bobby, you must sign hundreds of these?"

"Yes, I do son," he said, and carried on. This guy went outside, then reappeared and joined the back of the queue. When he came back to the front of the line, he had tears running down his face. Bobby had signed the book, 'Best wishes, Bobby Hundreds'. It's probably worth a few quid now.

Bobby's sacking by the club in August 2004, just four matches into the season, was a massive blow to him and also to us. I think towards the end of his time there, some of the players had begun to tune out of his style and his way of managing. He was that involved in every aspect of the club, maybe some players just didn't listen as much as they once had.

It was all very sad for him personally. The year we finished fifth, pens were already being sharpened, which is mental looking back. "Those bastards chased me out of the England job," he said to me about the press one day. "And they're trying to chase me out of this one."

I think part of him was still, even then, hurting about Italia '90 and the way his international career had ended and how he'd been hounded out.

After the news broke, Bobby came in to see the players and we were all in the same room where he'd had that pop at Bellamy. He walked in looking as white as a ghost, completely lost, completely devastated. All of a sudden, that spring and bounce he had was missing. He explained what had happened and that he was on his way.

"I don't agree with it but I have to respect it," he told us. "Good luck lads, all the best. Go and beat Blackburn tomorrow." And that was it. Another managerial legend gone.

Sir Bobby Robson got sacked by Newcastle United Football Club.

When you think about that now, that's unreal.

We finished just one spot outside the Champions League places and Sir Bobby Robson had given the club its pride, its identity and its spirit back. And then he was sacked. Crazy.

Fair enough, we failed to win a trophy under Bobby, just as we hadn't won one under Kenny before him, but, again, what would most football teams in the world give for a manager of his pedigree?

And what would Newcastle fans give to finish fourth, third and then fifth in the Premier League these days?

Bobby was a magnificent Geordie, a real character, a real football man, a real winner and a real person.

To have known him, to have played for him and to have watched him close up will always remain one of the greatest privileges of my career.

## 13

# FIGHT CLUB

LOOKING back now, I suppose the Graeme Souness era at Newcastle is best remembered for a fight between two Newcastle United Football Club players during a match. That's not exactly setting the bar *that* high, is it?

When Bobby left there was talk that he'd lost the dressing room but I don't think that's true. Did some players have a problem with Bobby because they weren't playing every week? Yes, of course, but that's football and that's footballers – that wasn't anything specific to Bobby and we'd just finished fifth as well, don't forget.

As a result, when Souness came in he wasn't exactly coming to a club falling to pieces on the park. Souness also brought in Dean Saunders and he was the perfect partner for Graeme because he was a bit of a Terry Mac figure for us. Dean wanted to lift us and keep things light and it worked well with Graeme, who was a more serious manager than Bobby had been.

Terry himself was soon back with us as well after contacting Graeme once he'd been appointed. Having him back at the club was a boost for those of us who remembered him from his first spell and, as with Kenny, it was good for Souness to have one of his old Anfield team-mates around.

I'll get to what happened between Kieron Dyer and Lee Bowyer in a while as there was already plenty going off at the club with Souness and Craig Bellamy falling out pretty much from the start.

Souness arrived in September 2004 and Bellamy was wearing Celtic's colours by the following January which tells its own story about what had gone on between the two of them.

Craig wasn't happy that Bobby had left, nor that we'd sold Gary Speed to Bolton Wanderers either, and he was coming to the boil too often and too quickly for Souness's liking. I think Graeme felt like he needed to let Craig and the rest of us know that he could handle himself and he was in charge. Graeme is solidly built and one look at *YouTube* will tell you that he was hard as nails as a player, so it had to come to a head eventually.

Craig was subbed in a match against Charlton in October and he called Souness 'a fucking prick' when he walked past him.

The following week we were having a meeting and, as expected, it was about to go off between them. Bellamy is opinionated and can get under people's skin but I think it was more that Graeme wanted to show his strength early on. He called Bellamy out for the abuse and that was it, he was fully into him.

"Call me that again and I'll fucking knock you out," he told Craig and he made this big lunge for him, trying to drag him out of his chair.

"In the gym now, me and you," Souness carried on, really up for it. It soon calmed down – but before long Craig was on his way to Scotland and we'd lost a really solid goalscorer and somebody who worked his bollocks off every single day. We couldn't afford to lose players like that.

To me it felt like we'd brought in too many players who just couldn't cut it while at the same time letting the likes of Speedo move to Bolton. Speedo was the ultimate professional and ultimate winner but you can't let quality like him slip out of a club, replace him with nobody and expect to get away with it. Bobby was actually still the boss when he left and the move was against his wishes as well as everyone else in the dressing room who still felt he had plenty to give.

Patrick Kluivert was one who came in during the summer of 2004 and although his arrival caused excitement for the fans and the player – he'd been a goalscoring machine all his life – by the time he joined us it felt to me that the spark he'd shown at Barcelona was on the wane.

Ironically enough, Kluivert rented Speedo's house in Northumberland. It was in the middle of nowhere and a beautiful house but he spent most of his time in the city centre, enjoying the various delights of Newcastle's late-night economy.

During that 2004/05 season, we had Blackburn away on Boxing Day and when Kluivert turned up for the trip down there it was clear he'd had a very enjoyable Christmas Day.

"Let's stop for a McDonald's," he kept shouting. "I want to use the drive-thru." He was subbed that day at half-time.

Jean-Alain Boumsong was another who came in to the club on a big contract. He cost the club £8m which raised a lot of eyebrows at the time and he couldn't justify that kind of money. I don't know if he was a confidence player because he just couldn't click and just seemed to get outmuscled more and more as the weeks went on. In training he wouldn't get revved up or aggressive, he just let the games pass him by. Somehow, he left us for Juventus; I think his agent was Harry Houdini.

It wasn't all bad news though, as lads like Nicky Butt and James Milner also arrived. Both were excellent players who gave it everything. They were very strong and determined to show they were good enough. James was at the start of his career, Nicky towards the end but they were driven and so committed.

Milner was only a young lad but he was the ultimate pro and one of those lads who was good at everything because he practised and practised and practised. He would stand there for hours, repeating the same moves over and over again until he perfected whatever he was trying to do. And that was just on the dartboard at the training ground.

He was nicknamed 'Machine Gun Milner' at the darts because he would throw fast and straight all day long. I wasn't much of a darts player but Harps loved it and set up two leagues, the 'Premier League' dartboard where you had to be one of the top eight players and then the other board was called the 'Moroccan Open' (no disrespect to Morocco!)

At training and at dead-ball practice Milner was just as hard-working and dedicated and it's no surprise to see how well liked he's remained throughout his career no matter where he's been.

There were plenty of characters in the squad and most were given a nickname. We used to call Titus Bramble, 'Dan Marino' because you just knew he'd zing it as far up the pitch as he could. He'd even look up like Marino and then send it. I think he had some new boots made, the 'Adidas Terrace Finders' because, boy, did he find them. The hand would come up automatically afterwards as the crowd ducked – sorry lads!

Andy O'Brien was nicknamed 'Postman Pat' – have you seen the size of the nose on him? – and he was a fans' favourite up there. He was quite quiet but was solid and scored a very important goal at Sunderland so he'll never buy a pint in town for as long as he lives.

We were all still socialising fairly regularly together and you would always bump into somebody somewhere. A restaurant called Smithy Bistro was next door to The Diamond Inn in Ponteland and on a Sunday it would be full of families and half the squad would be in there having a roast dinner.

Mark Devlin knew the chef pretty well so would drive round to the side door, it would open and the chef would plonk a roast dinner on the passenger seat with a jug of gravy and Mark would throw him a fiver. There was no need to go in and queue and wait and all that. I wasn't having it but Mark was adamant you could do it so I began to try it myself. I drove up to the side door, beeped the horn, it opened and, sure enough, this roast beef dinner was through the car window and I was away.

Before long, half the Newcastle United squad were turning up for a drive-thru Sunday roast and all the trimmings. In the end Mark rang me. "Shay, you need to stop doing that," he said. "I've had the chef on and the place is running out of plates! None of the lads are taking them back."

\*\*\*\*\*

Graeme's management style was pretty basic. He was an unbelievable player, he won three European Cups and was a stunning midfielder but his tactical information amounted to, "At Liverpool, we went out and worked it out ourselves."

Well, they had the best players in the world then, so that was why that was easy to do. Saying that though, I understood what he meant. When we crossed the white line, Graeme wasn't with us and we had to work matches out for ourselves. You can't stand there looking at the dugout going, "What now boss?" can you?

He also used to make a great point about the mental strength needed to compete at the highest level. Before a match he'd remind us what was at stake and what it took to be a winner. "Anyone can waltz around St James' Park when you're 1-0 up," he'd say. "But have you got the bollocks to turn up when you're losing? Have you got the bollocks to go and get the ball after giving it away when you're 1-0 down? That's the kind of player I want. That was my job at Anfield. I'd get the ball and give it to someone who could play." Bloody hell, that's a bit harsh on yourself Graeme! But he meant it; he wanted tough men with tough mentalities.

One of those who did get the nod of approval on that front from Graeme – at least until he started chucking punches at his team-mate – was Lee Bowyer. Lee actually joined when Bobby was still manager and we got on straight away.

Lee got a lot of bad press but it didn't bother him at all. He might've gone home and cried into his pillow at night but he certainly never gave that impression to me. He had a house in London and would travel up and down quite a lot but he also had a place in Morpeth.

"Shay, can you pop round and feed the dog for me?" he asked one day. I went round to his house, opened the gate and walked up to the front door and as I walked up, there was this banging coming from inside the house. Oh God, Lee Bowyer has the world's most dangerous, angry dog – some massive boxer or something. There was no way I was going in there.

I rang Lee and he was laughing. "Don't worry, he's as soft as they come, you'll be fine," he told me, as the dog continued to headbutt the door, grab at the letterbox and basically let me know that I wasn't welcome. "There's no fucking way I'm going in there mate, he'll kill me," I told Lee, who decided there was only one thing for it. Lee instructed me to open the letterbox and shout, "Down boy, down boy" at this beast (if anybody in Morpeth walking past has wondered in the years since why a grown man was shouting this through a letterbox then they have their answer now).

Eventually, after the dog refused to listen, Lee had an even wiser idea. "Shay, put me on speakerphone and I'll speak to him." This was getting more ridiculous by the second. In the end, you had Lee Bowyer on a phone 200 miles away screaming, "Down boy, down boy" into his phone while I propped it up in the door letterbox, hoping to get away with at least three of my four limbs.

Lee was super-fit and was one of those freaks who managed to be that way despite eating absolute garbage. His engine was incredible, he was like another Terry Mac, but he stuffed his face with crap every day. We'd get beasted in fitness sessions and he'd have a McDonald's on the way home, his place in the changing room would be surrounded by pic'n'mix, bags of Haribo and all sorts. The sports science lads today would have a heart attack if they had seen the stuff he shovelled down. Maybe he was on a sugar rush when he and Dyer started knocking the shit out of each other.

When Graeme came in we had a good run of wins and our

victories tended to come in bursts. We won five on the bounce early on and then eight consecutive wins later in the season so we must have been doing something right, somewhere. The problem tended to be that for every peak there would be a trough coming up and it would feel like there was no chance we were ever going to win again. The fans started to turn, slowly, against Graeme, and then the downward spiral gathered pace and became hard to stop.

Mad sideshows like Kieron and Lee's fight didn't help anybody either. Against Aston Villa at home in April 2005, we really did become the laughing stock of the Premier League.

How do you sum that afternoon up? We ended up with only eight men that day because Steven Taylor had done a 'Platoon' impression on the goal-line, pretending he'd been shot after handling the ball to stop Villa scoring with about 20 minutes to go. It was a noble sacrifice by Taylor and would probably have been applauded in the *Evening Chronicle* that night but the match, and the world, then went bananas.

My main memory of it all is just seeing this blur of black and white arms throwing haymakers and then seeing Gareth Barry fly in to try and split it up. The whole stadium was just in disbelief. When we got to the bottom of it later, it turned out it was over the two of them falling out over passing the ball to each other. Crazy.

When Dyer and Bowyer got sent off, the pitch was getting seriously short of black and white shirts. I just couldn't wait to get off the field that day myself. Not only had we been done 3-0 at home, two of my team-mates, two of those entrusted with representing the club alongside me, had completely disgraced themselves and us, massively.

We trudged back to the dressing room and I was chewing about the loss as much as what those idiots had just done. The whole day had been Sunday League. It was madness. You don't even see footballers punch opposition players these days so to have two team-mates going for it was ridiculous.

I was fuming but I was far, far calmer than Al was. He got back in the dressing room and was as mad as I've ever seen him. "What the fuck was that, what the fuck were you doing?" he was shouting at the two of them. "You're both a fucking joke, you're a disgrace to the club."

He was the captain and he was also a local boy and a fan. I think he was embarrassed for the club and for the shirt as much as they were.

Newcastle were making headlines for ridiculous reasons and he was dumbfounded by it all. He was absolutely right to go for them. It was ridiculous, a farce. Two team-mates fighting? What next? Football is hard enough when it's 11 v 11 never mind 11 v 8. Al didn't always say something after a match but when he did, we listened – and we listened that day all right.

Both Bowyer and Dyer were still fuming afterwards and they would probably have had another fight there and then to sort it out.

Boumsong told them to get on with it and get it out of their systems but then Souness put it all to bed in no time. "If you two think you can fucking fight, I'll show you," he said. "I'll take the pair of you on whenever you want. Come on then, if you're so tough. You two couldn't fight fucking anyone."

On the Monday, the two of them had to give a press conference and shake hands for the cameras. The positive thing for us was that there genuinely was no animosity between them. The bad blood didn't last a second longer after Souness offered to give both of them a hiding. They were genuinely embarrassed and were even laughing about it together in no time, the way two mates sometimes do after firing up against one another in a bar.

All in all though, April 2005 is not one for the highlights reel as in the space of four days, we lost in both the UEFA Cup and FA Cup to bring any hopes of a trophy to an end.

Against Sporting Lisbon at St James' Park in the first leg of our quarter-final, we won 1-0 but I had to come off with a hip problem so Harps played the second half. The win was massive for us, Bowyer actually came on for Dyer − which summed the entire episode up − and it was a relief to get back on the field and play football again in order to forget what had happened.

The only downside for us was Laurent Robert raging when he was subbed for Milner, which was another example of a player not getting on with Souness.

The two of them had been at it for a while because Robert − and quite a large section of fans to be fair − were upset that he wasn't playing every week. He was a wonderful footballer but Graeme had made his mind up he wasn't what he wanted − and that was the end of it.

I don't know what happened next but somehow Robert ended up talking to a bunch of reporters after the match − for European games you have to walk through a roped-off area where the media can ask you questions − and he absolutely nailed Souness, slagging him for not starting, for our style of play, the lot. I think they must have put the quotes up their sleeves for a bit because on the morning of the second-leg match, it was everywhere in the press. We were already in Portugal by then and as we got on the bus to train on the morning of the game, Robert came on and slumped in a seat at the back.

Souness got on and was searching for him straight away, a big wad of Fleet Street's finest newsprint in his hands.

"Where is he?" he barked. We all knew who he meant. He walked down the bus, lashed the papers at Lauren and threw him off the bus. Was that the right call? Is that what Bobby would've done? I don't think so. I think Bobby would've realised that Laurent was a wizard on his day, this was the morning of a UEFA Cup quarter-final and some things were more important than words on a page.

Either way, we played the match, went 1-0 up through Dyer and then completely crumbled. We lost Kieron Dyer, Jermaine Jenas and Titus Bramble to injury and after that they just kept coming at us. We eventually lost 4-1 on the night and 4-2 on aggregate.

I'd recovered in time to play the match but I was sickened by it. We'd had a good run in the UEFA Cup that season, we'd been a solid side, thrashing good teams like Olympiakos home and away and yet it all came to a halt that night.

The FA Cup was the same a few days later. I think we flew straight to Cardiff for the semi-final against Manchester United and we were terrible, losing 4-1. I'd always enjoyed semi-finals more than the actual big day but after conceding four goals again for the second time in 72 hours, I was starting to lose it and our season pretty much ended there and then.

Soon after the United loss in the FA Cup, we were again beaten by them at Old Trafford when Wayne Rooney scored one of the best goals of his career, smashing in a volley from miles away. He just caught it so sweet and it flew in. You always try and look at wonder goals from a goalkeeper's point of view and part of me thought I should've gone with the other hand really. He was proper arguing with the referee about 10 seconds before but he then looked up, the ball dropped and he just slammed it while still half-swearing at the ref! It was a great strike and he was pumped up – and Wayne is a dangerous man when he's wound up.

At the time, he was on the verge of being substituted because he had a dead leg and then he produced that moment of class. That seemed to sum up our fortune, or lack of it.

I made a save earlier in that match from him – I was always a busy man at Old Trafford – and he came up and grabbed me from behind afterwards. "Any chance mate?" he grinned, laughing. It was one bright moment in an otherwise tough day.

Another positive though was my continued good relationship with Harps. After he'd come off the bench against Sporting and performed well in the first leg, Souness could easily have kept him in for the second tie and the rest of the season but I went back in straight away. Harps never complained, never took it personally and never stopped trying to help me get better.

Someone would come in on trial and it didn't matter how young or old they were, we'd look at each other and wink – "Right, let's fucking sort him out." He was coming in to take our positions and our jobs but we've got bills to pay as well you know! Top corner, bottom corner, this way, that way – they wouldn't save a thing. We'd be high-fiving ourselves afterwards. "That's another one seen off Harps."

My footwork was always extremely quick and Harps used to take the piss about it as often as he could. When we were doing drills, if I stopped a shot by simply moving super-quick to one

**LEGENDS:** (*Left*) Presenting Alan Shearer with a Player of the Month award in 2003 while Sir Bobby Robson gives Gary Speed an award for his 400th Premier League appearance in 2004

**PARIS MATCH:** Applauding a clean sheet and a hard earned point in France. It was a bright start but we couldn't maintain momentum for the 2006 World Cup

**BAPTISM OF FIRE:** No wonder Steve Staunton has his finger in his ear while speaking to the press. He didn't deserve such a hard time during his spell as manager

**THAT INJURY:** Marlon Harewood collides with me at Upton Park in 2006. I've never known pain like it

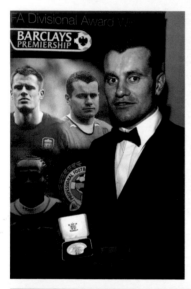

**RECOGNITION:** (*Left*) Named in the PFA Team of the Year 2005/06. (*Above*) training with Harps – Steve Harper – a great friend and a brilliant goalkeeper

**MY BALL:** Coming out to deny Cristiano Ronaldo during a Manchester United game in January, 2008

**END OF AN ERA:** Waving to the crowd after the Euro 2008 qualifying match against San Marino – the last time we would play at Lansdowne Road

**ALWAYS ON MY SIDE:** Liam's famous banner – it was the first thing I looked for before a game

**IN THE SPOTLIGHT:** Striding out for a training session ahead of a Euro qualifier against Italy and (*right*) saluting the fans on reaching 100 caps

**TAKING CARE:** Kevin Keegan was a first class man-manager but didn't really get a chance

**DAY AT THE RACES:** Relaxing with team-mate Michael Owen

**SHUT-OUT:** John Terry shows his frustration as I stop the ball crossing the line at Stamford Bridge

**THE LAST STRAW:** The 5-1 defeat to Liverpool in December 2008 was one humiliation too many

**NEW START:** Signing for City with boss Mark Hughes

**SPOT ON:** (*Below left*) Delight after a win over Chelsea – I saved a Frank Lampard penalty that day – and (*below right*) a hero in the penalty shootout against Aalborg

**NO WAY ROO:** Denying Wayne Rooney (*above*) in the Carling Cup semi-final

**WHO, ME?:** Flashpoints with referees Andre Marriner and Mark Halsey

**THAT MOMENT:** Thierry Henry disappears behind our goal after the infamous handball goal from the World Cup second leg play-off in November, 2009. The look of disbelief on my face says it all

**INJUSTICE:** I plead with the referee – but somehow Martin Hansson missed it

**CAUGHT IN A TRAP:** Enjoying a laugh with the man we called the Trap – who was a real character. (*Above*) Making sure Duffer – Damien Duff – looks the part

**PUT IT THERE:** But I just didn't see eye to eye with Roberto Mancini

**NO FEAR:** Plucking the ball out of the air to deny Chelsea's prolific Didier Drogba in 2010/11

**BODY ON THE LINE:** I took a risk playing against Arsenal in April, 2010 and I suffered a fully dislocated shoulder – the injury paved the way for my departure

**FULL VOLUME:** Communicating and organising defenders has always been one of my biggest strengths

**WINNING FEELING:** Celebrating on the Wembley pitch with Joe Hart and goalkeeping coach Massimo Battara after the FA Cup win in May, 2011. I couldn't have been happier for Joe. (*Left*) a picture with my good mate Patrick Vieira

side rather than diving for the ball – I used to be that fast I could do that easily – when it was Harps' turn to do the same drill, he'd set his feet off going like a jackhammer and then just keep running sideways until he hit the car park.

We were always laughing and taking the piss out of ourselves and each other. Sometimes we played golf together and on one occasion we went up to St Andrews in Scotland for a couple of rounds. We played then hit the town for a drink afterwards. A few beers were sunk and soon I was dying for the toilet. In between bars, I ran down this alleyway and let nature take its course. Next thing, the blue lights are flashing. I was called over and was sat in the back of this police van getting a dressing down from a copper when Harps turned, sat in the passenger seat and tried to plead my case. "Look mate," he told this copper. "That's Shay Given in the back from Newcastle United. If this gets out it will make all the papers. Is there any chances you can just tick him off and let him go, it was only a piss."

"That's Shay Given in the back?" the copper asked. "No it's not, that's not Shay Given!" He wouldn't believe him at first.

"It fucking is," Harps piped up. "I should know, I can't get a game off him!" This did the trick, the back door opened and I was allowed on my way, owing Harps a very large drink for using his 'charm' to get me off.

It was a different outcome to the first time the police stopped me in Newcastle when I was going a little bit too fast in my Audi TT, trying to get back home to watch the second half of an Old Firm game. On that occasion, the copper told me: "I know a lot of lads would let you off Mr Given. But I'm a Manchester United fan and I don't give a shit!"

The end of the 2004/05 season came and went and we

finished 14th, which was a hell of a slide from fifth under Bobby and the pressure was certainly on Souness and the club by now to sort it out.

I'd played 52 matches, the most of any player in the club, but that didn't bring any real satisfaction, not when I looked at the Premier League table.

I wasn't the only one dissatisfied either.

Over the summer we sold Craig Bellamy to Celtic while the likes of Laurent Robert and James Milner were loaned out and despite signing Michael Owen for £17m, we couldn't stop sliding under Graeme.

Eventually, after the noise from the fans became too loud for the club to ignore, Souness was sacked in February 2006 when we were only just above the relegation zone.

Souness was – is – a strong and proud man and I'm certain his dismissal would've disappointed him a lot. He certainly had a lot to deal with during his time at the club and he deserves a lot of respect for how he managed us during some tough times.

Ultimately though, Newcastle's board and fans will only put up with mediocre results for so long and if anybody was going to pay the price for our form, and our style of play, then Graeme was that person.

# 14

# WORLD CUP
# WANNABE

AFTER the 2002 World Cup, the end of Mick as our manager was on the horizon. He remained caught up in the post-Saipan inquest that the whole country was obsessed with.

The World Cup changed how we were reported on in the media. It all got a lot more negative and cynical and when we lost to Russia and Switzerland in the Euro 2004 qualifiers, that was the end·for him, especially when the Lansdowne Road crowd let their feelings be known by chanting Roy Keane's name during the Switzerland loss.

Mick has since said that he should've gone earlier. I don't know about that but I do know I was sad to see him go. He'd given me my first cap and had trusted me at a World Cup and that meant a lot. I texted him to say: 'Sorry to see you go. Thanks for the opportunity you gave me to represent Ireland. You deserve to be remembered as a great manager.'

Mick had been the captain of Ireland under Jack Charlton, he was a real leader and wore his heart on his sleeve out on the pitch. He was a no-nonsense player, he is a no-nonsense talker and I felt he was a great fit.

Mick had always managed the lads well, he knew when to push and pull you and when to let you enjoy yourselves. He's such an honest bloke – and you can only respect that. He would tell you things straight and always had the country's best interests at heart. Some managers go around the houses and bullshit you but Mick was never like that. He would look you straight in the eye, pick his team and then explain it to you. That hasn't always been the case in my career and it was nice to work for a manager who was so open. Mick has now been at Ipswich Town for about five seasons which is pretty much a miracle in modern-day football. He's doing the same job for them as he did for us; no-nonsense, honest and totally likeable.

Mick's replacement was Brian Kerr, a man we would come to call 'The Flamer' because he used to send everybody a text after a game, thanking them for their efforts. He used to sign them off, 'Thanks B.K' and that's how he became named after Burger King's finest.

Brian had done really well for Ireland as part of the youth set-up which he'd initially joined way back in 1982. He was a massively passionate Dubliner and like Mick, all he wanted to do was help Ireland get better and hold their own.

"Don't just throw this in your locker or in your attic," he would say when he was handing caps out. "Have this on display. This should be pride of place in your home. Millions would do anything to have the chance to win these. Don't forget what it means to play for Ireland."

When it came to Brian's managerial style, I felt it was a wee bit naïve and basic for the very highest level. I don't mean to do him a disservice but it seemed a bit up-and-at-'em – just get stuck in and see what happens. He had only worked with young players and, for me, it felt like he was a bit too inexperienced in getting the best out of lads who'd played in the Premier League.

We watched a lot of videos of the opposition and sometimes I felt we watched too many. We gave them more credit than they probably deserved.

In the Euro 2004 qualifiers, we beat Georgia on a night in Tbilisi where knives and bricks were very kindly thrown at us from the stands – I thought I was back in Tehran for a minute or two – and we then scrapped our way to a point against Albania in Tirana before beating the same two teams in June 2003 as Robbie kept scoring goals for fun. He had obviously had an amazing World Cup in 2002 and he led from the front in everything we did.

When Robbie used to go home to Tallaght – which he called 'Talla-fornia' – he could often be found having a kick-around on the streets with any young lads about. Ireland's World Cup goal-machine, famous forever for his Germany strike, would drop his bag at home, and take a ball straight out onto the streets, looking for a match.

Robbie was a scrapper, a street footballer who never stopped running and trying and he carried that throughout his entire career. He was a fighter and his will to win and his energy levels were unbelievable. He was such an important player and such a role model in the side for everybody.

In training we would finish with a first-to-five competition and when it was over, some lads would head for the showers, but not Robbie. "Let's stay out, first to seven." We'd have some right tussles, full-blooded games where he never wanted to give an inch. It was that mindset that made him so lethal and so valuable to all the managers he played under, not least Brian.

Thanks to the efforts of Robbie and the rest of the lads, at this stage, our qualification for Euro 2004 was still in our hands but we needed to beat Russia at Lansdowne Road and then Switzerland if we wanted to get out of Group 10.

There was nothing in it against the Russians, who were fast and well-disciplined but we just couldn't break them down until Duffer chanced his arm from a mile out and it took a deflection and snuck inside the post.

Again, Lansdowne Road sounded like there was twice as many as the 36,000 who were there, the stands behind both goals were covered in flags and we were doing great until I tipped over a decent effort from Alexander Kerzhakov. From the resulting corner, I came off my line to punch the ball clear but I had to come through a lot of bodies, got no distance on the punch and it fell to Sergei Ignashevich, who smashed into the net, again through a load of legs and bodies.

There's no two ways about it, it was poor goalkeeping from me, I should've got more on the ball and I had to just accept it. That's part of the job I'm afraid – on another day I manage to punch it further or it doesn't fall to one of their players or we manage to block the shot. Football doesn't go to plan too often.

I was down about the incident but mainly I was still trying to focus on the Switzerland match that was following it a few days later in Basel. Yet not for the first time we got outplayed at just the wrong moment and on a day when we needed to be sharp and competitive, we barely got a look in.

They took the lead through Hakan Yakin. In the second half, I stopped a Stephane Chapuisat header but I could only parry the ball, it landed at the feet of Alexander Frei and that was it, another major tournament evaporated before our very eyes.

After the Switzerland match, life could have gone from bad to seriously worse for the Ireland side when we were caught up in the kind of incident that could only happen to us.

The night before a friendly against Canada at Lansdowne Road in November 2003, we were all sat in the Portmarnock Hotel having dinner downstairs underneath the reception. It was about 7pm and we're halfway through the starters. Next thing, there's all this commotion. "Give us yer fucking money," could be heard from upstairs. And no, it wasn't Bob Geldof either. You could hear people screaming and panicking. We were all sat around, wondering what the fuck was going on. These guns went off and we all looked at each other, eyes wider than saucers! We all took our watches off, thinking they were about to get lifted. "Fuck this, come on," I said and we were off. Me, Robbie and Duffer were gone, bang, through this back exit and we were away. It was certainly the quickest I'd ever moved in my life!

Duffer never had much luck in Portmarnock. The hotel is right next to Portmarnock beach and has a golf course. Duffer's favourite thing in the world is sleeping – he'd do it for 25 hours a day if he could – so while me and a few others nipped out for a round of golf, he relaxed in the hotel and then wandered down to the sea to take a quick dip to freshen his legs up for the next day's training. The Irish Sea is plenty cold enough to act as an effective ice-bath so Duffer thought this was a good plan.

He wandered into the sea and he's still got his training gear on, leggings on underneath and this old training top. Unfortunately, he's also got headphones in as well. As he wades in up to his chest, a woman walking her dog on the beach sees him and thinks he's trying to commit suicide.

She shouts and waves at him, "Don't do it, DON'T DO IT" but Duffer can't hear her because of these earphones, thinks nothing else of it and carries on going in. Two minutes later, he's out, back into the hotel for a shower, job done.

Meanwhile, this amazing woman has legged it to a phonebox and rang the Irish Coast Guard.

We're on the sixth tee of the golf course and next thing, this helicopter flies over and the beach is full of police and the Coast Guard, searching for this 'suicidal' man. Flashing lights everywhere, people running up and down the dunes panicking and all the while Duffer is sat in his room having a cup of tea. Before another nap.

One of Brian's best moves after we failed to get to Euro 2004 was bringing Roy Keane back into the team.

I think nobody – whether that be Roy, Brian or the rest of Ireland – wanted Roy's international career to be remembered for Saipan and for what happened in the ballroom after dinner that night. Roy was too big a player, too good a player, to be last seen jumping a flight home to walk Triggs.

Brian never discussed it with the players but he flew to Manchester to meet Roy and offered him a way back. Roy also spoke to the media about how he had missed playing international football. I was pleased. Nobody was bigger than the team and having Roy back was undoubtedly going to strengthen us again.

We played Romania in a friendly in May 2004 and, yes, it was a bit of a circus but then it was always going to be one wasn't it? Press lads and photographers were all over us but Roy was pretty unfazed by it all as were we. "Bet you never thought you'd see me again eh lads?" he joked and it was good to get him back, even if his efforts to get us to the 2006 World Cup fell short.

To fail to qualify for another major tournament was gutting. I played in all 10 matches in Group 4, something I'm proud of as it underlines the consistency I had brought to my game by 2004/05 but in the grand scheme of things that counted for little.

What killed us in that qualifying group was the numbers of draws we got. We actually only lost once in that entire campaign – to France at Lansdowne Road – but draws with Switzerland twice, France and Israel – also twice – meant we only ever limped along and eventually that meant someone was going to pull away from us.

The Israel draws were real killers, especially the 2-2 at home in June 2005 because we were 2-0 up before throwing it away. You just can't afford to do that at the highest level.

After the match we were due to play the Faroe Islands, away, on the Wednesday. On the Sunday night, Alan Lee and Gary Doherty fancied a night out. We were staying at the Portmarnock Hotel and they snuck out of their room, dressed in their best dancing gear, about to head to Tamango nightclub down the road.

It was like some shit *Mission Impossible* film, they were hiding around corners, dodging security and sneaking around the floors of this hotel. Next thing, the Flamer has popped upstairs in the lift, the doors open and he's confronted by two of his players in their best clobber. "Lads, lads, where the fuck are you going?" "Oh hi gaffer," Gary says, as quick as flash. "Erm, yeah, we're just trying our clothes on in case we get a night out in the Faroes." Good thinking that from the Doc! "Fuck off and get to bed," Brian said, raging!

Gary was a real character and became an important player for us during the early 2000s.

We played a training match at Malahide once and the farmer next door to the training ground was burning loads of rubbish. You couldn't see your hand in front of your face for smoke and we're all coughing as this shit is getting torched. The Doc was in the team and you couldn't see the goals at the other end it was that smoky. "Fackin' hell, fackin' hell," he was shouting. "It's like the fackin' San Siro in here."

Towards the end of the 2006 World Cup qualifying campaign I got a lot of praise for one save from a Zinedine Zidane free-kick during our match at home but, being honest, it meant nothing to me then or now because we still lost 1-0 and that was the crucial turning point in the group. If we'd gone into the last two matches having beaten them then we might just have made it to the 2006 World Cup – so who cares about one save?

I also think most of the attention was more to do with Zidane than me. He was probably the best player in the world at that moment – one of the greatest ever in fact – and it did look spectacular, me diving high and up to my right to claw away his effort but, actually, it wasn't that difficult a save to make technically. I just had to get there, the speed of the shot helped parry it away pretty quickly. It was a good save but it definitely got hyped up.

My best performance in those qualifiers actually came against Cyprus in the game after the Zidane stop and one we needed to win to keep whatever slim chances we had of getting through alive. They absolutely battered us at their place in Nicosia.

They should have run away with it but we managed to sneak a 1-0 win with me saving a penalty from Ioannis Okkas after Dunney had chopped him down in the area.

It was a busy night for me, I remember that much. Chrysostomos Michail and Alexandros Garpozis also went close for them but I kept out their efforts and it was nice to be making headlines for the right reasons, especially with the penalty save. He hit it pretty well to my right but I'd guessed that way and got a good hand to it. Out came the fist pump. I knew we needed that desperately to try and stay on top.

Mind you, I didn't always enjoy myself in Cyprus. A few years ago I was on Mark Devlin's stag do in Protaras, sipping drinks on a yacht in the sun and life was grand. Gavin James, the Irish singer, was on board the boat and we were having a great time, the craic was flying and you couldn't ask for more. After mooring back up, I walked across the red-hot sand to try and get involved in a volleyball match with some locals.

They were all tanned and athletic and sober, I was an Irishman out in the blazing hot sunshine on a stag do. Form your own conclusions.

After about 10 minutes of me being extremely bad, they asked me what I did for a job and I let them know I was a footballer. After being probed a bit more I told them who I was but they wouldn't have it, probably wondering why somebody bright red was pretending to be a professional goalkeeper. Eventually they tried to test my skills and this guy kicked a ball at me. Which I dropped.

"YOU NO SHAY GIVEN, GO AWAY YOU SHAY GIVEN WANNABE," this bloke started shouting.

"I am Shay Given, I AM," I was shouting back, scarpering

back across this sand, the rest of the stag do lying on the floor in tears…

Back in 2005, the Cyprus result couldn't really disguise the fact that we weren't really clicking as a team by this stage. For me, the conveyor belt of good, young, hungry talent had begun to dry up. Where was the next generation of Robbie Keanes or Damien Duffs? We needed some big personalities. We'd lost the likes of Quinny and Stan and it just didn't feel like we had replaced them with lads who could do the same job.

Everybody who came in took massive pride in the shirt and tried their bollocks off, there's no question about that whatsoever, but we'd begun to lack a bit of quality here and there and at international level, that will catch up with you.

In the final qualifier, we drew 0-0 at home to Switzerland. It was a bit of a nothing performance really and the Lansdowne Road crowd began to let us know about that towards the end. Ian Harte had one decent chance but we looked shapeless and the Swiss were happy to just sit there and watch us run around with no real sharp edge.

We had needed to win to stand any mathematical chance of making the play-offs but we ended up finishing fourth in the group and that was that.

After getting to the knockout stages in 2002 to then missing out in 2006 was a huge blow. I was older now, obviously, than the Belgium loss before France '98 when I cried hard on the pitch but this one hurt just as much, even if, as a more mature man, I showed my public feelings a bit less.

A player gets maybe three attempts at getting to a World Cup – if that – and I thought I'd used up all my lifelines by this point. Part of me thought that these were the best years of my career and it was a shame I wouldn't be able to show what I could do on the biggest stage. What can you do though? It's a team game.

It was a shame for Brian too. He was a good man but there was no way he was going to survive failing to qualify for two major tournaments.

It was ironic, too, how the press treated him. When he'd been announced at the new manager at the Shelbourne Hotel in Dublin, the media were virtually cheering the roof off the joint but during the 2006 World Cup qualifiers, he'd actually ended up barring newspapers from the hotels. He was determined not to read what was being said about him and his team. Brian had bills to pay, the same as we all do, and I've never liked a manager getting sacked but, in the same breath, it comes with the territory.

The failure to qualify for the World Cup also saw the end of Roy as a player. He wasn't getting any younger and he decided to retire from international duty to preserve himself for the Premier League which was a decision we all respected. He'd given his all for Manchester United in the middle of the park for a long, long time and his hip was starting to give him trouble. We all have to stop at some point.

Roy will be remembered as an Ireland great, no matter what happened in 2002.

# 15

# THE PAIN
# GAME

WHEN we beat Portsmouth at home in February 2006, two things happened.

Firstly, Glenn Roeder sat in the dug-out as Newcastle manager for the first time while Alan Shearer finally beat Jackie Milburn's goalscoring record with his 201st goal for the club.

Glenn had been doing well at West Ham United but collapsed with a brain tumour in April 2003 after a match against Middlesbrough. His life that day was saved by Ges Steinbergs, the West Ham club doctor, who quickly called an ambulance and got Glenn to hospital in time.

Glenn was out of football for a bit, came to us as youth director and was picked to replace Souness on a temporary basis. We didn't really know too much about him but it was clear he was a pretty composed kind of manager. In public he always came across as thoughtful. He answered the press quietly and politely and he was pretty much like that behind closed doors too.

Al's historic Portsmouth goal came at the Gallowgate End where he'd stood as a boy. I was delighted for him. Like Jackie, he has a bronze statue now – I'm still waiting for mine! – and he'll never be forgotten. It was a special game. It felt like a big occasion for Al, Glenn and the rest of us. The noise when he scored past Dean Kiely was deafening; 50,000 Geordies saluting their hero, one of their own.

Al was just a one-off, a true phenomenon. He was just an absolute hero in Newcastle – an idol – and our leader. He was the lightning rod from the stands to the dressing room. He never shirked a tackle or a header and he gave everything for the club. Once he was out on the pitch, the adrenaline would take over and he'd be away.

If he was totally committed on game day, training was the same. We'd be doing drills and he'd be shouting, "Hit the target, hit the target" at other players, desperate to see the goalkeepers worked hard. I reckon nine out of 10 of his shots would force you into a save.

I remember in Bobby Robson's first game, the 8-0 win over Sheffield Wednesday, we had a young striker called Paul Robinson who won us a penalty late on.

Al already had four goals to his name and some strikers might have thought about handing the ball to someone else to spread the scoring around. But Al wasn't just some striker, he was the Newcastle captain and had the chance to score another goal for his club. Didn't matter if it was his first or his fifth, he was never going to give that chance up. Robinson looked at Al to see if he could take the spot-kick but Al just stared at him as if to say, 'You must be joking?' and smashed it in.

We used to normally have Wednesdays off and we'd have

a golf day. Al would normally win because he's got a dodgy handicap. He hits it a mile and low off the tee. Since he's finished he's improved and he's off a single figures handicap now so you wouldn't want to play him for money. The boys would throw £20 in each and Al would win but he'd then have to buy dinner with the winnings. We'd sit down and say, "I'll have the lobster and caviar please Al!"

His place in Portugal was always good for a week of beers and a few rounds even if Al would spoil it with his singing. We'd all pile into Montys karaoke and spend the night in there.

Al would sing Lionel Ritchie's *All Night Long* – he loves doing that, knows it word for word and likes to think he's good but he's horrendous. He used to time it to perfection and announce himself as Lionel just at the stage of the night where everyone was too far gone to protest. I used to do a Ronan Keating song, *Life is a Rollercoaster* and I was no crowd pleaser either. We went to Al's place for about seven years, from 2001. We had a week to recover then 51 weeks to look forward to it again although some, like Terry Mac, could probably have stayed there all year round!

One of the biggest question marks over Al is whether he regrets not leaving St James' Park when the offers came pouring in. At one stage, there wasn't a club in the world who would have said no if Al was offered to them. Alex Ferguson has said that not signing Al is one of his only regrets at Old Trafford (what about me before Celtic?!)

But, when Al looks in the mirror, I don't think he regrets staying at Newcastle in the slightest. Life is too short to think about ifs and maybes. Al's lived the boyhood dream, he went from the stands to the pitch, he wore the captain's armband

and he became Newcastle's record goalscorer. Life can't be too bad if you have a statue to show for it.

Going back to Glenn, I don't think he was ever meant to get the manager's gig full-time but he'd played at Newcastle and he knew what the fans wanted. "Just give it everything, it's that easy – they'll get behind you."

We beat Portsmouth 2-0 and followed it up with a win at Aston Villa to lift the doom and gloom. Glenn then took us on a great run towards the end of the season that saw us qualify for the Intertoto Cup.

Towards the end of that campaign, we travelled to Sunderland. We were 1-0 down at half-time and Glenn absolutely smashed us in the dressing room, telling us what a let-down we were and how we just couldn't afford to lose to our big rivals. He questioned our pride and our desire and whether we cared about the shirt we were wearing. This wasn't really his style. If anything, I'd wanted him to blow up before this point – he was maybe a bit too analytical and cool for me. That night he really gave it to us. We reacted well, winning 4-1 with Al scoring before damaging knee ligaments. It was to be his last contribution in a Newcastle shirt. It was an apt way for him to go out, a warrior to the last against the Mackems, the side he and every Geordie absolutely loved beating.

The club did some decent work in the transfer market over the summer, bringing in Damien Duff and Obafemi Martins. Duffer probably isn't remembered very fondly by Newcastle fans because we weren't playing well as a team when he joined. Maybe his confidence took a hit as well, which was a massive shame. I obviously knew Duffer really well by this point. We couldn't play in a way that brought the best out of him and unfortunately I don't think he will have great memories of his time there. He could easily have stayed at Chelsea, but he was another who just wanted consistent game time, to spend more minutes on the park.

Duffer might not have loved every minute in Newcastle – but his dad Gerry certainly did. We played one game at home and Gerry was in a box for the match. We met him afterwards and he'd certainly enjoyed his afternoon. "We're to be off out lads, come on," he said. We jumped in a taxi to Jesmond and tried to play catch-up but Gerry was flying. We went into this one bar, he was propping it up and then the next minute he did what can only be described as a 'Del Boy' and fell straight through the bar. I swear on my life, it was just like that scene on *Only Fools and Horses*. I don't think I've ever, ever seen anything as funny as Duffer's old man climbing back to his feet, wondering who on earth had opened the flap on the bar!

Another friendly face at the club was Pav, who came back to the club as cover for me. It was great to have him there again and I think Harps played a hand in his return. We all knew how great a professional he was, he was such a genuine guy and the fans obviously loved him. It was so, so awful what happened to him a couple of years ago. I was so upset; just devastated for him and his family. He called his book '*Pavel is a Geordie*' which goes to show you how much he loved his time at Newcastle.

Another 'Geordie' who was always entertaining was Steven Taylor. In every interview he made it sound like he was born on the shores of the Tyne, was weaned on Newcastle Brown Ale and crawled across St James' Park as a baby when, in fact, he'd been born in London. He would get so much abuse, especially off Harps.

Off the pitch, the era of players going out together and social-ising was pretty much over. I was no longer one of the newer squad members so the quayside wasn't the draw it once was. The Steve Watsons of the world, keen to lead those of us fresh off the boat astray, were no more.

Also, by Roeder's time at the club, the good times – when the city loved mixing with its players and the players loved mixing with the city – were on the wane. This wasn't King Kev and the Entertainers now, St James' Park had had its fill of trophy-less seasons and going into town might have led to an earful rather than a friendly chat.

At the end of the 2005/06 season, I'd played 50 games for Newcastle that season – including every Premier League game. I was pleased with that level of consistency and the fact I was still trusted with the No.1 position. With Al retiring, we needed solid performers and old heads.

Unfortunately, the season after, my appearance count dipped to just 33 matches as I suffered a freak injury that could have ended my career. It was the kind of injury that made you realise that your body – and your life – is on the line as a goalkeeper.

*****

Until we visited Upton Park in mid-September, our Premier League form had been patchy to say the least, having won just once. In the second half of the game, we were 2-0 up and I was buzzing; this was a turning point, a good, hard victory on the road at Glenn's old club. As the clock ticked down I was thinking this could be exactly what we needed to get going.

With about five minutes left, Marlon Harewood was put

through. I assessed it quickly in my head. I just had to beat him to the ball and keep things tidy. It was probably a 60-40 in my favour against Marlon, who is a very well-built lad.

I came sliding out and to be fair to Marlon, he realised he wasn't going to get the ball and tried to pull his feet out but his knees went crashing into my ribcage. *Fuck, that hurt.*

It knocked all the wind out of me straight away. You know that feeling when you'd pay a tenner for a breath of air, there's nothing there? You panic and you try and get the air on board as quickly as possible. I couldn't play on. It felt pointless battling through it so late on. I was substituted and taken straight down the tunnel.

A couple of minutes later the boys filtered back in, buzzing, but I still didn't feel too good. Scotty Parker asked me how I was but I just told him I was fine. "I feel alright boys, it's nothing too serious," I told him. How wrong can you be?

I spoke to the doctor Roddy MacDonald about this funny feeling in my stomach and he sent me for a shower and told me to take it slowly. I had my breath back. It was just thought to be an impact blow, nothing major.

I jumped in the shower and I swear to God, for a split second I thought I'd been knifed. BANG! It felt like I was getting stabbed. I've never known a feeling like it. Waves of burning pain started filling me up. I thought I was going to pass out.

"Roddy, RODDY," I started screaming. "Something is wrong here, get in here, get the fuck in here." It was pure torture. Roddy grabbed me and managed to get me onto a bed and that was it, I passed out. Gone. Now you don't pass out unless there's really something bad with you. At that point, apparently Scotty went racing out of the changing room door screaming for an ambulance because my eyes were rolling in the back of my head. It must've been pretty scary for the boys.

I finally came round again but immediately I was in agony. I can still taste the pain now.

It turns out that the tackle had actually perforated my bowel, causing a one centimetre tear in the lining which was leading to stuff leaking out inside me. Now you may be thinking, 'What's one centimetre? That's nothing.' All I'll say is I pray you never get to find out how enormous one centimetre can be!

After that, it's all a bit of a blur. I was surrounded by doctors and stretchered into another room – only to find out that the stadium ambulance had already left. Perfect. The head injury to Petr Cech at Chelsea that changed all the rules on ambulances and paramedics was still a month away so back then, when the ambulance upped and left, it well and truly upped and left.

Roddy was really concerned but by now he was getting lots of help and advice from a certain Dr Steinbergs – the same West Ham doctor who had saved Glenn's life three years earlier. It's a small world at times isn't it? I'd spent my career keeping my mouth shut when I was injured so for me to be making so much noise worried Roddy a lot. I was still undiagnosed at that stage.

Upton Park is not easy to get to and another 40 minutes passed before the ambulance managed to come back. I was in a world of trouble. Even the West Ham fans could see that. I remember getting wheeled out of the stadium and the fans applauded me onto the ambulance, which was a nice touch.

The paramedics pumped me with morphine and tried to calm me down. I was clinging to the stretcher bed, screaming, knuckles turning white. It was the worst pain I'd ever been in. All I had over me was a towel.

# THE PAIN GAME

Madly enough, there was a stomach specialist in the crowd that day called Steven Snooks and he met us straight at the hospital. This guy was actually off work but came in and tried to see what was going on. I'll always be grateful to him for that.

When I got to hospital they stuck a camera through my belly-button to try and diagnose what was causing so much pain. It was then that the problem became clear. The doctors later described it to me as a 'car crash injury' because it's usually caused by a steering wheel crushing into somebody's stomach. The shit was hitting the fan. Well, it was hitting somewhere anyhow. The perforated bowel was leaking into my system and my body was basically poisoning itself.

No wonder I was in complete and utter agony. I was knocked out with more drugs and they opened me up there and then, cutting through my stomach from my belly-button downwards, in order to stitch the bowel up and stop the leak.

The next thing I knew, I was waking up in hospital, I had tubes hanging out of my nose, everywhere and I had a drip – the works. It was very surreal and I just couldn't piece it all together. One minute I'm playing football, the next I'm in a London hospital, clueless about where I was and what happened. I took one look down at all the bandages across my stomach and knew it must've been bad.

I try and always see the positives in any situation and this was another one. My first thoughts were, 'Well at least I'm not dead' and my second one was, 'Thank fuck this happened when it did.' Like every other team, we often flew to games. If the bowel tear had started causing trouble at 35,000 feet, the chances are very high indeed that I would've died right there on the plane.

I was in hospital for about a week and for most of that time I was off my head on drugs; eyes rolling, not knowing what day it was. Mark Devlin came and visited me and asked for me to be moved because people were trying to get autographs and all sorts. Luckily the nurse was actually from Donegal so she helped get me into a sideroom.

Marlon came into hospital to visit me and we had a laugh about it. He was probably a bit shook up but it wasn't his fault really. I was coming out at pace, he was coming in at pace and it was a pretty hefty collision.

Dr Steinbergs came to see me every single day as well, which was an amazing thing to do and I'm still so grateful to him for that. Robbie Keane also popped in because he was at Tottenham at the time. He cracked me up when he arrived with two bags under his hands that were full of jellies, chocolate, Coke tins – you name it. My stomach was in bits and there's Robbie with half a tuckshop under his arms. "Ah shit, I never realised!" he said. He stayed for about six hours, chatting, and that was the worst thing we could do as I had stitches in and it hurt every time I laughed – which was a lot! He's a busy man is Robbie but he found the time anyhow to come in for so long and that shows the class of the man.

When I checked my phone after the surgery, I had messages and texts from loads of players, especially goalkeepers. There's always been a strong 'goalkeepers' union' as it's known. We stick together. Petr Cech and Edwin van der Sar both texted, telling me to stay positive. They didn't have to, they had busy lives and were are at the top of their profession. Packie Bonner also got in touch and the Newcastle lads messaged me. They had been genuinely concerned – Scotty Parker turned whiter than I did when I collapsed.

I'm not a great patient and as I was lying in hospital, all I cared about was how quickly I could get back on the pitch. I sent a text to Harps from hospital one day to take the piss. 'I've got wires and tubes hanging out of everywhere,' I wrote. 'Hoping for a late fitness test Friday morning.'

After I was released, I had to take it so, so slowly. I found some of the old doubts creeping back into my mind. *Will I get back in? I'm no good to anyone here.* During the recovery, I felt like I was letting everyone down, drawing a wage for absolutely nothing. Nobody at Newcastle ever gave me any reason to feel that way – I suppose it's just the way I was brought up. You get nothing for free in this world, certainly not in football. Glenn was great, telling me to take all the time I needed. "You're mentally tough and physically tough," he said. "Come into the training ground to stay around the group but take your time."

The frustrating thing for me was that it was an injury you couldn't work on. How do you stretch or physio your way out of a bowel tear? How do you ice bath a deep internal injury? You simply can't. I'd be sat around looking and feeling ok but I knew I could do nothing at all to speed things up.

While I was injured, Albert Luque was also out with a chipped nail or something so we had to go to the pool to do some fitness work. On the pitch he'd be breathing out of his arse while I'd be fine but it was the other way around in the water. He was gliding from end to end while I was all over the place, like an octopus trying to do my washing, arms and legs splashing about. "Football?" I said to him. "You want to try fucking water polo!"

Eventually I could train again. I missed just less than two months. My first match back was a 5-0 win for Ireland against San Marino which was a nice way to return. I was just so relieved to get through it in one piece and was back playing for Newcastle the following Saturday.

One of the main problems for Newcastle by this time, and my biggest source of frustration, was the dip in the club's prestige and attraction to players. When I had joined, Newcastle were on every player's wishlist – I should know, I was one of them – but by the time Glenn was manager, that had all changed. How do you replace an Alan Shearer or a Gary Speed? Newcastle United needed quality but we were no longer the attraction we had once been. The likes of Chelsea, Manchester United, Manchester City and Arsenal were flying. They had money to spend and a winning mentality, as if their dressing rooms didn't know how to fail. Ours was the opposite – and who wants to join a club like that? We'd become a team that had perfected the art of teasing our fans, raising their hopes and then letting them down at the last second. Look what had happened in the FA Cup or against Sporting Lisbon and Marseille in Europe.

History repeated itself under Glenn and in the UEFA Cup, we steamed into the last 16, beat AZ Alkmaar 4-2 in the first leg at St James' Park but lost 2-0 on the night in Holland and went out on away goals. All you could do was watch the Newcastle fans file out of the stadium, shoulders slumped, gutted that they'd again believed in us and again we had let them down.

Ridiculously enough, we actually 'won' the Intertoto Cup that season. We'd beaten Lillestrom 4-1 over two legs at the start of the season and that put us in the hat. They changed the format of the competition that year which meant that the last surviving Intertoto entrants in the UEFA Cup were awarded the trophy. Scott Parker picked up the silverware before the first leg against AZ Alkmaar. It was a bizarre moment that meant and still means absolutely nothing. It's a Mickey Mouse Cup – I'm never putting it on my CV, put it that way. I wanted to win a trophy on the pitch, I wanted to hear a referee's whistle blow and to jump on my team-mates and race over to celebrate with our fans. To read in the paper that we'd 'won' something was never going to compare.

Before the AZ Alkmaar loss we'd been totally humiliated at home to Birmingham City in the FA Cup, getting hammered 5-1, and the writing was on the wall for Glenn. We just couldn't score. From February until the end of the season we won one Premier League game. The knives were out and in May, Glenn resigned.

Sam Allardyce, my sixth permanent manager, was next through the door. It was a case of a new face but the same old story.

*****

I've just checked and Big Sam was brought in on May 15, 2007 and his bags were packed on January 9, 2008.

A bit like Craig Bellamy under Souness, that tells you pretty much everything.

If life can be tough on the pitch for Newcastle, it can be even harder for the bloke on the touchline but Sam has never been short of self belief and confidence and I was pleased he had been given the job. He was big in every way, and Newcastle needed someone with broad shoulders to take on the position.

Big Sam was straight talking and he knew precisely how he wanted us to play – which caused some friction from the off. We had players like Emre Belözoğlu, who wanted to get on the ball, and Stephen Carr, who was always looking to pick his man out precisely but Big Sam was not keen on that.

In training one day, Stephen was looking for the centre forward but Sam boomed, "No, NO! Stop, stop! Get it into the corner, squeeze up behind." It was the way he'd worked. He'd been unbelievably successful at Bolton but it just wasn't a style we could adapt to. Emre was a brilliant little Turkish playmaker with the ball at his feet but he was about 5ft 7in; there was no way he was physically built to play the way Sam wanted us to. We should've gone with the ball on the floor and through the defence but our orders were to play a super-disciplined, high-pressing game.

Sam loved his physios and sports scientists. He brought in loads of new staff and deserves credit for that. Sam wanted to squeeze every extra percentage he could out of players – we were swigging protein shakes and getting ice baths and massages constantly. Sam's philosophy was that if you've had the perfect preparation and you perform badly on the Saturday then there's nobody to blame but yourself.

A strength and fitness coach came in from Canada to speak to the players. By the time he left we had to take so many fish oil capsules and vitamins that if I jumped in training you could hear me rattle. During a meal you'd have to pop a pill halfway through your meal and zero light was allowed in your bedroom at night, that sort of thing. He got the callipers out and did a fat test on us all and then came back two months later to see how we'd gone on.

I'm quite open to all that stuff so I was smashing these pills down and doing what he asked. When he tested me again, I'd lost three per cent fat. Next, he got to Obafemi Martins, who is always ripped. "You've lost two per cent, this is very good," he said to him. Only problem was, Obafemi had never touched a single pill the whole time. He'd just lashed them in his locker and continued doing his own thing. Basically, this so-called expert was just talking shit – the tablets did absolutely nothing really! Obafemi was a good lad but he used to drive a Ferrari around Newcastle – you know, something subtle that wouldn't stand out.

Geremi was signed in July 2007 which was exciting but only for a short while. He was a Champions League winner with Real Madrid and had also won the Premier League title with Chelsea. Finally, I thought we were bringing in some quality players. Still, the fact his fee was only £1.5m was an idea of what market we were now looking at.

Geremi wasn't what you'd class as a man overly concerned by putting a shift in during training.

Duffer was supposedly the same age as him but at training Geremi could barely run he'd be that stiff and sore. Duffer used to say, "If that fucker is the same age as me, I'll eat my own arse!" He hated running and never stopped moaning about it. At pre-season he had a right face on. "At Madrid, we got the balls out on the first day," he said. "All you English do is run, run, run. We play football not athletics."

Alan Smith also joined us from Manchester United. The minute he walked through the dressing room door he got battered for dressing like a student. He had this clapped out BMW 3 Series car that was on its last legs – a convertible with a canvas roof that looked like it was stuck together with Sellotape.

Alan never liked to spend money. He'd dress in indie gear and I think he even lived in Jesmond where all the cool students live.

His problem on the pitch for us was he never knew whether he was meant to be a centre forward or an attacking midfielder, he kind of fell through the gap between the two and a bad ankle injury didn't help him either.

Mark Viduka was Sam's first signing. He was another really talented player but I got the impression he only fancied it on certain days. If he was ticking then he was superb but some days he just wasn't on it.

But it was the leavers more than the new recruits that bothered me. For instance, why were we selling Scotty Parker to West Ham United? He had been picked as club captain after Al retired, he was a solid professional, a great club man and somebody who gave it everything. What were we doing letting him go to a club in and around us in the Premier League?

Scotty was a really quiet lad, a family man and totally under-rated in my opinion. Years ago he'd been in a McDonald's advert and I murdered him for it. "Fucking hell lad, you used to be good looking as a kid," I said. "What happened, too many Big Macs?" He'd come up from London and would always wear loads of trendy gear, really tight trousers and skin-tight tops. "You need a hand getting out of your shirt mate? Quick, you're going purple, undo your top button!" He had to jump off his wardrobe to get into his jeans. He loved it and he loved Newcastle so why we were selling him baffled me.

The 2007/08 season started with us winning 3-1 at Bolton, but we never got a foothold in the season, never built up any momentum or spirit. I hurt my groin in a pre-season match against Sampdoria so missed the start and it was tough to watch. We needed to get off to a flying start but we struggled and – crucially – Sam never won the fans over.

# THE PAIN GAME

There are few venues in the world that can let a manager know what the fans think better than St James' Park. Sam's style just wasn't that popular with the supporters and they let him know it. I felt sorry for him really because it had been successful elsewhere – getting Bolton into Europe was no fluke – but Newcastle fans wanted to be entertained.

I was becoming increasingly frustrated and would happily let my feelings be known when we had one of the many, many, meetings that Sam enjoyed having. "You always want to get the last word in – you have too much to say," Sam would say to me. I think, I hope, that was meant as a back-handed compliment. Sam took on board what his advisors and what the players were saying but ultimately he was strong enough to go with what he wanted. He could give it back too and would let rip at us when he felt he needed to. He had thick skin – which he sometimes needed. "Fucking some head on your shoulders there Sam lad," an Everton fan said to him one day as we walked into the ground. We all stood behind Sam and pissed ourselves laughing.

During that first half of 2007/08, we were only ever 90 minutes way from a crisis and the pressure just piled on Sam, especially as the press was again full of stories questioning his relationship with the players. The papers quoted 'friends' or 'sources' who were saying 'senior players' had turned against Sam. Well, me and Harps were the most senior players and we weren't saying a word to anybody so we felt we needed to support the manager. There were phone-ins and talk shows constantly winding up the fans. Newcastle were either world beaters or we were relegation fodder and a disgrace to the city. Me and Harps released a joint statement saying it was all

255

bollocks. The only issue after that was we were also bollocks on the pitch, the fans were still going crazy and the spirit at the club was as low as I'd known it.

After losing at home to Manchester City just after New Year, Sam was sacked.

I hated this time. We had no new talent on the horizon, we weren't clicking as a unit, nobody knew what was going on at the club and the results were an embarrassment, none more so than when we got smashed 6-0 by Manchester United at Old Trafford. It was Nigel Pearson's only game in charge as a caretaker and somehow it was still 0-0 at half-time even though Cristiano Ronaldo, Carlos Tevez and Wayne Rooney had been queuing up in the first half.

After the break, they cut loose and I just wanted to get off that pitch as quickly as I could. Newcastle United Football Club should not and should never lose 6-0 to anyone and it showed exactly where we were as a club when Harry Redknapp was offered the job and told the board they could stick it.

Where do we go from here? In the last 12 months I'd seen another two bosses off and wondered, the same as everybody else, who'd be next through the door. If we couldn't get Harry, we needed someone equally as charismatic and respected and someone who wanted to give the fans some hope.

Who was out there?

# 16

# MY SIDE

WHAT'S that phrase, 'It's the hope that kills you'?

Tell me about it.

After the 6-0 defeat to Manchester United, we needed a miracle to lift the club and the fans and on January 16, 2008, I thought we'd got one.

I'd just had an afternoon nap before an FA Cup replay with Stoke City that night. I came downstairs in the hotel, bleary-eyed, and turned on the news and there it was: KEVIN KEEGAN RETURNS TO NEWCASTLE.

This was news to me! The Messiah was back. Newcastle's ability to always be a club full of surprises had even caught me out this time. His message to the fans that day was classic Kevin and perfectly judged: "I'm home. It's great to be back." His name was sung all night as we beat Stoke 4-1.

I was absolutely delighted that Kevin was coming back. I'd always heard stories about what the club had been like during his first spell. I missed it by only 12 months or so but I'd watched and admired the football Newcastle played. They looked like they didn't have a care in the world. Now, in 2008, Newcastle had plenty of cares and we hoped he'd be the man to end them.

Meeting him for the first time was great. He was very normal and polite but he was one of these people who oozed charisma and personality. He just had that something, a special aura that only a handful of others in the game have.

For me, Kevin was a brilliant man-manager. In his first match there was a problem with my goalkeeping kit, some mix-up which meant I had to wear this awful looking top. It looked terrible and I wasn't bothered at all but Kev, being Kev, wanted everybody to feel completely positive before a match. "That kit is shit," he said. "It's the keeper inside it that counts – and he's superb." He did the same with Michael Owen. Michael was struggling at the time and he gave him the captain's armband to spur him on.

Before his first training session, Kev had given us a bit of a rallying cry. "I've come back to get the club challenging at the top again," he told us. It was great to hear.

His team-talks before a game were straight from the heart. "You're playing for Newcastle," he would say, and you could hear the emotion in his voice. "It means so much to these fans, these people, show them what it means to you." He'd look at both squad lists on the wall then look at us all. "That's their team," he'd say. "But this is our team. You're better, go out and beat them." He made you feel 10 feet tall. You could sense people puffing out their chests. He knew what he needed to say to get the best out of us. It was often a word in the ear, here and there, nothing flash or loud. "You've got this today mate, they're nothing," he'd tell me. He'd walk up to the strikers and tell them they were flying and nailed on for at least a goal or he'd tell our defenders they were the hardest in the league.

You see it now with Jurgen Klopp and the way he loves his Liverpool players, hugs them after games and boosts them up. Kevin was the same. In the changing room after a match, he'd praise and hug you. You'd feel amazing. I suppose management is sometimes about disguising your emotions but I liked his honesty. If he had to let rip at half-time, he would do, he would lose his cool and let us have it.

Ironically enough, for all that the club and the players loved having him back, we still couldn't buy a win and after another heavy defeat against Manchester United when we lost 5-1 in February, my season was over due to a groin problem that needed surgery. Harps, Al and Michael Owen had all used a specialist groin surgeon called Ulrike Muschaweck in Munich and I did the same. It was a nagging problem that needed fixing.

When they performed the emergency surgery on my bowel after Marlon nailed me, they had to cut through a lot of stomach and groin muscle to fix the problem and that had left me with a tendency to pick up small hernias and constant groin niggles and I found I couldn't set off and dive quickly enough, which wouldn't do. I knew the procedure was a season-finisher but it was the right call, I needed to get sorted. Harps was playing really well and even though I was in hospital and out of the team, I still felt confident about the direction we were now going in. If anybody could fix Newcastle, Kevin Keegan could.

This was March 2008.

How then, was Kev gone by September?

*****

At the same time that Sam Allardyce was moving to Newcastle, the club was sold to Mike Ashley for £133m. We didn't get informed about it or really know too much about what was going on. I knew that Freddy Shepherd and John Hall loved the club, were massive fans and would only sell if they thought it was the right thing to do to the right person, so when Ashley's name was announced it set no real alarm bells ringing at all.

But as time went along with Kev in charge, I think he felt he was slowly losing grip of the club. Ashley brought in Dennis Wise, Tony Jimenez, Derek Llambias and Jeff Vetere as chief scout.

It was a strange set-up. Who was the boss? Who decided transfers? Was Dennis, as director of football, the main man or was Kevin? Who signed the cheques on new players? Who decided who came and who went?

You'd meet fans in the street and they'd desperately ask what was going on. "Fucking hell, don't know pal," you'd tell them. They wouldn't believe you. "No pal, genuinely, we don't have a clue what's happening."

With some clear leadership and the right backing, Kev could've got us back up there but I don't think Ashley understood the situation or what Kev wanted. He brought a massive hero back to the club but then didn't back him up. It made perfect business sense as a brand to bring Kev in but to not then let him sign who he wanted, or match his ambition, was a real shame.

I actually think there is a place for directors of football in a club because they take pressure off the man in the dugout and they can concentrate on the business side of things while the manager sorts the squad out. However, no player should be signed or sold without the manager's say-so. To my eyes, that was clearly not happening and Kev started clashing too much with Lambias and Dennis Wise. They were bringing in players he didn't want, bidding for players he had no interest in and although he bit his lip a few times, I think the pressure cooker inside him was building up and ready to pop.

As players we had nothing to do with Wise at all. He was never at the training ground. From what I knew, he seemed like he could be a feisty character and maybe that's another reason why he clashed with Keegan.

The calibre of players we were bringing in just didn't live up to what Kevin thought we needed if he was to turn the club around. Ignacio Gonzalez or Xisco, with respect, were never going to fire us up the table and although we forked out a few quid for Fabio Coloccini, he was a central defender.

If the club was going to put their trust in Dennis Wise, Tony Jimenez and Derek Lambias to attract and purchase the best players, they were looking at the wrong end of the pitch to start with. We also allowed James Milner, a great player, to join Aston Villa because we were apparently on the verge of signing Bastian Schweinsteiger from Bayern Munich. Guess what? Were we fuck, it was never on the cards. Kev was being told to watch videos on *YouTube* so he could check out players that those above him wanted to sign. You couldn't make it up.

The manager has to get the players he wants otherwise he's just a puppet. If you sign Joe Bloggs and he's had a beast then it's on your neck. If Dennis Wise signs him and he has a beast, it's still on your neck! It's still your fault! You have to take all the flak, whether you want the player or not. The crying shame is Kev would have taken all the flak in the world for Newcastle, he loved the place but when your hands are being tied by those upstairs then what can you do?

Kevin eventually had enough and walked out in the September. We were devastated as a squad and as a club as a whole. Ashley had pulled a rabbit out of a hat by getting Kevin back and now we'd somehow messed it all up in less than a season. Kev wanted us challenging for the Premier League but I don't think that the club matched his dreams.

Once again, the club I loved was splashed everywhere in the media and we were looking like idiots all over again. This was as low as we could get as a club, right?

*****

Wrong. Chris Hughton came in for a short while as caretaker before we were all called into a meeting at the training ground. Who was going to be next through the revolving door? In the meeting, there was a piece of paper with the new manager's name on it and Hughton said, "Joe Kinnear is coming in as manager?" You could hear a pin drop.

One staff member in the meeting, who I won't name, somehow came up with the following bit of inspiration and broke the ice – Dean Kiely style – with, "Joe Kinnear? Is there a fucking joke in here!" It's a great line but I swear it's the truth. We just could not believe it. I was shellshocked.

Joe was the interim manager while Chris stayed as first-team coach but whether it be for one game or a thousand, I never believed Kinnear was the right fit.

No disrespect to Joe but he'd been out of football a long, long time. The foreign lads didn't have a clue who he was. Everyone felt down after the appointment. There was a general feeling of absolute despair. I feel for Joe when I say this because he's not a bad bloke but, basically, this was Newcastle United and he was a guy who hadn't worked at the top level for 10 years. It just sort of summed up Mike Ashley's tenure, it felt like everything he was doing was on the cheap, to wind the fans and players up.

It felt like we were drifting, inch by inch, week by week, from being a club that wanted to win and succeed in the Premier League to becoming a club that just wanted to survive in the Premier League. There's a world of difference between those two approaches, those two ideas, and I only had one career and one chance. I started to think that I would have to move on.

Joe began his Newcastle career by sounding off in a press conference about all the negative coverage we were getting. It was done with good intentions but it wasn't the smartest move. It just annoyed all the reporters. I was sick of us being slammed all the time too but the truth was we were a comedy club and Ashley had just made it worse.

Someone once counted how many times Joe swore in team-talks and let's just say they ran out of fingers and toes before the second sentence. He was like Mike Bassett, effing and jeffing everywhere. I don't even know what the foreign lads were thinking when this began.

As 2008 went on under Joe, it was clear that my time at Newcastle was up. I'd become tired of fighting for the team. It felt like nobody else cared. I was so ambitious and I just didn't feel others at the club matched that. We had an owner with quite a bit of money but we let our best players go and who was coming in? Free transfers, unknown players and players who couldn't cut it.

Eventually the chance to join City came up. They were everything Newcastle were not at the time – ambitious, clear about their plans, willing to spend and attract big players and they wanted success. What footballer doesn't want that in his life?

Against Liverpool at St James' Park in December 2008, I reached the tipping point and endured one of the lowest moments of my career. I genuinely didn't want to leave the club but we were stuffed 5-1. It was an embarrassment, a disgrace, as bad and as careless a performance as you can imagine.

I was the busiest man in England in the first half and kept the score to single figures but I just couldn't do it alone and eventually Liverpool – with Gerrard on fire – stuffed us. I shook Steve's hand at the end and his look said it all.

At the final whistle Paul Barron, the goalkeeping coach, ran on and said, "Go and thank the fans, Shay" but I just couldn't. I ran down the tunnel, the emotion was getting too much. There had to be more to life than this, getting battered every week.

I was trying to do my best week in, week out but the club wasn't doing their best by us. They were selling our best players and, in my eyes, nobody gave a fuck. It felt like I cared more than anybody else – maybe that's what nearly 12 years at the same place does for you.

It felt like some players were just coming in, getting their wages and going home. Fuck that. I lived in the area, I'd been there a long time and I'd committed my career to Newcastle. And now it was all coming undone, week by week. I felt the pain of the fans because I was a fan myself at the end. It was just totally demoralising.

After the Liverpool loss I released a statement through my solicitor, Michael Kennedy, and it still says it all today:

*Shay is very despondent following the very poor per-*
*formance last weekend. It was the lowest point of his*
*football career and a performance he would not wish*
*to be repeated. When he signed a five-year contract in*
*2006, it was on the basis that the club would challenge*
*for major honours. But on the present evidence all that*
*he can see ahead with the turmoil on and off the pitch*
*is a battle for survival. Having served the club loyally*
*for over 11 years, Shay feels compelled to consider his*
*position in the light of the interest being expressed in*
*him by Manchester City, Arsenal and Tottenham.*

In other words, put simply: "Shay can no longer feel like he's one of only a handful of people in the building who gives a shit."

The die-hards will point the finger at me, but I played 462 times for that club, I missed two Premier League matches in five seasons; I'd earned the right by then to make my feelings known and look elsewhere. Eventually, me and Michael had a meeting with Mike Ashley about what the future held.

It was at the manager's office at the training ground and Lambias was there as well. I was willing to listen to what they had to say but ultimately I left it all up to Michael. This is what usually happens with contract and transfer issues, the player leaves it in the hands of someone they trust.

I went out of the room soon after the meeting had begun and returned to the car. Michael was back out, sat in the passenger seat, soon after. "We're not staying," he said. "That was not a serious offer in any way, shape or form."

Mike Ashley had told Michael the deal being proposed but it was considerably lower than what we were offering new players at the time, who were coming in on huge long-term contracts that would secure them for life.

My deal did not do that and just confirmed what I already suspected – they weren't going to pull out the stops to keep me at the club.

I was prepared to stay for the rest of my career but, ultimately, I was in my prime, a potential Premier League winning team wanted to sign me and Newcastle did not give any impression they wanted to chase silverware.

The sad thing was I'd placed serious, long-term roots down in Newcastle, my children were in school there and I would easily and happily have stayed forever. How much did they really want to keep me though? How much did they want to be challenging? Did the boardroom care about keeping their most loyal players? In a word, no.

Staying at a club for a long time is sometimes to your detriment because they offer you a much lesser contract than the new lads, who get the red carpet rolled out and receive double what you're on. You can be taken for granted by clubs and that is not a wise situation to get in.

In the end, with me unhappy at what was going on and the lack of ambition shown by the club, a gun was put to my head. They said they would not allow me to leave unless I signed a transfer request.

By making me hand in a formal written request, it meant they could waive 10 per cent of the fee I otherwise would've picked up after moving. With the fee being around £6-8m, it effectively meant I was waiving £600,000 to go. It says everything that they were more keen on saving themselves £600,000 than they were keeping hold of a player who had given his absolute all for the club for over a decade. I'd literally spilt blood for Newcastle, pushed myself hard every day, even when times were so tough and quality players were leaving by the second.

The least the club could've done, in my opinion, is prove I was wanted. Instead, they were more interested in the transfer fee than they were me – a proven Premier League player, a dedicated team-man and a good professional.

If they were letting me go, and they were more than happy to let the likes of Milner go as well, what does that tell you? It tells me that the economics of the club were a bigger priority than success on the pitch. That saddened me a lot then and it saddens me a lot now.

When you're involved in a transfer, you do take more notice of the media and more notice of what is being said. BREAKING NEWS is flashed across the telly and you do start to wonder if it's going to happen.

When me and Harps nipped for a beer one afternoon, I knew that it was. His contract was up in the summer and he had been speaking to Harry Redknapp and Kevin Bond at Tottenham Hotspur. We were in The Diamond Inn and Harps took a call to say that Newcastle were offering him a new long-term deal. He wanted his future sorted out because he had a family and young kids and it wasn't fair that he didn't know what was happening. He walked outside the pub to take the call and came back in.

"What's happening?" I asked.

"They've just offered me three years," he said.

Well, if Harps was staying, that meant I was going.

It all then happened very quickly.

I didn't have chance to say goodbye to the lads, say goodbye to the staff at the training ground or even clear out my stuff. Fair enough, that's life. I just wanted to get out and get playing again and move to a club that was going places. It was a fresh start and a chance to go again. I could've signed the deal offered and lived on Easy Street but I knew we wouldn't have been challenging for anything anytime soon. In the end, it came down to the January 2009 deadline day. They had to get it done quickly to hit the Europa League cut-off.

What really pissed me off – and one of the reasons I'm doing this book – is the way the club treated me after I 'demanded a move.'

The club was leaking stuff against me, left right and centre, telling the media: 'We couldn't keep him, unfortunately, because he forced us into the deal with his transfer request' when, actually, it was the club that made me sign it in the first place. They made it sound like I was holding them to ransom and that poor little Newcastle were being stitched up by just another greedy footballer when, in actual fact, I wanted to stay – but only if Newcastle gave me a competitive contract and, by doing so, proved the club had big plans for the future.

The way the club portrayed me was a disgrace and the money it cost me wasn't – and isn't – the issue; the issue was I'd given nearly 12 years of my life to that football club, given everything. They'd quadrupled what they paid for me and when it came down to it, they couldn't care less about me, the future of the club or the direction it was going in. To then read in the papers that I was effectively the one 'desperate to go' made me so mad.

In one press conference, Joe Kinnear said, "We bent over backwards to try and keep him at Newcastle United and offered him a longer contract to stay at the club. He has been with Newcastle United for a long time and has been a great servant but he felt the time was right to move on and so, realistically, we had no choice but to reluctantly agree to allow him to make this move."

Hang on a minute…

Not only did the club play bullshit politics behind my back, claiming it was all me, after I'd gone, they were no better.

All it would've taken was for them to say, 'We place on record our thanks to Shay Given for his service to this football club.' One sentence would've done me but no, I got nothing. I was hurting at the time and, to be honest, I'm still mad because it could've been dealt with a million times better. Not 10 times better, a million. As a player and as an individual I deserved so much more than that. I didn't have the chance to say goodbye to the fans and the club hung me out to dry in the media.

The odd time I've been out in Newcastle since I left, I've had a few negative comments about me leaving and it kind of angers you, you know? Maybe this chapter will set the record straight and help dispel a few of those myths about why I left; at least they will get my angle to the story.

Newcastle United Football Club will always be a part of my story and I will always love the place, no matter the ups and downs. The club gave me everything but I gave the club everything back in return and, thankfully, it will be around a lot longer than Mike Ashley will.

I don't actually know why he bought the club to be honest. Legend is he just bought it on a whim, to show he was a billionaire and could do what he wanted. I think he wanted to be liked by the fans but at the end of the day, he's a businessman and he still has to make money out of Newcastle United. It's his club and he can do what he likes with it ultimately.

Despite all that, I just think that if you buy a club, you've already got money. Why worry about making any more? Why are you trying to balance the books? I don't know. Maybe that's over-simplifying it. But, to me, you either buy a club and accept it's going to hammer your wallet – which is a price worth paying for glory – or you don't buy a club and balance your books.

You can't do both.

From where I was standing, Mike Ashley tried to do just that, it gave him and the club problems and I think he'd sell up in a heartbeat if he could.

When I left the north-east and moved to Manchester City I left with my conscience clear, knowing it was the right decision at the right time.

And, sadly, looking at the club in the time since has done nothing to convince me otherwise.

## 17

# OVER AND OUT

AFTER Brian Kerr left the job, everybody was linked with the Ireland position from Alex Ferguson to Kenny Dalglish and Martin O'Neill. David O'Leary was also in the frame for a while before John Delaney at the FAI announced that Steve Staunton, Stan, would be the national manager.

I was delighted for him in one sense because he was as passionate and as patriotic as they come.

Steve is one of the best left-backs to ever play for Ireland. He set a great example for us younger lads and seemed to be around forever. I remember watching him at USA '94. During the anthem before the Italy game, he had a cap on his head and was covered in suncream because it was so hot. It looked like white emulsion paint it was that thick!

As you would expect, questions were asked about how right he was for the job because he was only young and he didn't have much managerial experience at all. He had been at Walsall for a while as Paul Merson's assistant and was only 36. A four-year deal for a man still learning the ropes was a great result for Stan. We all had high hopes that it could work and he could get us back into major tournaments – and quickly.

Stan becoming the manager was a tricky one for those of us who'd known him as a player. All of a sudden, 'Stan' is now 'Boss' and anybody who says a mate becoming a manager doesn't change their relationship is lying.

In every international team I played in, the players and the manager were tight but there was another even tighter group that consisted of everybody but the manager. I'm not saying the boss was ever isolated, not at all, but it's like the manager is the headmaster and you're the pupils, seeing what you can get away with. All of a sudden, one of the naughtiest schoolboys Ireland ever had is now telling us what we could and couldn't do – and that was always going to be a bit weird for everybody involved, including Stan himself, I suppose.

Let me give you an example of what I mean.

Back in 2002, on the day before the FAI dinner in Dublin, we all met up as a squad for a few beers in the city centre. There was hardly a bar in Dublin untouched by us that night. At the end of the evening, Stan and Quinny went missing, they could not be found anywhere. We all staggered back home and thought nothing more of it.

We didn't have to do anything on the Sunday before the dinner so we spent all morning nursing our sore heads, waiting for the awards, and as the afternoon passed on, there was still no sign of either Stan or Quinny. At about half five, both of them staggered through the reception of the hotel, rocking. Stan was up for player of the year that night but he could barely talk.

# OVER AND OUT

Turns out that Stan and Quinny had had a bet at about 4am in the morning because – surprise surprise – Quinny was still thirsty. "Stan, I will find us a pub still serving," Quinny told Stan. "Nothing, no chance, let's go back," Stan had told him, before they put 50 euros on it. They walked around Dublin for a bit but couldn't find anywhere that was open so Quinny, using the kind of logic that only exists when rocking, came up with a genius plan. They ended up going to Heuston Station and jumped on the first train to Waterford out of Dublin – because you could drink on the train. The two of them carried on boozing all the way to Waterford, got there, turned right around, drank all the way back to Dublin and by the time they were back on O'Connell Street all the pubs were open again and ready for business.

A few hours later, they poured themselves back through the front door of the hotel. Stan was in the worst shape I'd ever seen him and we had no time to fix him. Quinny on the other hand – you'd never have guessed he'd had a drink!

Quinny rang the room. "Kev, get my suit," he barked at Kev Kilbane. He had 20 minutes to get ready. His eyes were tiny, bloodshot and cross-eyed. He jumped in the shower, jumped out, threw his suit on, fixed his hair and he was out of the door, absolutely fine. It was like somebody flicked a switch. The shower in his room must be magic. "I'm grand, I'm grand," he kept saying. Stan was anything but grand. "I'm done, I'm retiring," he was saying, still plastered.

Fast forward a few years. And now Stan is the manager.

It can't help but blur the lines a little.

When I think back to his time in charge, two things strike me. One is that I think Stan worked too hard, too quickly, in trying to blood too many youngsters. The second is that the way he was treated by the media and some sections of the public was an absolute disgrace.

As I've said before, with the loss of the likes of Stan himself (ironically enough), Quinny and now Roy, I could understand the need to bring in new faces. I get the logic but some lads got a cap who would never have been anywhere near one four or five years earlier.

No disrespect to players like Joe Lapira, who was a college footballer for Notre Dame in America, but he got a cap against Ecuador in a friendly in the summer of 2007 and that just would not have happened in an earlier era, no chance.

Ireland did need to rebuild and reach out to younger and fresher legs but Stan did not go about it the right way. I thought he experimented a bit too much.

In his very first squad, for a friendly against Sweden, he picked five new players. The problem is, international football will find you out; it can be absolutely brutal. You cannot expect young lads with barely any domestic experience to be able to go straight in and perform for their country.

Although I disagreed with the new policy, I was massively in favour of a couple of moves made when Steve came in.

One time, he got all the lads together.

"There's someone here who wants to meet you," Stan said.

The next thing, Mick Byrne – who had been removed by Brian Kerr – walked into the room. The place erupted. We were all giving him loads of stick. It was great to have him back in the set-up. It was a massive boost for the lads.

He was only back two minutes and he was already banging on doors, leading the lads in a sing-song and generally being himself. Mick's title was physio but I don't think he did much actual work on you physically, he was more interested in seeing how you were mentally. He'd plonk you down, pour oil on your back and rub it about three times and that was it.

Mick had a brilliant manner and could see inside your head to find out how you were coping. If somebody had something on their mind, Mick would often knock on their door before they even knew there was a problem themselves. He had a way of knowing how footballers ticked and solved many an issue for the lads. He had the absolute faith and trust of all the players and he probably kept a million secrets from firstly Mick and then Stan in order to protect the players. Every good set-up has a guy like that, a guy who was a buffer, a confidante, a mate and a comedian.

One of his usual jobs was getting everybody up after our afternoon sleep. We always had a walk in the morning and then a nap later on. But if we were meant to be getting up at 3.30pm, Mick would get bored and he'd be knocking on the doors at 3pm, wanting some company and a laugh with the lads.

Mick reckoned he was big mates with *U2* and never missed a chance to let us know. We'd be in the dressing room before a match and he'd go, "Lads, just had Bono and Larry on the phone and they said fucking do it for them."

Yeah, alright Mick, whatever...

"I'm telling youse boys, *U2* are on the speed-dial!"

Larry Mullin did actually come into the dressing room after the match a few times. He'd bring his lad in, have a chat and talk to the boys. He wasn't this world famous superstar inside the dressing room, he was just another Irishman, another Ireland fan, happy to see us do well.

Before games, Mick would be on the bus climbing down from one end to the other in the luggage racks above our heads, shouting at us all to get ready for a big day, generally taking the piss and letting himself be the butt of the jokes so we would all relax.

Another old friend, Bobby Robson, was also brought into the fray by Steve. Now this appointment raised a fair few eyebrows in Ireland as to who exactly was in charge and whose decision it had been to bring Bobby in but it made perfect sense. Steve had very little managerial experience whereas Bobby was the most charismatic and experienced manager around.

Bobby and Stan had only met the week before and the press pounced on Bobby's appointment, claiming he was there because the FAI wanted somebody to show Stan how to cope with managing at international level.

That was harsh on Stan – he'd played over 100 times for Ireland and was a legend to us – but Bobby's appointment alongside him immediately put the pair of them on the back foot and Stan in particular was always playing catch-up with the press and the public after that. He sounded confident and defiant when he told everybody, "I'm the gaffer, what I say goes" but it wasn't the steadiest of footings to get off on.

To be honest, we didn't see much of Bobby and he didn't really have any say on the training ground or in the dressing room.

I don't know what went on behind the scenes in terms of team selection but he was not hands-on with the players. He occasionally shouted something to us in training but the Bobby of old at Newcastle – where he was the life and soul, the heart-beat of the place – was not evident, simply because Stan was the manager.

# OVER AND OUT

Bobby was also ill at the time. After Stan was appointed in 2006, Bobby's cancers returned and so he was away a lot getting treatment.

*****

In Stan's first match in charge we beat Sweden 3-0 and the omens looked really good but we then lost to Chile and Holland in further friendlies and it just seemed to get harder and harder.

We put in a decent performance against Germany in our first 2008 Euro qualifier but lost 1-0 before Marlon Harewood tap-danced on my bowel which meant I missed the next match, a 5-2 destruction by Cyprus in Nicosia. Poor Paddy Kenny, who had replaced me, must've wondered what the hell was going on – I sure know I was.

The 5-2 defeat was just a really poor night and I felt for Steve and the players. We always seem to get drawn against Cyprus and a trip to Nicosia was never an easy game. The night I saved a penalty against them I was man of the match, so what does that tell you about how good they can be?

The day after that loss, Stan opened the papers to see that the *Irish Sun* had labelled him and his players as the Muppets and the next day at Malahide, someone dressed in a Miss Piggy outfit, also sent by the *Irish Sun*, turned up to take the piss. There was even talk that they went to Stan's mum's house in the outfit, trying to get a comment.

Whichever way you look at it, that is totally out of order. That is wrong on every level.

The treatment Stan got by the media when things started going wrong was terrible in my opinion. Stan bleeds green, he gave everything for his country and he was a great, great defender for us. You don't get to be the first man to play 100 times for your country by being a poor player. How can you go from that, an Irish legend, to being completely slated by the press? To having Miss Piggy rocking up at your mum's house? If I'd played in that game and they'd turned up in Lifford like that, my Dad would've punched them one, and rightly so.

I missed the draw with the Czech Republic at home but was back in time for the 5-0 thrashing of San Marino when Robbie got a hat-trick and for a brief period all seemed to be ok. Until the San Marino away game, that is. Again, I was injured so Wayne Henderson played ahead of Paddy and we only just squeezed past them 2-1. The writing was on the wall for Stan after that as the media and most of the fans blamed him, Bobby and John Delaney for the state of the national team.

In one sense, the next match against Wales came at a good time for all of us because a lot of the spotlight ahead of the match wasn't on us but was on the ground we'd be playing at. Lansdowne Road was being knocked down and rebuilt so after plenty of talk, we moved to Croke Park for the Wales qualifier.

It was a big, historic game. Ireland's history with the UK is well known and I'm not going to go over it here but, basically, soccer was an English game that the GAA had always said would never be played at Croke Park.

We needed to play somewhere, though, and there was talk of the Millennium Stadium or even Anfield at the time – which would've been a huge shame for Irish fans. To walk out at Croke Park, the venue of so many All-Ireland finals, was a real honour for me personally. We were just footballers – it wasn't for us to get involved in the history or the politics.

# OVER AND OUT

When the game eventually came around, the first thing I noticed was it was hard to re-enact the atmosphere from Lansdowne Road. A Gaelic pitch is a lot bigger than a football pitch so it felt like the fans were a long way from us. Croke Park is one of the biggest stadiums in Europe and it seemed to swamp the amount of people in there whereas Lansdowne Road was tight and you heard every cough and spit because the supporters were on top of you.

We won the match 1-0 thanks to a Stephen Ireland goal before we prepared again for Slovakia, a match that was my 80th – the same amount as Packie Bonner.

To equal his record was something I was extremely proud of and not even some comments from Roy Keane before the game were going to take that away from me. Roy had been quoted in the papers as saying, "Maybe the players want to get 50 or 100 caps and a pat on the back for it. I think Shay's one of those – he wants to get 200 caps."

At the time, I couldn't believe it even made the papers but at the same time I understood why – everything Roy Keane says is a headline.

The year before, if players were pulling out of squads it was all, "They're picking and choosing games" and all this kind of stuff but I'll say now what I said at the time – I never thought I'd play one game for Ireland, it was everything to me so he could say what he liked, it really didn't bother me whatsoever. I'd travel anywhere, at any time, with any notice to play for Ireland and if some people thought I had a deeper 'agenda' then they were wrong. My agenda was lining up next to my team-mates, singing the national anthem and winning football matches for my country. End of.

We had another narrow win at Croke Park over Slovakia, we drew against them in Bratislava before a loss to the Czech Republic and a draw against Germany meant we were in real trouble ahead of another match against Cyprus.

They were desperate to do the double after the 5-2 game and they got close, leading until the last kick of the game when Steve Finnan equalised. The FAI bosses had seen enough and Steve was sacked but for me, a lot of the blame for his 21 months in charge has to lie with the FAI itself. They were the ones who threw him in at the deep end by offering him a job he could never refuse at such an age.

To put it in perspective, Steve was five years younger than I am now when he got the Ireland job, which is insane. He was offered a position no Irishman could turn down but he was offered it 15 years too early. He hasn't really had a chance at a proper club since then and that's very unfair on him.

Steve didn't have the opportunity to do an apprenticeship and learn how to do the job. He'd played a lot of top-flight football but being a coach is completely different. I learnt that myself at Aston Villa. The difference was, I got the chance to learn surrounded by the security blanket of only being an assistant coach, whereas the FAI ensured Steve never got that option.

Steve's not the only one to have struggled with the way the FAI works from time to time. While I am grateful for some of the things they did over the course of my international career, there are a couple of incidents that have left a bitter taste in the mouth.

Over the years I've done some work for the Beechwood Cancer Care Centre in Stockport and also tried to help Macmillan Cancer Support. The Beechwood Cancer Care Centre is a place that supports people who are suffering from cancer and also their families. After what happened to Mum it was something I felt I wanted to do. I'm proud to have raised money for them over the years as well as over £1.3m for Macmillan.

In 2016, ahead of a special Christmas auction to raise funds, I promised Beechwood that I would get them some matchday tickets and some player lounge passes for the Ireland v Wales match at the Aviva in March. They auctioned them off for quite a lot of money but when it was time for me to get the prizes for the winning bidder, I started encountering problems.

I bought six tickets for the game – I personally think that ex-players should get some match tickets but I didn't really mind – and I then rang the FAI and asked for two lounge pass tickets for after the match. "Sorry Shay, there's nothing we can do," I was told down the phone. Twenty years of playing for your country and they could not even rustle up a couple of spare passes? That doesn't sit comfortably with me at all. Surely they could've done something.

As I understand, there are about about 3,000 passes available at every match. It's not as if the lounge passes are just you and the players; there are thousands of people in those rooms but the FAI could not find just two for an ex-player who was trying to do something worthwhile for charity. I'd been signing autographs in player lounges for two decades but that no longer stood for anything by the looks of things.

In the end, I had to practically beg and thankfully Jon Walters gave me two of his that I could then pass on along with the match tickets. That meant at least two of Jon's friends and family were inconvenienced by the FAI's stance. It didn't paint the FAI in the best light – and that wasn't the first time either.

A few years earlier, my Dad was in a pub and was asked a

question by a bloke about loads of FAI staff losing their jobs. Dad innocently told this guy that if people were getting made redundant then John Delaney should also see his pay and bonuses cut. It turned out that the man in the pub was a reporter who stitched Dad up. He turned his opinion into big news and shortly afterwards we had to have a meeting with John about the players' bonuses.

Early on in the meeting, where he sat on one end of a long table and me, Robbie Keane and John O'Shea sat at the other, Delaney criticised Dad's opinion and I exploded. "What the fuck's that got to do with me?" I asked. "That's my Dad – he's a free man and he can say what the fuck he likes." I was boiling and it's a good job the table between us was so long.

After 20 years of service, not a single person from the FAI hierarchy has ever picked the phone up and thanked me for my efforts and that is a massive disappointment to me and my family, especially Dad. He'd watched his son proudly wear the shirt for so many years and just couldn't get his head around it.

The thought had also crossed my mind that I could have a testimonial where I could say farewell to the fans and give all the money to the Irish Cancer Society, but the offer never came.

The closest I got to any formal recognition was when Robbie Keane played his final time for Ireland against Oman in August 2016. Martin O'Neill rang me and said I should come out at half-time to wave to the fans but I was never going to do that. It was Robbie's big night and he rightly deserved it; what right did I have to gatecrash his farewell?

Instead, I've received zip, zilch, nothing. It was hurtful and upsetting for me and my family, who have supported Ireland all their lives.

# 18

# NOISY NEIGHBOURS

IT was a big decision to move to Manchester City because I never really thought I was going to leave Newcastle. I was settled up there, my brother Marcus and sister Sinead lived close and I loved the area. It was purely a football decision that needed to be taken.

The move to City freshened me up, gave me a new goal and a new sense of direction. I knew they could afford any goalkeeper in the world – their chequebook had no last page in it – so for them to come in for me felt great.

Originally when I moved down, I stayed in the Radisson in the middle of Manchester. There are a couple of little apartments at the top where I lived before I then rented a place in Alderley Edge, which wasn't too far from Carrington.

One thing I did notice when I moved to Manchester and the surrounding area was that I was now in a two-club town, so the goldfish bowl element of life wasn't as intense.

You could grab a coffee and a bite to eat without feeling like you'd got the world looking at you. Don't get me wrong, I loved Newcastle, I've never forgotten how privileged I was to play in front of those fans for so many years – I'm always grateful for that – but moving to Manchester just took a bit of pressure off me in a nice way. Mostly, the move was exciting.

I went to the Etihad Stadium to sign the contract and saw Mark Hughes. It was good to meet him. You hear stories about people getting tapped up but that didn't happen with me; the first time we met was at the stadium. We just chatted about mutual mates and what City had planned for the future. He was somebody I had huge respect for. Growing up as a kid, we watched him playing for Manchester United. His CV as a player was phenomenal. Meeting him for the first time added to my enthusiasm for the move; this was something fresh to embrace and get stuck into.

Everything, obviously, was totally different; the players, the training ground, the regime itself. I enjoyed the change. Even the drive in to work every day was new and refreshing.

At City, Joe Hart and Kasper Schmeichel were already bedded in so there was strong competition. Mark Hughes had brought me in to be his first choice but I still felt like I had to prove I was worthy of that. Joe had done very little wrong, really, to warrant me coming in. He was only 21 at the time but he was a seriously good goalkeeper even then so I knew I would have my work cut out to stay ahead of him.

On one of my first mornings at Carrington I was warming up on an exercise bike and Joe came in to say hello. "I don't know what to say really mate," he said to me. "I suppose my chance is gone for now."

# NOISY NEIGHBOURS

"To be honest Joe, I don't know what to say either," I replied, honestly. "The chance was there to come and I had to take it. We'll work together, we'll work well but neither of us pick the team so we have to make the best of it."

Fair play to Joe, he agreed, he respected that and we've always had a brilliant relationship. I went to his birthday party earlier this year and we have always had a laugh.

Whereas at Newcastle I'd been the No.1 for a long time, it was now time for me to impress my new employers and, for once, the clean slate I had was of benefit. I had a new set of players, staff and fans to impress and that was a motivation for me. Newcastle fans had seen me for a long time – I was part of the furniture – but City would've only seen me the odd time we played against each other. That meant that now, week in and week out, I had to prove and convince people I was good enough and hungry enough to be at a club whose ambitions were as big as City's were.

Changing allegiance from Newcastle to City was easy enough because you have to be a professional. From Lifford Celtic onwards, I've always had fond memories of all the clubs I've played for. I think I'll always have a soft spot for Newcastle because I was there for so long. But when I joined City, I wanted to win every game for them from that second onwards – the same as at Villa, Stoke, Middlesbrough, you name it.

My debut was against Middlesbrough on February 7, 2009 and in the end it couldn't have gone any better.

I'd been nervous before that match because it had been a long time since I'd made a debut for anybody and I was desperate for it to go well.

I made a few decent saves from Afonso Alves and I was named

man of the match. We won 1-0 and Craig Bellamy, who'd also just joined the club for £12m from West Ham United, scored. It was good to be reunited with Craig – I think Sparky wanted more niggle and more passion in his side and Craig certainly provided that.

For me, the Middlesbrough performance was a great way to show anyone who still doubted me that I was the man for the job. Players from other clubs might have watched me on *Match of the Day* but you never get to know another player until you've lined up next to them and I wanted to show the likes of Pablo Zabaleta, Vinny Kompany and also Mark Hughes himself that their faith in me would be paid back.

Gaining respect early on was important and I felt I killed any potential scepticism about my suitability for the role. Joe Hart was a great young goalkeeper with bags of potential but I wanted early on for people to go, 'Bloody hell, he is good this guy.'

*****

Joining a new club is no different to changing your job in the 'real' world, by the way. For the first few weeks you're trying to feel your way around the training ground, learn everybody's name and just get used to things. It soon became clear to me just how focused the entire place was.

This was the time of the 'noisy neighbours'. The entire squad felt like we were getting ever closer to United and the others at the top of the table. Fergie knew we were coming after them, that's why we managed to get under his skin enough for him to make his famous comment about us.

# NOISY NEIGHBOURS

You can say what you want about City's owners but Sheikh Mansour and Khaldoon Al Mubarak are in for the long haul. Look what they have done in terms of the Eastlands set-up and revitalising that area of Manchester. They didn't have to take that extra step but I honestly think they want to give back to the city – and they have done that.

Shortly after I joined the club I met Khaldoon before a game. He made me feel really welcome and seemed a genuine, nice bloke. "I don't get involved in too many transfers," he told me. "But, yours, I wanted it done. I really wanted you here. This is a project and you're a part of that and the future." That made me feel amazing. From hot air in Newcastle to proper, definable ambitions and goals at City. They had the finances to buy anyone they wanted so I felt privileged that they chose me to help out. The names we brought in that first season I was there, 2008/2009, set the tone for City's future and showed how serious they were.

My good mate Richard Dunne, who I obviously knew from Ireland, was also at the club. That was a big help. He was a massive player for City at the time and I was delighted to be playing alongside him. I knew all about him and his character and I thought he was seriously underrated as a defender. A lot of people thought he was just a massive brute who scored own goals! But he was an intelligent, skilful player. And if he did score own goals what did that mean? It meant he was often the last line of defence, putting his head and body in places I'd never dream of in a bid to stop goals; and you can't ask more than that from any team-mate.

All in, City spent about £120m on new players that season. I came in, as did the likes of Bellers, Wayne Bridge, Nigel de Jong and Vincent Kompany. These were top class performers, players who expected and demanded the best from those around them. It was a pleasure to be working with them and to have a squad around me that wasn't second-rate, wasn't coasting. The entire City set-up, from the manager down, was focused on success.

One player we did bring in who didn't quite work out was Robinho. He'd signed for the club three or four months before me for big, big money.

Robinho, Jo – another 2008/09 signing – and Elano very much kept themselves to themselves. Because they had the language connection, they could stick in a little group and not mingle too much. I could understand why in a way. If I was in the middle of a different country and two or three other Irish fellas were in the squad then I reckon it's only natural I would've been drawn to them as mates, so I had no problem with it. They were all nice lads and they'd say hello to you when they first got in but you didn't – or couldn't – start a conversation with them because their English was pretty scratchy.

Robinho was similar to Tino Asprilla at Newcastle. He was always messing about in training, doing tricks and flicks and stuff. He just never seemed that bothered.

On matchday, we all wondered which Robinho was going to show up. We'd seen him play for Real Madrid and rip teams apart on his own. His head just wasn't on it for most of the time yet on some days he could do stuff with the ball that most people could only dream of.

Another signing cut from the same cloth as Robinho was Emmanuel Adebayor for £25m which, for City, at that time, amounted to about £2.50. He was a bit of an enigma, really, and you always thought you could get more out of him if he fancied it. On his day, when he was in the mood, he was as good as any striker in the country but it just seemed to me that those good days weren't often enough for us. That used to frustrate me.

I suppose his most famous moment in a City shirt came when he ran the length of the pitch at the Etihad to give Arsenal's fans some stick after scoring against them when we beat them 4-2 in September 2009. He'd been getting dog's abuse all day from the supporters of his old club so I was buzzing for him when the goal went in. I was obviously at the other end and was delighted    until he set off in my direction. Mmm, this was a long way to run just to give me a hug. He was going absolutely crazy. I went over, told him well done and tried to pull him away from the carnage he was causing. Technically speaking, he never left the pitch so didn't break the FA's encroachment rules but they hammered him anyway. He ran further celebrating that goal than he ever did in training, incidentally!

Coaching sessions under Mark were not long but we did lots of high-intensity stuff. There was no slacking off and most of the players seemed committed, especially Pablo. Zabaleta is a great lad and I think that came over when he left City last season. He really settled into Manchester life and the City fans took him to their heart. He was a dedicated, funny, down-to-earth bloke and he made an effort to really fit in.

Apparently he told his wife that she would only have to move to Manchester for a couple of years and that anybody could put up with the rain that long – and then nine years later he was still there! He wasn't an Aguero or a Tevez – he wasn't a South American playmaker type – but there was nobody more committed than he was. He gave absolutely everything.

In my early days at City, before they both left, me, Joe and Kasper used to always go early before training for a yoga session with Sarah Ramsden at Carrington. She used to do the Manchester United players at their training ground, which is virtually next door, and then pop round to us. We'd ask for any inside information but she'd never give anything away!

The yoga was a great addition to my week's training because it certainly helped keep me more flexible and prepared for games. Ryan Giggs was the first big name to use it and I suppose we all followed in his footsteps a bit. I know Brad Friedel was a big fan of it at Spurs. He was using it at 40 – and he seemed to get better with age. Kevin Hitchcock was the City goalkeeping coach at the time and we'd do 45 minutes together before we'd go over and join the main group.

Hughes didn't say much in training, he preferred to leave it to his coaches while he circled the training pitch, quietly observing what was going on. He's not a loud, outgoing character, he prefers to keep himself in check. You won't see him regularly effing and bawling like Joe Kinnear. He would have the odd mad moment but Sparky was all about keeping a level head whether we won or lost. He was exactly the same when I was with him at Stoke.

Joe and Kasper were as keen as I was to keep on learning.

When I first saw Joe close up, I noticed that his hands were really low. "Joe, just work on lifting them a bit," I told him. "See if that helps you get up quicker." Because he is so tall and because his hands were so low, if he was crouched and ready to spring then it would be easier if his hands were higher.

Joe, like me, was always keen to take anything on board – I wasn't his coach or trying to be his coach but he always listened and he'd give me the odd bit of advice too. You're never too good or too old to learn new tips.

Me and Kasper got on great and one day he told me he looked up to me a bit because we're a similar stature. That felt very strange indeed. I was stood there thinking, 'Your dad is one of my biggest heroes and now you're telling me this.' It felt like the world had gone full circle! Kasper was happy to be around me and Joe and to see how we worked. When any of us made great saves in training or if I'd had a good performance, we'd all talk about it and compliment each other.

Probably because of who his dad is, Kasper has felt the need to prove himself even more than he really needs to. He deserves credit for that because Peter Schmeichel's shadow could've been too big to ever escape but look how amazing he's been. Peter is a legend but I bet even he has to buy his own drinks in Leicester and his son doesn't.

We worked well together and I got the impression that he knew he'd be out of City soon because he was unlikely to get many starting chances in the near future. It was a bit like me at Blackburn. Kasper showed the same determination that I had done to get out on the road and get some football under his belt and he joined Notts County in August 2009, a move that paid off brilliantly. He eventually moved on to Leicester City, of course, and now has a Premier League winner's medal, so he clearly did the right thing. I texted him after Leicester had won the title. It was unreal, fairytale stuff wasn't it?

Joe and Kasper are still close. When Leicester won at the Etihad on their way to the title, Joe grabbed him on the final whistle, hugged him and told him that this was the biggest, best chance he'd ever have to win the Premier League and that he couldn't mess it up. Joe was as passionate about Leicester winning it as Kasper was and that friendship and relationship between those two, with each other and with me, started at Carrington when we were all there together.

At the end of May in my first season at City, 2008/09, I'd played 21 matches for the club and kept Joe out of the team since January. It was clear to me that he was going to go out on loan. He went to Birmingham City, who couldn't sign him quick enough and rightly so.

Both Joe and Kasper were like I'd been at 21 – headstrong, determined and desperate for matches so in one sense I was glad he'd got fixed up with a club. There are players at clubs the length and breadth of the country who are 23 or 24 and never tied their boots on a first-team pitch. They're just happy to sit there and collect their wages. I knew that neither Joe nor Kasper were like that and it was Joe's season at Birmingham that arguably set him up for the rest of his career.

We finished the season in tenth spot in the Premier League. We'd lost to Nottingham Forest in the FA Cup before I'd arrived but what stung the most was the UEFA Cup loss when we were doing so well. Just a fortnight or so after joining City we played FC Copenhagen who we squeezed past 4-3 on aggregate over two legs and in the next round, we won the first leg against Aalborg at home after goals from Felipe Caicedo and Shaun Wright-Phillips.

After that we lost to Chelsea in the league but travelled to Denmark for the second leg. Everything was going fine until the last six or so minutes when we fell to bits, conceding to Luton Shelton and Michael Jakobsen.

Eventually it went to penalties. *Oh good.* Those of you who have been following closely will know I've not exactly had much luck from 12 yards, but this night was thankfully very different.

Goalkeepers don't get much chance to send the fans mad but that night was one of only a handful in my career where that happened. Aalborg had never been in a penalty shootout before and I was hoping that would go in my favour, as it did. I managed to guess right, twice, and got down to stop Thomas Augustinussen and Shelton from knocking us out.

It was a really great feeling. There were about 600 fans behind my goal to my right and you could hear them shouting and screaming advice and encouragement; *go this way, go that way.*

I tried to delay the odd penalty, walking out to the six-yard line, making myself look big in the goalmouth, trying to psyche them out. It worked a dream early on as they scored the first two but Ched Evans and Elano also kept things level for us.

The noise as the lads ran up to take their spot-kicks was huge but the boys kept their nerve. Augustinussen looked nervous and twitchy as he picked the ball up, he hit it low to my right and it was quite a comfortable save in the end. Shaun Wright-Phillips nailed his effort; one of their lads cheekily chipped their fourth passed me; Dunney smashed one in to make it 4-3 to us before Shelton stepped up for them. I held the ball in my hand for as long as I could, standing on my six-yard line. Fuck it, I've got nothing to lose here, the pressure was all on him. Again he went to the right and I followed him, blocking the shot and the ball dribbled away to safety.

Before I knew it, the boys were on me and we were all in the crowd with the City fans, all of us going mad.

We hoped that the win would give us the bounce we wanted for the rest of the competition but at the time we were really struggling away from home and by the time the quarter-final came about, we just couldn't seem to perform. We lost 3-1 to Hamburg at their place. Back at the Etihad, the place was rocking and Elano was brilliant that night but the damage had been done in the first leg and although we won the match, we went out 4-3 on aggregate.

To have ended the season with nothing to show for it hurt but City's owners again spent big in the summer of 2009.

I think the signing that excited me the most during my early time at City was enticing Carlos Tevez from United, where he was one of the best players. It was a massive coup for us and proved we could compete in the transfer window and bring the best players to the club. It felt like a big statement.

Carlos was a quality player and a big personality but he was not a great trainer at all. He seemed to go through the motions yet when the matchday arrived and the ref blew the whistle, he was like a man possessed. I didn't think you could switch your energy on and off but he certainly could. He set the tempo for all the outfield players. One minute he'd be playing centre-half, the next he'd be chasing their keeper down. He couldn't speak any English at all so he used to set an example to us by the way he played. He brought goals, and he scored some great ones, but I was more impressed by his dedication to the dirty work during a game. He never let the opposition settle.

Quality just seemed to flood into Carrington with people like Kolo Toure and Gareth Barry arriving by the day.

I was really pleased to see Gareth Barry sign for us. He is a really good guy. People say he is a bit quiet but he isn't when you get to know him. We used to go out and play golf all the time at Mottram Hall or Mere and he loved a few beers; he was just one of the lads. On the pitch, he always seemed to have time on the ball and always picked the right pass.

Kolo was another amazing signing. He'd been rock-solid for Arsenal, he was a legend there, and he would bring some strength to our defence and deepen our squad. He had not been at City long when he threw a dinner in town. I think it was for his birthday so I turned up looking smart with a bottle of champagne and a card to the restaurant, Rosso, in Manchester city centre. I handed him his card and champagne – the only player who'd brought him anything by the way! – and he looked at me a bit funny.

He's such a nice guy, a really great bloke, but I sensed something was up. "Shay," he said. "Only an Irishman would bring a Muslim a bottle of champagne for his birthday."

I'm such a fast learner that a short time later Kolo threw another bash.

"Lads, I want you all to come to my house," he said. "You are my guests, there will be food and it will be excellent."

"Any drink?" I asked him, straight to the point.

"I can't let alcohol in my house," Kolo said.

"Ok, what about the front step?" I said, half joking.

"If you stay outside then ok," Kolo said. "I will not look and you can get on with it."

I turned up at his gaff in Prestbury with a 24 deck – no Irishman arrives at a party with two arms the same length. "Hiya lads," I said, rocking. Next thing, there's more City players outside with me than there is inside the house, all of us tucking into the beer. The front garden was the VIP lounge!

*****

When we went back into training before the 2009/10 season, one player I really felt for was Michael Johnson because he just had so many injuries. His knee seemed to go all the time.

On the odd time he was fit enough to train with us, he was genuinely phenomenal. But the next day he'd come in and his knee was twice the size it should have been. He piled a lot of weight on and he tried to shift it but he just couldn't stay fit long enough to do anything.

It was a real shame actually. We lost a player who was class but so did England. I know he's dropped out of the game now and that is a massive loss. He could've been a great.

The dressing room before the start of that year had plenty of new faces but, unfortunately for us, after a good start which saw us win our first five matches – three away from home – it was our away form that started to let us down badly. We lost 3-0 at Spurs, 2-0 at Everton and 2-1 at Hull.

One trip that everyone remembers for the wrong reasons came in late September at Old Trafford. It was a see-saw game but we looked like we were going to get the draw after Craig Bellamy made it 3-3 in the 90th minute. There should have been about four minutes of injury time but we played 97 minutes I think. In the 96th minute, of course, Michael Owen pops up and wins it for them. Fergie-time strikes again. Why was there that much time played? It felt like we were really hard done by that afternoon. We were sick and it was devastating.

Owen had done that all his career, he never missed many one-on-ones. In training at Newcastle he nearly always scored. Maybe I should've stayed off a yard, who knows. He slotted it by me as I tried to get in his face. Typical striker. He didn't do much else but got the headlines the next day.

After that defeat, we became experts at drawing matches. We beat West Ham at home but then took just a point from every one of our next seven games. With the size of City's squad and the stellar names we'd brought in, the fans and media expected more.

But you can't just wave a magic wand and turn a side into champions overnight. Moulding a winning side was always going to take a while – you name me one successful team that has clicked right away – and the poor results kept coming until we faced Sunderland at home on December 19. There'd been an article in a paper that morning saying Mark Hughes was going and that Roberto Mancini was coming in and that totally changed the atmosphere in the ground that day.

We beat Sunderland 4-3 but the entire game had this surreal edge to it. The Etihad felt flat and uncomfortable and the dressing room was the same. What was going on? What was happening? Who was going to come and explain it to us, the players?

Usually after winning 4-3 there would be a buzz in the dressing room but nobody seemed that bothered that we'd just edged a thrilling match and, eventually, Sparky was called away for 20 minutes. He finally came back into the dressing room and called me, Vincent Kompany and Kolo Toure to one side.

"I've been sacked lads, I'm off," he just said, very quietly and calmly. "I'm not really sure what else there is to say."

It felt harsh. We were growing and building as a squad, we were on course to reach the targets we'd set pre-season but by binning Hughes in December, that at least gave the club's owners the chance to get a new man in and let him have a go in the transfer window – I suppose that was the thinking behind it.

I really felt for the gaffer and the rest of the dressing room was very much the same. Many of players had been brought to the club with the promise of stability, a new way of doing things and they all respected Hughes for the player he'd been and the manager he was. All that was now out of the window.

Garry Cook worked as a liaison between Khaldoon and the players. I spoke to him about it but it was too late by then. Garry had a nice way about him and listened but it didn't go anywhere, as it couldn't do really because the decision had already been made.

Part of me also thought, 'Oh, here we go again'. I'd just left one club five minutes ago because they were changing their manager constantly and now it was happening all over again plus Mancini was coming over from Italy – was he about to bring Buffon with him? All the unknowns were back in my life and I didn't need that.

Ultimately though, you play for the badge and the shirt and your team-mates, so we had no say in the matter. It was time to get used to Roberto Mancini. Or at least try to...

# 19

# THE MADNESS OF MANCINI

FOR the love of me, I couldn't work Mancini out.

We heard that when he was sacked by Inter Milan in 2008, the entire squad had a massive night out to celebrate.

By the time I left Manchester City in July 2011, I was ready to throw a party myself.

Surely, the first and most important job a manager has is to get the most out of those around him. Whether you rate a player or not, if he's on your books then surely you want the best for him, you want the best from him and you want your entire club to move forward. Otherwise, why bother wasting everybody's time even being there?

Roberto Mancini saw the world differently to Shay Given, that's for sure. He fell out with everyone.

And when I say everyone, I mean everyone. The players, the back-up staff, the physios, the kitman, the press officers, the canteen workers, the car park lads, the lot. He probably even swung a punch or two at his own reflection for looking at him funny.

Every single morning, he'd sit on an exercise bike and the physio would come to him to report what condition the squad was in. That was the start of World War Three every day. The physios would deliver a standard list of who was and wasn't fit and he would erupt in anger, accusing them of shielding fit players or not working hard enough to get injured players back. Tell me, how does that get the best out of people?

Life is not meant to be that difficult.

The maddest thing was, after causing chaos with everybody in the week, I'd then go off to St Pius X Church in Alderley Edge on a Sunday morning and he'd be in there, as devout a Roman Catholic as could be!

After Hughes was sacked, the first meeting with Mancini came at Carrington with Garry Cook and also a translator. He spoke really scratchy English and was reading from a piece of paper. "I'm…'ere… to 'elp Manchester Citee…" and we knew it was going to be tough from then on.

We won our first four matches under Mancini and I kept a clean sheet in three of them so maybe his introduction to the club did strengthen us up a bit at the back and, don't get me wrong, he won the Premier League for City but, personally, I just don't think he needed to be so volatile.

Initially, I was Mancini's first-choice − or, at the very least, he preferred me to Stuart Taylor, the back-up now Joe was at Birmingham − and I did well, as did the rest of the boys. We began turning draws into wins and away losses into at least a point so Mancini, on one level, was justifying his existence even if his training sessions were very strange, to say the least.

# THE MADNESS OF MANCINI

At most clubs I've been at, you do a bit of team shape on a Thursday to lead into the weekend and you play 11v11.

The two teams would be the rough starting XI v the 'Custard Pies' who were on the bench. But at City it would just be the starting XI against nobody. Ghosts. Nothing.

I'd roll the ball out to the right-back, he'd pass it back. I'd pass it to the centre-half, and he'd pass it back. I'd kick to Bellamy or Stephen Ireland and he'd dribble, at walking speed, towards their goal. Then they passed it to Tevez or whoever and he'd have to score. Into an empty net. Fucking hell, even I'd score a hatful in those circumstances.

It was weird because it wasn't done at any great pace or intensity so I couldn't work out the point of it. Last time I checked, when you kicked off on a Saturday you had 11 men in front of you, but still we did it every week.

As the season progressed, the one really low moment was the loss to Manchester United in the Carling Cup semi-final about six weeks after Mancini had arrived.

City hadn't been in a cup final since sometime before I was thinning turnips but two Carlos Tevez goals following Ryan Giggs' opener for United in the first leg gave us a slight lead going into the away match at Old Trafford.

Don't let anyone tell you that the Carling Cup or whatever it is called now is 'only' the League Cup, especially when it's a Manchester derby. The competition might be used to blood a lot of youngsters but that night we were both at full strength and we threw everything at each other.

Paul Scholes hit a deflected effort past me just after half-time before Michael Carrick made it 3-2 to them on aggregate as he slotted into the far corner. Fuck.

Tevez put us level again and I then pulled off a great stop to prevent Darren Fletcher from stealing it in the 90th minute. Instead, Wayne Rooney stole it in the 91st, nodding in from point-blank range. Old Trafford went absolutely crazy and to be fair to Wayne it was a cool header thanks to a wonderful cross from Ryan Giggs. Rooney ran off to my left and was doing cartwheels, which showed you how much the League Cup could mean when it meant winning a semi-final.

We were all absolutely devastated by that defeat and it showed we still had some way to go as a squad to adopting a winning mentality and edging those matches where the margins are so fine.

But the real turning point for me that season – and what essentially paved the way for me leaving – was the shoulder dislocation that I picked up against Arsenal towards the end of the season. What happened was this…

We had lost at home to Manchester United the previous week when Paul Scholes scored a header down to my left. It was a classic Scholes finish, ghosting in from nowhere, although it was his head this time rather than his right foot.

I was gutted to concede – another sickening late winner – but the split-second I landed on the turf and as Scholes wheeled off to celebrate like a madman, I knew I was hurt and that I'd done something pretty serious to my shoulder. I didn't train all week but I was desperate to play the next weekend against Arsenal.

After losing, especially late on, I always just wanted the next game to arrive to get back out there and even though I'd strained and pulled some ligaments in my shoulder, I wouldn't listen to the advice of those around the club whose job it was to try and keep us healthy.

Jamie Murphy was the head of physio at City at the time and he was black and white with me about the risks I'd be taking if I played and that I shouldn't even be thinking about it. "I'm fine, I'm fine, I'll play," I told him. We travelled to the Emirates and my shoulder was wincing all the way there, which was never a good sign.

Before the match, I got it strapped and even in the warm-up I couldn't do my usual stuff, I was a bit tentative and it was still giving me lots of grief. Jamie is somebody I have a lot of time for, he is a superb physio, but I just couldn't let myself be injured at the time.

Joe was still with Birmingham and Stuart Taylor had a knee problem. If City were going to keep their Champions League hopes up then they needed an experienced goalkeeper and that meant me. Neither me or Manchester City could afford for me to be hurt so, in my mind, I wasn't. Simple as that – I just had to get out there.

When I was at Newcastle, Harps used to call me 'Lazarus' because I'd be bad all week and then the adrenaline would kick in on the morning of the game.

We were away at Manchester United one year. I had been struggling with a knock all week in training and it looked as if Harps was going to start. I asked for one more fitness test before the decision was made but we couldn't find anywhere to do it. The gym at the hotel was closed so we did it right there, in the hotel car park. I was always that desperate to play that any bumps or knocks would fade into the background. I was vomiting severely pre-match against West Ham United once yet got through it and played ok.

One of the things any goalkeeper will tell you, though, is that if you play with a knock or an injury then it will find you. Sure enough, with about 20 minutes to go against Arsenal, I dived for an Abou Diaby shot and, BANG, the shoulder popped straight out with a full dislocation. Turns out Jamie and his physio mates didn't go to university for nothing after all.

The pain at first was right up there with the Marlon Harewood injury. My entire shoulder went into a massive spasm and they couldn't pop the shoulder back in for ages, which is not exactly an experience I'm in a hurry to repeat.

Gunnar Neilsen replaced me for his one and only Manchester City appearance as I was stretchered off, season over.

The Arsenal injury obviously gave Mancini all the ammunition he needed to bring Joe back to the club and relegate me to the bench, yet I don't regret playing in that match. I'd do exactly the same tomorrow, no question.

It wasn't as if the shoulder dislocation was something I could never recover from. I was fit for the next pre-season; ready to go after the summer. I was still getting rehab on the shoulder, but that wasn't enough to warrant completely dropping me all together.

When Joe came back from Birmingham, it was clear he was Mancini's No.1.

I even spoke to Brian Kidd about playing in pre-season and I was as good as begging him for games. "Mancini doesn't think you're fit to play," Brian said. I was fit but for whatever reason, Mancini wasn't having any of it. He wanted me out of the club and to this day, I can't give you a straight reason as to what I'd done to justify that or warrant it.

Whatever club I've been at I've been exactly the same; approachable, committed, desperate to win and professional but all of a sudden I was on Mancini's shit-list and I couldn't get off it.

We even played a pre-season tournament in America and I saved two penalties in a shootout during one friendly which I thought proved my fitness and form were absolutely fine. But apparently not...

*****

Although that pre-season was an unhappy time for me, the one-way traffic of quality into Carrington continued as the likes of Patrick Vieira, David Silva and Yaya Toure all arrived.

Yaya has had some stick for the size of his contracts but he has delivered. Forget what he's on a week, think about what he's brought to the club. He's been paid the big bucks to do the business and he's done that. He used to just hang around with Kolo and didn't really interact with anybody else. But he was a pleasant guy and always asked how I was when we bumped into each other.

To play with Patrick Vieira was a fantastic experience. I mean, what do you say about him? He won everything you can win and he had a huge stature. He had some issues with his knees but he still trained with massive intensity and spirit.

Patrick would be getting changed for training with the lads and it was all smiles and laughs, taking the piss, the usual stuff and then he'd tie those laces and nobody was safe.

He trained like he played, with some massive tackles, complete commitment and a will to win. Good luck to you if you couldn't be arsed training that day or went into a tackle half-hearted because Patrick would be on you straight away, demanding more – and rightly so. He used to love putting himself about but the gentleman that was Patrick on the sidelines was replaced by a warrior on the field.

Vincent Kompany was also a shining light in terms of his preparation. He looked after himself very well off the field. Like Vieira, as he settled into City he trained like crazy, as did Nigel de Jong, who would fly in and nail anyone nearby as if it was a match. A good tackle in training can get the lads going sometimes and Nigel was never scared to get stuck in.

Vincent would stay behind and do extra work in the afternoon or injury-prevention stretching to try and keep himself in good nick. He was signed as a midfielder but he settled in at centre-half and he was brilliant on the ball.

When David Silva joined the club, the papers were full of stories about him being the final piece in the City jigsaw and when you think we 'only' paid £24m for him from Valencia then that looks like the bargain of the century these days.

I'd also like to think I played a personal role in his development at the club.

When he arrived, his favourite dessert was plain fruit salad without yoghurt. Dead healthy stuff like that. One day he sidled up to me in the canteen while I was sat eating my favourite dessert, which is several rungs lower on the health scale.

"Shay, what is this you are eating?" he asked.

"That David," I told him, licking my spoon. "Is apple crumble and custard."

Well, that was it! David Silva, who weighs about nine stone, went from fruit salads to as much apple crumble as he could get down his neck. He was hooked on the stuff. It's always nice to influence the careers of your fellow professionals.

Away from the canteen, my God what a footballer that man is. You can call it God-given or natural ability or whatever you want. Label it however you like; the stuff he can do with a football, the passes he can see, instinctively, and the way he makes that ball move is just mind-blowing. You just cannot teach what he has got.

In training you'd just stand there and admire the weight of his passing, the positions he dropped into naturally, the way he found space. He skills don't exist in any coaching manual. You've either got it or you haven't – and he has it. Hard work gets you everywhere in life but there will always be some things and some people you will never beat because they were just born with greatness – and Mr Apple Crumble and Custard is definitely one of them.

Another arrival, and one who sucked up plenty of publicity was Mario Balotelli. Mario was just daft, like a big daft Geordie. He was always messing, always looking to wind someone up. He was just a young lad who wanted to enjoy himself but he landed in Manchester at a time when the club was at the centre of world media and everything he did became a huge story.

Mind you, he didn't exactly help himself because he was another who never gave the impression he was that bothered. He had so much talent. In training he used to hit a ball and it would be a blur, it would be past you in no time but on the pitch he would try and show he was super arrogant and a bit aloof and you just wanted to shake his head and tell him to apply himself a bit more, to give a bit more, because it was all in there.

If we did nip out as a squad for a drink together – which was almost never by this point – Balotelli used to love standing behind you, lobbing ice cubes down the back of your shirt. We'd be in a nice bar somewhere quiet and you'd feel the ice hitting the back of your neck as he tried to get his aim right. I'd turn around and this big stupid grin would be plastered all over his face – although he and Mancini had that many arguments during his time at City he was never smiling for long.

As the 2010/11 season went on, and my arse rubbed the subs bench shiny, there was talk that I was too big a personality in the dressing room, too quick to say what I believed and what I thought and that Mancini didn't want that presence around. I picked up whispers here and there that this was why he wanted me out. I don't know, I don't suppose I'll ever know and to be honest I'm not that arsed now.

Back then though, I certainly was.

I went to see Mancini a few times about his plans for me. Ideally, he wanted Joe in goal and me on the bench because he wanted to avoid the emergency loan situation from the year before but I was too old to be sitting on a bench and still young enough to still be a No.1 somewhere else.

In his office I made it clear I wanted to go and it didn't bother him. "You can go," he said, sat behind his desk, cup of coffee on the side. "You can leave. It's no problem." He was that black and white. I wasn't calling his bluff but he never even attempted to make me stay. If he'd said, "Shay, Joe is in now but you'll get the cup games and keep pushing him hard" then I might've been tempted into sticking around but there was none of that.

In December 2009 he'd told the press I was, "One of the best five goalkeepers in the world" after I'd kept a clean sheet against Stoke City yet now, in the space of no time at all, I'd gone from the top five to top fuck all.

Mind you, I managed to get myself permanently removed from Mancini's Christmas card list when I was part of a trip that went up to St Andrews after we'd lost 3-0 at home to Arsenal in October 2010.

Firstly, why do I always get in trouble in St Andrews?! Secondly, I'm not going to apologise for having a few beers and enjoying my team-mates' company.

Mancini had given us a few days off so me, Joe, James Milner and Gareth all flew up to Edinburgh and went for a round of golf on a course not far from St Andrews.

So far, so boring.

After we played, we then entered a draw to play at St Andrews itself and luckily enough, our names came out of the hat so we knew we'd be playing the famous course the next day.

Before then, we had a night out to get stuck into. One beer turned into two or three and before we knew it we'd ended up in a nightclub called the Lizard Lounge on North Street, about a two minute walk from St Andrews. I know, classy.

It was a Monday night and the joint was deserted but I think word got round we were in there because it suddenly filled up. When it got to throwing out time, these students invited us for another drink. They took us to a place that was literally straight down the road from the pub. It wasn't another bar – it was just this grotty student digs. There was food everywhere, grubby old couches, sticky carpets, the lot – and it was rammed with people.

We were all rocking and a very drunk Gareth Barry decided to do a speech. He stood there for about two minutes, building it up until he came out with: "We've come a long way. It's windy. It's been raining. We're in St Andrews. Let's party!" Churchill wouldn't have much to worry about on the public speaking front!

The next morning we got up with some thick heads and headed off to play at St Andrews.

We got to the first tee with our caddies – you have to play with a caddie there – and as we started to tee-off, we noticed this guy with a big zoom camera, snapping away.

"Is he always here?" I asked the caddie. I thought that was his job, taking pictures of people on the first tee with the clubhouse in the background. I thought it was like a ride at Alton Towers where they try and make you buy the photo after. "A good wee business he's got himself there," I told this caddie who remained diplomatically quiet.

We got to the first green and this photographer is now up our arses, still snapping away. That's when the penny dropped that what we did yesterday might cause us some trouble tomorrow.

Eventually I asked my caddie to go and ask the photographer what he was doing and the snapper told him to fuck off, so that just confirmed it for me. Whoops. The next thing, Joe's phone goes and it's the Manchester City press officer on the phone as the shit slowly started hitting the fan.

As the round went on and on, I thought I'd dodged it all actually. Joe's phone kept ringing as face after face got identified in these *Sun* photos but my name wasn't cropping up. Just as I was starting to take the piss out of Joe, his phone went again and a big smile cropped up on his face. "Yes, yes, I'll tell him," he said, looking at me grinning. "I'll definitely tell him." Shit! Busted too!

What harm had we really done though? It was only bit of fun. Gaz had to make a big apology and we got a dressing down from Mancini when we got back but, if anything, that showed how big City had become – anything was now a story.

The irony for me really was the fact I was 34 by now so my chances of being able to drink and then train the next day were well and truly gone. It was literally impossible to go for a beer with the lads and then train at the right intensity the next day and if I had to choose a pint or a good performance then there was only ever going to be one winner. My earlier days of being up and out with the lads were behind me.

Christmas came and went, I still never got a look-in and it was time to go. I've always been more than happy to answer a straight media question with a straight answer and on Ireland duty one time I was perfectly honest and said I'd be on my way soon, even if it meant out on loan. There was talk of a move to Arsenal and Fulham but, hand on heart, nobody ever approached me directly and asked about whether I would join them.

On the pitch, meanwhile, Joe was playing superbly well and I did all I could in training to support him and push him. All my career I'd been used to being No.1 but I'd seen both Harps and Joe be superb understudies and I was determined to be the same.

Yes, I desperately wanted to play every week but what kind of bloke would I have been if I'd broken my own rule: *The manager picks the team, we just try our best and leave it to him.* There was no chance I was ever going to sulk or play up to Joe because, firstly, that's just not who I am and secondly, it would've been disrespectful to Joe and also to the club.

Let me stress, my own issues with Mancini were just that – with him. The rest of the staff at the club and all the other players and back-up staff were superb and I got on with them all. It was only the man who matters most who I cared for the least – and it was clear that the feeling was mutual.

*****

Joe kept playing well and by the time May came around, we were in an FA Cup final.

Being in yet another FA Cup final where I would not be playing was, once again, a strange feeling but at least this time I'd had chance to prepare for it. I'd barely got a match all year at City, Joe was doing really well and it was crystal clear I'd be on the bench again.

Once again I was also determined to be as much help to Joe as I could and the build-up to the game was great, he was loose and confident and warmed up really well. We returned to the dressing room and then something strange happened.

Mancini and his staff took one look at Vieira and walked out. Mancini wanted Vieira to deliver the team-talk. He sat down and looked around at all the lads, most of them with their heads down, sorting their laces and fixing their shinpads.

"This means so much to this city," he said. "We are going to win this today. This is a turning point in the history of this club. Right here, right now, you men sat in here are going to change, together, the history of Manchester City. From now on, Manchester City are going forward, we are winning and it begins here and it begins with you."

By the end everybody was up clapping, proper pumped up and from that second onwards I thought, 'There is a manager of the future.' That took our intensity up another level. Everybody had hung off every word. Aye, aye, this bloke knew how to talk to a group.

We beat Stoke in the final that day after Yaya Toure smashed home a winner and for the club it was an incredible moment. I'd be lying though if I said I enjoyed it as much as the 11 on the pitch. Of course I didn't. Who would or could?

It's a difficult one because I was happy for the fans, the club and the history of the club but, personally, I didn't do anything, I didn't contribute. I wasn't responsible for the win so I wasn't going to claim any credit – the credit all belonged with Joe.

When the whistle went, I raced on and he jumped into my arms, screaming his head off. I was honestly genuinely delighted for him. We worked hard together every day, I knew how dedicated he was and we were big mates by then. I just grabbed him and hugged him hard and we went crazy together.

About 20 minutes later, Carlos picked up the FA Cup and we headed down to the stage they had set up for the celebrations. Somebody thrust a bottle of champagne into my hands and everybody got a good lashing. I was really enjoying myself on the pitch but there was still that gap, that ache, that comes when your side does well but you did nothing yourself.

In fact, as I sit here now I can honestly say I don't even know where my FA Cup winner's medal is. I'm sure it's in the house somewhere but the fact it's not up pride of place probably tells you everything.

We finished that season with a win against Stoke City and then Bolton Wanderers and that was it, it was time for me to be on my way.

Incidentally, a year after I left the club, I went back to watch City v United in the FA Cup third round. As I took my seat I saw that Costel Pantilimon was in goal. I was sitting there thinking, 'Cheers'. The year before I hadn't been given a go when we played Notts County in the FA Cup – no disrespect intended – and yet 12 months on, Pantilimon was getting picked for a Manchester derby. If anything, that just confirmed to me what I already knew – Mancini had wanted me gone.

Despite my issues with the manager, I'd genuinely enjoyed my time at the club. Brian Marwood and Khaldoon Al Mubarak are still there, we always chat when we see each other and I have nothing but respect for the City set-up, the club's ambitions and the style of football they try and play.

I saw Khaldoon again last season in the City reception when I was at a game and he came and grabbed me from behind. "Shay, I want to get you back to the club at some point in the future," he said. He didn't have to say that and it was nice that he took the time out to come and say hello. Maybe somewhere later down the road I will go back in some capacity and I'd absolutely love to. Everybody there was a class act.

Well, almost everybody.

# 20

# THE HAND OF FATE

*"Right, this is it. This is our chance – let's just go out there and show them what playing for Ireland and against Ireland is all about. This is no time for caution, don't leave this field without fucking breaking yourselves for the next 90 minutes."*

*Robbie and me finish revving the lads up, the huddle breaks up and I run towards the goalmouth at the Stade de France. We're here to face France in the second leg of our 2010 World Cup play-off.*

*Those charmers at FIFA have decided to seed the play-off matches which means, to me, that they are happier seeing the big boys get through to the World Cup. France got a home draw for the second leg because they've been seeded higher than us.*

*Fine, whatever, throw as much shit our way as you can fit on a shovel, we can take it.*

*For a match as big as this, in a stadium as huge and noisy as this one, we should all be a bag of nerves.*

# SHAY

*But Giovanni Trappatoni's men are anything but.*
*We are hungry and we are aggressive and we are focused and*
*we are as relaxed as can be.*
*We're after ye France.*
*The boys in green are coming after ye.*

GIOVANNI Trappatoni's appointment as Ireland boss in 2008 was a surprise to me but I was as delighted as the rest of the country.

It was common knowledge that he had won Serie A about a hundred times with Juventus and he'd been a decent player himself so we appreciated his pedigree and knew that for Ireland, this was a quality name who was used to winning and was used to success.

It was a bit difficult to get to know him at first because he didn't have great English. It was hard to chat with him one-to-one. To his face he was always 'Mister' but amongst the lads he was and will forever be known as 'The Trap'.

You could tell he was a bubbly character, even when he was talking in Italian to himself. If the press were getting on his case about something he'd tell us, "No problems, let the birds tweet, tweet, tweet, they talk, talk, talk" and make little birdy signs with his hands, showing it was nothing to him. In one of his first meetings with the lads, he was talking about how he was too experienced to care what anybody said about him and pretended to wipe his arse with a newspaper, going, "Tomorrow, tomorrow, tomorrow…" The lads cracked up and you could tell straight away we had a bit of a character in as boss.

Trap had a thing about mushrooms. We were training for a friendly shortly after he was put in charge and he noticed that mushrooms were part of our diet as we scoffed some food down at Malahide. There was mushroom soup available one day after a session and he went absolutely off on one. "No. More. Mushrooms," was the cry and that was it – mushrooms were literally off the menu from then on. He was going nuts. It was like he'd have preferred us to have 20 pints over a single mushroom. We all looked at each other in confusion; who has anything against mushrooms? I'll tell you who, Giovanni Trappatoni.

Trap was pretty old school in a lot of his ways and he had the utmost respect from all of us. He was a world-renowned coach and, to some extent, we felt fortunate to have him as our manager. Everybody knew who he was, he was a figurehead and it helped that his assistant was Marco Tardelli, the Italian with the amazing celebration after scoring at the 1982 World Cup. Marco was a direct line to the manager from the players – the same as most assistants really – and we could always approach him if we felt we had to. Robbie Keane would go to Marco with any problems – maybe we were training too much or not enough – and Marco would feed that back to the Trap who would change his plans from there.

Marco was living in London at the time and had better English than the Trap so we all got on great. All the players listened to him and so they should. If you don't try and take on board the advice given by someone like him then what are you doing in the game? He was a winner, he'd been there and done it and we wanted to take advantage of that.

Trappatoni brought in Liam Brady as well and all the Irish players loved him too. I mean, how could you not? Liam Brady was Liam Brady. And the man who had taken me to Celtic when I was 16.

Back in Lifford, in between my brother Liam beating me up for taking up too much space in the double bed, I used to pore over football magazines and one day Liam Brady was the centre-page poster in *Shoot* or *Match*. He was there in the black and white stripes of Juventus, he had his hands behind his back and his chest jutting out with a big smile on his face. Under his image it said, 'THANKS TO FOOTBALL' in big letters. I taped it to the back of the bedroom door; he was a real big deal to us kids back home. That poster stayed up for years, even when the tape started to peel.

Liam's job in the set-up was more of a translating role for the Trap rather than anything too hands on. He didn't do much in training but he would come in and talk to the Trap then get his point over to us during the game or at half-time.

The strange thing about the Trap was he loved to talk – to the press, to his family and friends, to the players – but on the eve of a match, he would go into silent mode.

Brian McCarthy, the team analyst, would set up these videos for us to watch and understand the opposition and Trap would love them, trying to speak in English about what he expected and how he wanted us to set up – and then that would be it.

He never spoke to us before a game and never uttered a sentence at half-time. Literally the odd word here and there to individuals but Liam would be the only one you would hear at half-time. He would try and express a few ideas and give us a few tips but that was it, the Trap would stay out of it. And then, when Liam left, Alan Kelly used to say a bit but, again, not that much.

Liam eventually left the Ireland set-up in 2010 because he'd maintained his job as Arsenal's youth boss during his time with the Trap and it all got too much. It was a shame to lose his wealth of experience and knowledge. I never asked him about our time together at Celtic. He would ask after my dad, and he still always called him 'Mr Given' not Seamus – pretty much the only man on the planet who does – but we never brought up the 'what-if' element of my time in Paradise. He'd not lasted long as manager and probably wanted to discuss it less than I did!

After Stan's tenure, I think there was a general idea that we just needed to be a bit more solid, a bit more defensive and Trap was perfect for that. As an Italian, he knew better than probably anyone else in the game how to close down a match, how to tighten a defence and how to keep things uncomplicated. We needed to get results under the Trap, as simple as that, and he set us up in such a way to get them.

We had four defenders and two sitting midfielders who were basically chained to the halfway line, they weren't allowed to move, and then two wingers and two attackers. I think he thought that we weren't as good, either collectively or individually, as some of the teams and players he'd coached in the past so he wanted to simplify everything completely.

"Shay, get the ball," he'd tell me. "I want you to hit it as far up the pitch as you can."

We then hoped the ball would bounce favourably, we could pick up any scraps and second balls and then play from there. That was about it! I could kind of understand it when he explained it to me. He was saying that even if we did not win the aerial ball, we were in a decent spot on the pitch and in a good shape to ring the ball and then pick it up.

My main aim was to try and hit someone like Kevin Doyle

and then Keith Andrews and Glenn Whelan would be pushing in behind while the likes of Stephen Hunt, Aiden McGeady and Damien Duff would come in off their wings to try and pick up the loose ball. Occasionally, Robbie would gamble on it being flicked on and then set off, hovering just onside, but mainly it was all about hitting big Kevin and then the chances were it would fall to a green shirt. We created plenty of chances from it and then we'd watch those chances back on a DVD to cement them in for the next match and so on.

Trap never ever wanted me to play it out to the full-backs or one of the centre-halves. On a Thursday or Friday before a match we'd do shape training so each player knew who was where, who they should pass back to, who they shouldn't look to pass to and so on. I was always the start point for the play, obviously, and my instructions were to play in their half rather than ours – why make life difficult for yourself?

I personally felt we could've played a bit more football. We were very route one with him. I wanted us to lift our heads a bit and play what was in front of us but he wanted me to go direct and then see what what happened.

Fair enough, everyone is different. He swore by that and to be fair he got us to the Euros and one Thierry Henry handball was all that stopped us getting to a World Cup too, so maybe he had a point.

*****

Trap had a very Italian approach to alcohol and partying and it was down to Robbie to go to his hotel room and speak to him and request the odd night out for the lads in Malahide. Trap

**DRESSING UP FOR A GOOD CAUSE:** The Manchester City squad and many other celebrities helped us out at the Fashion Kicks event we staged for charity at Lancashire County Cricket Club. (*Right*) with City chairman Khaldoon Al Mubarak. He genuinely wanted me at the club

**DARK DAY:** I can't hold it in during the minute's silence for Speedo in 2011. He is so badly missed...

**FRIENDS REUNITED:** Coming up against my former team-mates was a regular occurrence!

**HEROES:** With the great Stiliyan Petrov and Henrik Larsson

**HEADING TO 'BORO:** Beating Leicester's Jamie Vardy to the ball. I enjoyed my time on loan at the Riverside

**TEAM SPIRIT:** (*Top*) In the dressing room after the win over Liverpool in the 2015 FA Cup semi-final. Sadly I picked up another loser's medal in the final...

**STEPPING UP:** Paul Lambert gave me a taste of life in the management team

**THUMBS UP:** Saluting the fans at a Euro 2012 training session – I was desperate to play despite not feeling 100 per cent fit. (*Right*) Looking up for some much-needed inspiration

**GOING HOME:** Consoled by Gianluigi Buffon after our final game in Euro 2012 – a 2-0 defeat to Italy. It was a poor tournament all round

**BACK:** Martin O'Neill presents me with my cap as I return to the fold in 2014 after calling it a day in the aftermath of Euro 2012

**THE NEXT GENERATION:** I was disappointed not to be No. 1 at Euro '16 but only too happy to give Darren Randolph whatever help he needed

**THIS REALLY IS GOODBYE:** With Robbie as we wave to the fans at Euro '16 (*also above left*)

**LEAGUE OF HIS OWN:** Meeting actor Tom Hanks – football has given me a great life. (*Right*) passing it on – giving advice to Jack Butland at Stoke

**LEARNING THE ROPES:** I enjoy working in the media – staying inside the game in some capacity is something that interests me

**KEEPING IN TOUCH:** Reunited with Robbie and Duffer for Michael Carrick's testimonial

**HOME, WHERE THE HEART IS:** I was so proud to receive the Freedom of Donegal in 2006. I am pictured (*right*) with Margaret and Dad

**THREE AMIGOS:** (*Left*) Me, Robbie and Mick Byrne. It turns out Mick did know U2 after all! (*Above*) A man named Horse...

**CHEERS:** Enjoying a pint of Guinness and (*above*) joining Eurovision singer Mickey Joe Harte on stage in Bannigan's

**I HOPE I DID YOU PROUD:**
A picture of Mum at her happiest

**HERE'S TO
THE FUTURE:**
With my wonderful
partner Rebecca

was never that pleased about it but, fair play, he would allow us out for a couple of beers to relax and get to know each other.

By this stage of my career I was one of the older players and was keen on keeping up the traditions that made the international team what it was. By that I mean massive commitment, aggression and pride in the shirt but also I wanted us to still forge a bond off the field that would hold us in good stead when times got tough.

If we weren't due to meet up formally until the Sunday, we'd try and fly over the night before for a few beers and then Trap would always let us loosen off after matches together.

After games there'd always be a red and white wine bottle on the table and a few bottles of beer. The Italian way of drinking was slow, civilised, adult-style sipping, preferably with a meal – so we had to introduce the Trap to the Ireland method of drinking. Within seconds, within the blink of an eye, the bottles would be drained.

In September 2008, it was time for Trap to take charge of us in our first World Cup 2010 qualifying match. We played Georgia in Germany and beat them 2-1 thanks to goals from Kevin Doyle and Glenn Whelan. We were all buzzing afterwards.

We had to play it in Germany because of some trouble in Georgia so after the game we were in the bar and having a bit of a sing-song. Andy Reid is a decent guitarist so he was knocking out some great tunes. We weren't pissed at all, we'd only had about three or four beers but for whatever reason, the Trap wasn't happy. He came into the bar and shouted, "Reid, no drink, NO MORE DRINK, NO BEER" and he tried to get the bar closed, even to all the other hotel guests! The owner of this hotel was looking at Trap as if he'd gone mad – like he was going to close his bar and wipe his profits out! It all calmed down but then later, apparently, Andy and Trap had another right pop at each other and it almost came to blows, which was not exactly the best way for them to get to know each other.

I don't think it was too much of a cultural leap for Trap to take the Irish team on and we did occasionally go out in Malahide but by this time, stuff would get back to him so quickly that you couldn't jump the train to Waterford and back like in Quinny's day. The camera on a mobile phone has a lot to answer for. It was different by now, you just couldn't go out as much as we once had. The days of Gary Kelly and "WHAT YOUSE HAVIN'?" were coming to an end.

The qualifiers for World Cup 2010 showed Ireland in a new light and, a bit like when Kenny was in charge at Newcastle, I'm not entirely sure how the fans felt about the super-tight disciplined performances we produced. Some sets of fans – the Geordie Nation being one and maybe the Irish another – quite like the rollercoaster ride that comes with following their team but fair play to Trap, he made us so much more secure, even if some of the shine went out of our play.

The way he wanted us to lash it up the field and then see how the cards dropped afterwards is one of the oldest managerial tactics going and, personally speaking, not conceding goals left right and centre was perfect for a goalkeeper, but part of me wonders if we'd stopped getting people out of their seats quite as often – and if playing for Ireland over 100 times has taught me one thing, there's always a drama or two following us about.

I played in all 10 qualifying matches which was something I was delighted about. We had some great back-ups in the shape of Dean Kiely – when he wasn't trying to play in midfield – and Kieren Westwood. But, for now, the No.1 shirt was still firmly mine, and that's how I liked it.

I made a couple of decent saves in that Georgia game and was just as sharp when we drew Montenegro a few days later.

In October 2008, we faced Cyprus at home and thankfully, the memory of our 5-2 collapse remained just that, a bad dream, as Robbie scored early on to give us a 1-0 win.

We were in a decent position in the qualifying group and my main memory of that campaign is that we weren't a bad side but, equally, we couldn't do enough, often enough, to break teams down. We became masters of the draw, earning points against Georgia, Bulgaria twice, Italy twice and Montenegro and that allowed Italy to slowly inch away and top Group 8.

Finishing second again meant we were heading once more for the play-offs and we'd be up against a France team that was decent but by no means world beaters.

The likes of Zidane, Vieira and Blanc were no more and although they had some good players, there was nobody who kept me awake at night apart from, maybe, Thierry Henry.

That's right. Thierry. Henry.

*****

We lost 1-0 in Dublin in the first play-off leg on November 8, 2009 and we were rubbish. Nicolas Anelka capped off a poor game with a poor goal, a deflected effort that just about summed up the night.

What disappointed me most – and the rest of the guys were the same – was that we were too rigid, we were too stiff, we were too by the numbers and predictable. Where had our spark gone, where had our mischief gone? We'd gone from a side that would gamble – and believe – that they could pull something from somewhere, like Robbie had done against Germany in 2002 for instance, to becoming a side that had lost its devilment, its fuck-this attitude, in essence its Irishness.

That was all about to change.

For the second leg in Paris, the Trap wanted us to remain as we had in the first match. He wanted us rigid and deep without pressing too much. He wanted us to nab a goal from somewhere and maybe force extra-time – and then who knows what might happen?

As a squad, though, we felt this was the time to roll the dice. On the day before the match, driving through the streets of Paris with *The Dubliners* blaring out, the message was the same.

*We're after ye France.*

*The boys in green are coming after ye.*

I'd said my piece in the build-up to the match and I was as black and white as I could be.

"Lads, I don't care what he says, we're going to go at these tonight," I said. "We're going to fucking go for it, we're going to press them, we're going to hurry them, we're going to throw everything at them. Whatever happens, if we get beat we get beat – but nobody gets back on this bus without giving it everything."

Even thinking about it now is making the hairs on my arms stand up. We weren't being disrespectful to the Trap at all and it wasn't like we were going to disobey him but we wanted the shackles to be off, we wanted to just go for broke.

"Lads, this is the chance of a lifetime," I said. "We're going for it." In the huddle before the game, the message was pressed home by Robbie. "This is why we play boys, this is where we want to be," he said. "We go out there now and we hit them with everything we've got until they don't know what the fuck's going on."

*We're after ye France.*

*The boys in green are coming after ye.*

Maybe because it was our last chance to get to the World Cup or maybe it was because I was older, I don't know, but I was so relaxed that night. We were sipping a Guinness in the last-chance saloon, you know? Why get tense, why play tense, when we have absolutely nothing to lose?

All the lads were the same. It's the least nervous I've ever been on a football pitch for Ireland – it was more a feeling of enjoyment and liberation. It was time for the Ireland team to play like the Ireland team and we came out and did exactly that. Everyone was at it and on it all night. Dunney had Henry asleep in his pocket, Duffer was class, Robbie was the same. We didn't overthink, we didn't overplay, we just crossed the white line and played with our hearts and finally, Robbie gave us the lead after about half an hour, beating Hugo Lloris.

After the break, Duffer missed a good chance but at 1-1 on aggregate after 90 minutes, we went into extra-time and still felt solid and strong.

We again spoke and the message stayed the same. *We've got these lads. We can do this. They don't know what's fucking hit them.*

Early on in extra-time, Anelka went down in the area as I challenged him but it was one of those that can go either way and the referee Martin Hansson waved away France's claims.

He'd just made the last decent call of the night.

Then it happened. France got a free-kick about 25 yards out, just to my left. Florent Malouda floated it into the back post. Lurking there was Thierry Henry. The worst thing we did was let the ball bounce in the box. We should've just headed it clear – somewhere, anywhere.

Anyhow, the ball fell across Henry and bang, straight away, the arm goes out to control it. Only for a split-second but it was blatant. I was so close to it that I could even see how the ball being touched by Henry had changed the spin and altered the pattern on the ball. Then he tapped it again, ever so slightly, knocked it past me with his right leg and William Gallas poked it in.

*You bastards.*

It all happened so fast but the moment Henry had done it, my first thought was, 'Get the ball for a free-kick, let's get up their end' but as I looked up, Hansson was pointing to the centre-circle.

*You're having a laugh here, surely?* I just couldn't believe it. He stopped the ball with his forearm from going out then pulled it back in with his hand! It was a double handball, how had the ref missed both? If you miss the first, you must see the second one?

Immediately I was off, sprinting over to him.

"HANDBALL, HANDBALL, REF, REF, HANDBALL!" I could see by the look on his face he was trapped with fear; he couldn't handle the moment, couldn't handle turning the goal down in front of so many French fans. I was like Usain Bolt after him and then the linesman but they just wouldn't have it.

It was the most blatant act of cheating I'd ever seen on a

football field, it was simply unbelievable that the goal had stood. It was my worst nightmare coming true. I just wouldn't and couldn't let it lie and the rest of the lads were the same.

I remember Kevin Kilbane hammering the referee, telling him he was a joke and that he'd just made the biggest mistake of his life. I was into him as well, giving him loads. "YOU'RE A DISGRACE, HE CHEATED, HE'S CHEATED US."

It was just so blatant. Watch the video back and you can tell straight away that Henry knew what he'd done because he immediately set off around the back of the goal celebrating, trying to buy one over the ref. It worked didn't it?

At the time, the Irish fans in the stadium didn't get a replay on the big screen and they hadn't realised what had happened, so when the final whistle went they just cheered us but the feeling inside me was desperately low, the lowest I've ever felt in an Ireland shirt.

Not qualifying for the 1998 World Cup was one thing and it was bad enough. But at least we got beaten fairly and on merit. Yet when that final whistle went in Paris, Ireland had been denied another World Cup and this time we'd been mugged, robbed, call it what you will. I was shattered by it.

*Fucking Henry.*

We must've had about 25,000 in the ground as we sloped over to them and they were all cheering us – the plucky, unlucky Irish once again – but then later on, when they got word from back home over their phones, they began raging with the rest of us.

The fans were there in their thousands that night and I can remember the noise now. I never talk about any of this stuff really but it's only now, as the memories come back, that I can feel the blood running quicker and the anger rising in me. I hope the Ireland fans realise what that night meant to us. When they read this book I hope it hits home to them. Sometimes, as a player, you get the impression that the fans think you don't care but one look inside the Ireland dressing room afterwards said it all.

It was carnage, as angry a dressing room as I've ever been in.

Robbie was raging, Kev was livid, Duffer was the same.

Everywhere you looked there were lads swearing, throwing and kicking boots and bags out of the way. Shinpads were hurled and power drinks lashed against walls.

Other losing play-off dressing rooms were silent and gloomy. We were heartbroken but resigned to our fate. This night we had a real, genuine and justified anger at being totally stitched up. "Brian, get the fucking match on, now," someone shouted at Brian McCarthy and when it was played back the anger just cranked up another notch or two. *The bastards. Robbing us of a World Cup.*

This was 18 months of our lives. This was our entire futures boiled down to 90 minutes (or 120 as it turned out) and we wanted it so much, yet we had nothing at all to show for it. If you get stitched up in the Premier League, that's difficult to take, it's not something you like, but you always have next week to make up for it. If you get a tough call, the luck will swing back in your favour sooner rather than later. But that night we had no chance of getting revenge, no opportunity to wait for luck to even itself out. That made it even more devastating. It had been do or die – and we'd been killed by the ref.

The Trap was going nuts along with the rest of us, half in Italian, half in broken English: "It has been a fucking murder."

# THE HAND OF FATE

Straight after the match, Henry had gone and sat next to Dunney on the pitch, like they were best mates. Henry admitted that he'd cheated but added, "I didn't mean it." Ok Thierry, that's fine then mate, that makes it all ok – what you drinking?

I reckon the reason he went and sat down with one of our lads was because he was feeling guilty. It's a good job he picked Dunney to sit with – he is a lovely, calm individual. There's a fair few in that team who would've told Mr Henry where he could shove his apology.

We spoke to the press. Duffer gave an interview and claimed it was all a big conspiracy. He told the papers, "Fifa want the big teams in the World Cup. They want France in the World Cup and, it may sound silly, but they want teams sponsored by Adidas. Adidas sponsor the World Cup and they sponsor France." No problem with that, apart from he's sponsored by Adidas himself and he had to apologise to them.

Where was our apology though? Where was our replay?

The media was filled with noise about what the FAI were going to do and what FIFA were going to do but, as usual, it was hot air. Sepp Blatter was happy enough to fly from five-star hotel to five-star hotel, but he couldn't be arsed getting his hands dirty with sorting out a real problem.

Before long, it was confirmed there would be no replay and that the goal would stand.

All these years on, what do I think about it now?

I suppose I've been around the game long enough to know how it all works and part of me thinks, 'Can you blame Henry for trying it?' If it had been Robbie, or Kev or Duffer doing that, would I have not gone to the World Cup on principle? What do you think? Maybe that's football for you.

# SHAY

I didn't see Thierry Henry for a long time after that night but I knew I'd eventually bump into him somewhere on the media circuit.

About two years ago I was doing some work for Premier League Productions in London and he was doing something for Sky at the same time. This was it. We shook hands and said hello and although everything was very polite, there was definitely an elephant in the room.

A fucking big elephant called the 2010 World Cup.

In a career lasting 25 years, he was responsible for the biggest injustice I've faced on the pitch and that is not something I'm likely to smile about any time soon. We're probably never going to really sit down and chat about it, although I do wonder what Thierry does think when he looks back on it. It feels like it's all been swept under the carpet a bit but the Irish players that night, and the fans, will struggle to forgive or forget.

## 21

# HEROES AND VILLANS

GROWING up, Aston Villa were a huge deal. They always seemed to be a great FA Cup side and were contenders for the Premier League in its early seasons. With their history, they were what you'd class as a 'proper' club with a massive fanbase.

When it was clear I had no future at City, my solicitor Michael spoke to the Villa chief executive Paul Faulkner and I spoke to the manager Alex McLeish, who wanted the deal done as soon as possible. "Shay, I want some experience here and I want some international players," he told me. "We have a good squad but we need help leading it. Brad is a fine goalkeeper but I need more experience at this level."

I was more than happy to hear that and more than happy to be part of a wider picture. Alex believed that Villa could achieve something special with older players like me and Richard Dunne, also now at Villa, lining up alongside new signings like Charles N'Zogbia.

Leaving City was still sad because I knew I was leaving a club that was inevitably going to be challenging for titles and cups but if you're not a part of it, and the manager has no interest in making you part of it, then it's definitely better to pack up and go. I hold no grudges and Khaldoon Al Mubarak and Brian Marwood are still friends to this day. I just had to go.

When you get to 34 or 35, you hear the clock ticking. I felt I was still in my prime and I wanted to get out there and show I could still do a job. That hunger to compete was as strong as ever. I chose Celtic over Manchester United at 16 because there was a better chance of a game, why wouldn't I do it at this end of my career as well?

McLeish was so enthusiastic and the club doctor, Ian McGuinness, was somebody I knew from Newcastle. He was just as excited about the potential of the club. Villa had everything in place to compete. Their training ground at Bodymoor Heath is phenomenal, Villa Park is steeped in history and everybody was desperate for success. All the pieces of the jigsaw seemed to be in place to get the club going in the right direction.

I'd taken a huge pay-cut to join Villa and I was really excited about being a first choice again but my initial optimism was soon tempered by the realisation that the club wanted to do some major work in the accounts department. That usually leads to one thing on the pitch: pain.

Alex had only just replaced Gerard Houllier before I joined and it seemed like the days of spending big money on the likes of Darren Bent – and therefore competing with the top six in the Premier League – might be over before they had begun. Almost immediately, the likes of me, Charles N'Zogbia, Alan Hutton and Darren were told that Villa had to get decent players off the wage bill and replace them with younger and cheaper players. Ashley Young had already gone to Manchester United for £17m. That wasn't what we wanted to hear. We wanted to be attracting top-quality names, not selling them.

I think by the time I joined, Randy Lerner was already looking to sell up. Fair play to the guy, he'd poured money into the club over a few years but with nothing to show for it. Sometimes he threw good money after bad in a bid to get Villa back up the league but for whatever reason that hadn't worked. When I got there, he was keen to get the books in better shape so he could eventually sell the club. In other words, my timing was off, badly.

Villa had struggled under Houllier and we would again under Alex. He had a lot to deal with straight away and I felt for him. I've always liked Alex, I was his first signing and he's one of those guys in the game that everybody has respect for and everybody likes. Well, nearly everybody. He'd just walked down the road from St Andrew's, so the Birmingham City fans hated him and ultimately Villa fans used it against him.

McLeish is a tough man and he's managed at Rangers where the pressure every week to win is off the scale but Birmingham City and Villa are only three miles apart and you should never underestimate the hatred in that city. Other derbies might get more headlines and more column inches but the strength of feeling between the fans of those two clubs is unbelievable.

Alex was a good man-manager and he liked the senior lads to run the dressing room. He would only step in if somebody overstepped the mark. We had an on-the-spot fine system for being late for training, for using your mobile phone in the dressing room and a million other things.

I had a great debut against Fulham which helped me settle into the club and it showed that I was still capable of playing in the Premier League. When I walked out that day at Craven Cottage it had been 16 months since my last top-flight match. I'd actually played more games for Ireland than I had my club and the Fulham game was all the proof I needed that I'd made the right call. I did well to stop an Andrew Johnson effort and twice denied Bobby Zamora from close range. I was delighted and so was Alex.

"That's why you're here," he told me afterwards. "Games like that are exactly what you were brought here for." It felt great to be playing again for a manager who respected my accomplishments and spoke so positively about me to the press.

Sadly, that Fulham game was to be one of few highlights in a difficult season. One of our biggest problems was that we just could not stop drawing matches. We won only seven games all year but drew 17 and lost the remaining 14, finishing just two points above the relegation zone.

We did win at Stamford Bridge to prove we were not a bad side and although the effort could not be faulted, goals were in short supply. Darren Bent was top scorer with just nine in the league. You are never going to do much if your top scorer doesn't reach double figures.

The squad was also upset and affected by what happened to Stiliyan Petrov, our captain, and his serious illness did put everything else into perspective.

Against Arsenal at the Emirates in March 2012, he seemed leggy and looked to be struggling with a really bad fever. McLeish suggested he should come off at half-time. "I'm fine, I'm fine," he kept saying, and he battled on. He was our leader and he wanted to keep playing but, unfortunately, he was anything but fine. Stan went for tests that week ahead of a Chelsea game and the doctors at the club kept asking for more and more blood work until he was finally told the terrible truth: it was leukaemia.

It was desperate news and I was so upset for him and his family. It brought back memories of Mum. But I was so impressed with how he fought it head on. We were all in complete shock because he was so fit. "I will fight this Shay," he just kept saying over and over. "This will not get me, no chance!"

He would come to the training ground to see the lads and even though his face was swollen through the medication, he was always so bubbly. We were mates because we were a similar age and I still stay in touch with him now. He won the biggest match of his life, his strength of character was amazing and how he carried himself throughout all that, as a man and a father, was incredible.

I used to go and see him when he was in University College Hospital, hooked up to all these machines which were giving him chemotherapy, and his wife, Paulina, and sons, Kristiyan and Stiliyan would be there and they would be so strong too. It was obviously a dreadful thing to happen to Stan and although it ended his career, he still has his life, his family and the respect of everybody in world football. I never doubted you, Horse.

Towards the end of the season we had managed to get a draw against West Brom and I made one of the most crucial saves of the season to keep out Peter Odemwingie. It was literally the last seconds of the game, the ball fell nicely to him and he had the whole goal to aim at but I just managed to get across and block it. I fell into the back of the net but the ball didn't, and that's all that mattered. Dunney put his hands to his head and went, "How did you fucking do that?" It was an important stop, a big save and the point helped keep confidence in the squad just high enough to avoid going down.

Relegation battles are such a worry for most players, the manager and the staff because you understand all the consequences if you go down. The masseurs and kit-men and matchday staff all have kids and mortgages to pay and they are usually the first to get cut back in a relegation year. If you don't feel for them then you've no humanity about you and I was determined to do all I could to help us.

I felt for Alex and I felt for the lads because the spirit in the group was really good.

Robbie Keane joined us on loan from LA Galaxy which was a big result for us and there were some great characters in the dressing room. Fabian Delph was a machine in training. Every day was a cup final for him. He'd had a knee problem before I got there and he trained with the perspective of a man who had glimpsed early retirement on the horizon but managed to escape it. Sometimes, it's the players who've been closest to losing it all through injury who are the most determined and dedicated because their life – this amazing football life – was so nearly taken away from them.

Towards the end of the season, Delphy got hold of my washbag and winged it across the room after a match. Deodorants, vitamins, toothbrush, hair stuff, everything was splattered across the dressing room and I had to go round picking it all up. Nobody would cough up who'd done it but in the end I broke somebody and they let me know it was him. Right. "See this little black book," I told him. "Your name's in it."

We played Norwich at the end of the 2011/12 season and we all had lunch as a squad on the Saturday and travelled down to play the day after. Delphy pulled up that day with a brand new Range Rover and was showing it off to the lads. While he was talking shit, I sloped off to the kitchens and spoke to the chef. Two minutes later he delivered just what I'd asked for. A lovely big brown trout. With Delphy's back turned, I shoved it under the driver's seat and we set off as a team for Norwich.

Because it was the end of the season, it was boiling hot and Delphy didn't get back to his car until the Monday afternoon because he'd stayed down there an extra night. He got back, opened the car door and was nearly sick. I had about 12 voicemails from him. He said he'd had to drive home with his head out of the window, retching, and was cursing the good Given family name. But I didn't start the fire did I? I just put it out!

Alan Hutton loved messing about and would always give you stick, mainly about your partner. If he wanted a night out or even just a coffee and you were busy he'd ask, "Why, you not allowed? The missus stopping you?" Three years in and he was still giving me exactly the same stick — "You asked your missus if you can text?" It was the only line he had. I used to hammer him about everything. Scotland. Rangers. Being bald. Being Scottish. Being bald and Scottish. You name it.

That Norwich game had even more significance for us as it was to be Alex's last in charge.

Before the game he spoke to all the players in the dressing room. It was as if he might've known he didn't have much longer with us.

"Lads, you've given your all, you've given everything," he told us. "I couldn't ask more from any of you. It's not been the season we wanted but if we'd turned a few of those draws into wins then we'd look a lot better off. Thank you for your efforts, have a good summer."

Within days he had gone in to see Paul Faulkner about his plans for next season but he took one look at Paul's face, walked out and cleared his desk.

Villa were losing a fine man and a good manager. I was yet to know it but I was losing my biggest ally in the dressing room. I was also losing my No.1 spot.

*****

I'd had a poor summer at the Euros in 2012 and when I first met Paul Lambert after he came in to replace Alex, I got the feeling he wasn't too keen on me as his first-choice keeper.

I went in to his office a couple of times to see him but the vibe wasn't good. He asked me how the Euros had been. "How's your head, are you ok?" It wasn't positive stuff, he wasn't telling me he rated me or that he wanted me as his No.1 and I'll be honest, I probably needed to hear some reassurance at that stage, especially after a difficult summer.

I felt like he was just waiting for me to make a mistake and when Marouane Fellaini scored a goal for Everton early in the season that squirmed underneath me, he had his chance. After something like that, a goalkeeper wants their manager to go, "Forget that, look forward now, it's finished." Paul wasn't like that and it wasn't in his nature to take a player to one side for a quiet chat.

I got the feeling he wanted me off the wage bill and away from the club. I don't say that in a malicious way, Paul was feeling the squeeze from the boardroom to shift their big earners and I was one of those. I think it was probably more a financial decision than a football one. That 3-1 home defeat to Everton in late August summed up what was wrong with us. Apart from me, N'Zogbia and Bent, we lacked Premier League experience and Everton were ruthless enough to expose that.

The next match was a Carling Cup game against Tranmere. Brad Guzan came in for me but I expected to come back in for the next game against Newcastle and when I didn't, the deja vu hit me, big time.

I'd already sat on the bench at Manchester City for a season, I wasn't getting any younger, I was as desperate as ever to play but I'd joined a club whose priorities – a bit like Newcastle's – seemed to be asset and talent stripping rather than trying to make the Holte End bounce. I wanted the Holte End to bounce. Everybody in the Holte End wanted the players to be bouncing. It was just the suits who stopped it happening.

Mentally I was at a real low point. I didn't really speak to anybody about it but I was hurting. I had taken a massive wage cut because I wanted to play at Villa. I could've been paid more to sit on a bench, doing nothing at City, and now, here I was doing exactly that.

Brad did really well when he came in. It was now all over the press and out in the open that Lambert had been ordered to get some of the highest earners in the club off the wage bill, so things looked bleak.

We got labelled 'The Bomb Squad' – lads like me, Darren Bent, Charles N'Zogbia, Stephen Ireland and Alan Hutton. I somehow kept my place in the first-team changing room but they'd be down the corridor with the reserves, split from the rest of the lads. I'd walk past them in the morning on the way to the canteen and we'd raise a grin and a smile, as if to say, 'What the fuck is happening here?' It was all a bit weird.

When it became clear that I wasn't wanted by Lambert, I decided in my mind that if the chance came, I would go out on loan. But I'd struggled a bit at the Euros and I think people were questioning whether I was still good enough. I just had to get my head down and hope for a break at Villa.

Working with Brad was actually really good. I'd been a No.1 for a long time and I'd also been an understudy at City so I knew I had to say and do the right things. We got on great – Brad is very American. Everything is "awesome". You couldn't fault what he did on the pitch but for me, I'd gone from playing 33 matches in one season under Alex McLeish to just nine the year after – having done nothing wrong. It felt ludicrous.

In the summer of 2013, it got worse. Jed Steer joined us from Norwich City so I was effectively relegated to third-choice goal-keeper. By this point I just wanted out and at one stage it looked like I would be joining Liverpool, a move that would've been absolutely incredible.

Brendan Rodgers wanted me to come in and challenge Simon Mignolet, keep him on his toes, and maybe even nip ahead of him. I was delighted by the thought of that and desperate to go. I'd always loved playing at Anfield, the Kop had always given me a great reception – I don't know if that was an Irish thing or whether we were usually losing by then! – and I was really excited by the opportunity.

In the end, though, it didn't come off. We waited and waited and waited by the phone, expecting Villa to allow me to leave, but the call never came.

It was all completely baffling and frustrating. The reasons why Villa wouldn't let me go have never been made clear to me. I'm as in the dark about it today as I was then. I don't know if it was my wages that stopped the deal or whether it was the fact Randy Lerner was American, like Liverpool's owners. Had they had some beef in the past? I've no idea, you'll have to ask them.

What I do know is that chances to move to clubs like Liverpool do not come around every day and it remains a massive disappointment that I couldn't go. Villa supposedly wanted me off the wage bill, here was the chance to do it, yet the offer wasn't taken up. It seemed a no-brainer to me.

The Bomb Squad didn't make much sense at all when you think about it. If you want to sell a car or a coat, do you put it on *eBay* or bury it at the back of the wardrobe or leave it shut away in the garage? If you want to sell players, don't isolate them, don't make them train with the reserves – put them in the first-team every week, get the best out of them, let people know they're available and then you will get more interest. I could never understand it from a business of point of view why they wouldn't let us go. Nobody was seeing us, nobody was match-fit, nobody was going on loan – but we were still getting paid our full wages. How does that add up? There's no point putting something in the shop window then closing the curtains.

What made it worse was the fact that the players brought in to the club over the previous 18 months just couldn't compare with what we were leaving out every week.

No disrespect to the likes of Brett Holman, Jordan Bowery or quite a few others, but they were too young, too inexperienced and too lightweight to be thrown straight into the Premier

League. The league eats you alive if you show any weaknesses at all and Villa seemed to have them everywhere you looked.

I think Paul wanted to play a mobile, rapid game with a team full of fresh young legs that can run all day and I absolutely get the thinking behind that but you also need an Alan Hutton, a Stephen Ireland, a Darren Bent to add experience and clout. But they were with me, twiddling their thumbs.

I think the only signing Paul got the best out of was Christian Benteke who we picked up from Genk. He was clearly a talented footballer and Lambert worked hard on him. I think he was nervous on his first training session because he was all over the place and couldn't trap a bag of cement. He wouldn't really speak to anyone either, but he soon settled down and proved what a good player he was.

I eventually got the chance to go and joined Middlesbrough in November 2013 on an emergency loan and I really loved it up there. You never know how you're going to be received at a new club, especially one so close to Newcastle, but they were class. Due to league rules, I could only stay for 93 days, which was a shame. I would have stayed longer.

I felt I had again proven a point to Villa – and anybody else watching – that I was still worthy of more regular football. At Boro, I kept 10 clean sheets in 16 games and only conceded 10 goals in all while I was there. Unfortunately, a deal to take me there could not be worked out so I had to return to Villa.

I wasn't happy about that but fortunately, by the end of March 2014, an offer I hadn't seen coming was presented to me and it was too good to refuse.

*****

To fill the time over the summer of 2013, I'd done my UEFA A and B-licence exams in Belfast. It's real 12-hour classroom stuff, no messing about, but I'd been thinking about the future and I decided to get it in my back pocket. Terry Gennoe, who was with me after I'd persuaded him into taking on one more job rather than chilling out in Spain – he'd swapped a villa for Villa – approached me at the training ground one Tuesday lunchtime and told me Paul wanted to go and see him in the office.

"Shay, take a seat," Paul said. "I want you to come on board as a member of the coaching staff for the last six weeks of the season." Paul's assistants, Ian Culverhouse and Gary Karsa, had been suspended and he wanted me to step in.

Some people have said that I should have told him where to go but I was looking at the bigger picture. We were in a situation where we needed results, so there was a lot of pressure and I enjoyed that and knew I'd learn a lot from it.

It was a big eye-opener seeing what went into being a manager. There's a lot of meetings, put it that way. I stopped training to focus solely on helping to prepare the team – I well and truly went to the dark side for that six weeks!

We would meet in the morning at 9am for a preparation meeting in the office, we'd debrief at lunch after the morning's training and then there would be a video session at 3pm with Scott Marshall, Terry Gennoe and Gordon Cowan. It was a great learning curve from a coaching point of view although I remember one session where Gordon nodded off and I had to give him a nudge to wake him up!

It undoubtedly had a little bit of impact with the lads in the dressing room. Was I still one of them? I decided to front it head on so I walked into the changing room with a clipboard before the first match against Southampton and told Brad and Jed they were both dropped!

"Right lads, any messing about and it goes straight back to the gaffer," I told the rest of them. I got loads of stick for that but it was the best thing to do as everyone took the piss. It felt like bygones were bygones with Paul too – I wasn't there to hold grudges with him then or now and was happy to help out.

The 2013/14 season ended with Villa in 15th place and over the summer, Paul rang me and asked me to come on board permanently but I wasn't ready to pack in the playing side. I still felt I had enough to offer playing wise and that there was plenty of time ahead of me if I wanted to coach. He respected my decision and I returned to the ranks. One Irishman who didn't say no to the offer of a coaching job was a certain Mr Roy Keane, who arrived in July 2014.

I think Roy turning up at the club surprised everybody but personally speaking I was delighted he had decided to join Lambert. I really mean that as well. Saipan was a long, long time in the past, there was no animosity or ill will there and Roy Keane is a winner; a man driven to getting the best out of others.

Roy was eager to get back involved at club level, alongside his role as Martin O'Neill's right-hand man with Ireland. I think most of the Villa players were excited about it, although I'm sure some were nervous too. Roy tells it how it is and doesn't care who takes offence.

It didn't take long for the sparks to fly. Fabian Delph and Gabby Agbonlahor took a pretty much instant dislike to Roy – and he returned the favour. Fabian argued one day with Roy after a bollocking in training. As I've said, Delphy loves training and always works hard so Roy obviously touched a nerve.

Then, towards the end of Roy's time at Villa – he left as quickly as he arrived, finishing with Villa in November 2014 – Gabby was talking to Paul about something and Roy added his thoughts only for Gabby to give him a mouthful along the lines of, "I wasn't talking to you."

It didn't escalate to pushing or shoving but there were plenty of verbals and it got heated.

Roy had high demands and players today have opinions which I'm not sure Roy liked, even though he had his own opinions in his day too. I didn't really know much about his reasons for leaving and he certainly wasn't the type to come in and say goodbye to the squad but players with the knowledge Roy had are rare indeed and it was a shame it didn't work out.

Lambert followed not long after Roy as he was sacked in February 2015. Just before he went, we dropped into the relegation zone after losing 2-0 at Hull City. We'd gone 10 Premier League matches without a win and scored 12 goals in 25 league games all season.

It just felt like Paul's race had been run. Those statistics tell their own tale. We just couldn't find a winning formula.

*****

The feeling of being at a club where a manager is sacked was getting a bit much now. I was like the Grim Reaper. Sign Shay Given and clear your desk. I've played for 18 managers in the Premier League which is a record for any player. If you want your P45 in no time at all, give me a ring and the countdown is on.

Tim Sherwood replaced Paul and I was pleased because I

knew him from my Blackburn days. He'd been the guy in the Selhurst Park tunnel telling me not to be afraid of Wimbledon's giants when I made my Premier League debut.

Tim had a few challenges to get his head around at Villa. He tried, like a fair few others had done, to get the best out of Charles N'Zogbia but for one reason or another he never gave the impression of being a player who was that arsed.

Alex had signed Charles at roughly the same time as me and he'd cost £9.5m which was a lot of cash back then. However, it always seemed as if that was it, he'd made his money, he had his long contract, it was feet-up time from then on and you couldn't get the best from him.

He was also one of those players who absolutely loved being a Premier League footballer with all the bullshit and bling that comes with it. He had a Porsche with blacked-out windows and his registration plate had 'BOSS' in it in big capitals.

And the clothes he used to wear; fuck me, he had some rascal outfits. He came into training one day with a suit on covered in flowers. It caused a migraine the moment you looked at it.

He started getting changed and I sat there and said, "Well that's me not training today then."

"Why not Shay?" he asked.

"Well, I can't leave your fucking suit in here on its own can I? Who's going to water it?"

"Gucci man," he shouted. "This is Gucci."

"I don't care what it is, it needs going in that bin over there."

That's just how he was. No Villa manager ever seemed to be able to drum any dress sense or motivation into him.

Tim stuck by me in the FA Cup, picking me for a 2-1 win over Leicester City in the fifth round, and I actually played in every

FA Cup game that season. It felt brilliant to be back in the side and able to help out the club by doing what I was ultimately paid for, which is playing.

Brad was still the recognised league No.1 but I was desperate to get to another FA Cup final. After beating Blackpool, Bournemouth, Leicester and then West Brom, we had a semi-final against Liverpool.

The Liverpool match build-up was all about them, not us. In fact, it was all about Steven Gerrard. I've played against him a few times obviously and he was a phenomenal player, it was his last season at Liverpool and I think the final was due to be on his birthday.

It was set up to be a Roy of the Rovers scenario where Gerrard was going to pick up the trophy on his birthday but we all know – and I know more than most – that football is not fairytale stuff! We played really well that day, Jack Grealish had a fantastic game, as did Benteke, and to see the Villa fans without a care in the world was a real pleasure.

The semi-final was my first time playing at the new Wembley and it was class; I was coming towards the end of my career and it was great to walk out and see all the Villa fans. I didn't know if I'd ever be back when we walked out into the middle and I told the guys beforehand that it was days like this that would stand out when they were as old as I was! I remember the 1998 semi-final like it was yesterday because it was my first.

I just wanted us to go out and play in a brave way and we did that, we beat the favourites to book a first FA Cup final place in 15 years. At the same time, Tim had done wonders in virtually securing our survival in the league so for the first time in a long time, Villa Park was a happy place to be.

It didn't last. It couldn't last.

The FA Cup final of 2015 was another grim one for me.

The final was dreadful, again, and although they didn't batter us completely, 4-0 looks like an absolute hammering, doesn't it? In 20 years' time people will forget that we played ok, they will just see the scoreline and see that we were heavy losers.

When the final whistle went I was fuming because some of the boys seemed to already be on the bus. 1-0 or 2-0 is respectable but 4-0 in a final is unacceptable. Some lads just didn't perform on the day. We never tested them, we never got into them, we never got going and you can't afford to do that in any match, never mind an FA Cup final.

They had done the double on us in the Premier League and were miles out of sight but on a cup final day, anybody stands a chance. Ask Sunderland fans, or Wimbledon – anybody on the day can pull off a shock.

Again, it wasn't my day.

Picking up another FA Cup loser's medal was not how I'd dreamt the afternoon would end. It was another bit of silverware to chuck in a drawer and never look at again.

I sat on the pitch, feeling disconsolate after the game. When I eventually got up, I bumped into Arsene Wenger who shook my hand and told me I'd played well but that was about it. At that moment it wasn't the time for polite chat.

I went back to the dressing room and Tim was devastated, not so much by the final score but by the fact we hadn't given ourselves even half a chance of pulling off a result. If you've done all you can and you lose then fair enough, open a beer and sleep comfy in your bed at night. Not many Villa players slept comfy after that performance.

Not long into the next season, Tim was sacked.

I think he was harshly treated by Aston Villa and he only spent eight months at the club. He felt like a good fit, he was a bubbly fella with a thick skin and you need that at Villa. If he'd been backed right then he would have made a good manager. I think he still will be.

After the FA Cup final, I remember walking back down the tunnel after the game, desperate to soak it all in. I managed the odd wave here and there to the amazing supporters before disappearing down into Wembley's dressing room. I kicked my boots off, looked at a broken dressing room and started to get changed.

That was the last time I ever wore a Villa shirt.

I was devastated by the result and as it turned out, that was my last chance to claim one of English football's greatest prizes.

That is a disappointment for me, of course it is.

But saying that, along with what had happened to Stan, another event during my time at Villa had shown me that no matter how devastating a football match could be, events in the real world were always far more important.

# 22

# ONE SUNDAY

IF you want an idea of who Gary Speed was, you should've been in the away dressing room at Fratton Park on Sunday February 29, 2004. Covered in sweat and mud, one sock rolled down, he was absolutely fuming, raging.

Speedo was as mad as I'd ever seen him or for that matter any other professional footballer; sounding off in all directions, to anybody and everybody who would listen. In fact, you had no choice but to listen – most of the south of England would've heard him that afternoon.

Newcastle had just played Portsmouth and, with all due respect, they were absolutely dross. We were winning 1-0 thanks to a Craig Bellamy goal until Lomana LuaLua, who'd arrived late to the match in his blue Porsche, scored in the last minute to grab Pompey a point.

A late goal, especially on the road and especially against a side in the relegation zone like Portsmouth, is always going to be a sickener but Speedo's rage went much further and deeper than that. LuaLua was still a Newcastle player, he'd been loaned out to Pompey until the end of the season yet somebody had forgotten to add a clause in the deal which meant he shouldn't play against his parent club. It was a thoughtless balls-up that had cost us two points. Newcastle feels an awfully long way up the A1 when you've slipped up like we just had. For Speedo, the irony of LuaLua scoring just added to his rage at the final whistle – and didn't we know about it.

"It's a FUCKING disgrace," he started. "It's a FUCKING JOKE. That was nailed on going to happen. I KNEW he would score." Speedo was pulling no punches. All this anger and frustration that had clearly been building up inside came flooding out. He didn't care who heard him. "Some CLOWN has messed up here. How hard is it to DO YOUR JOB? I'm packing in, FUCK this!"

We were ducking and diving, watching out for the flying furniture. Bobby Robson, the manager at the time, just stood there and let him get on with it. Bobby knew Speedo was absolutely spot on and there wasn't much he could say about it. In fact, Bobby probably loved the fact Speedo was showing his passion so much.

That is what Speedo was all about; professionalism and complete and utter commitment to his team and his team-mates. He demanded and expected the best from himself and he demanded and expected the best from everybody around him – from players on the pitch to the people who arrange the finer detail of loan deals.

I first met Gary at St James' Park in September 1997. We won 1-0 thanks to a late Rob Lee goal but what stands out more is the way Speedo was before the game. It sums up his qualities as a human being.

# ONE SUNDAY

As we lined up to come out of the tunnel, I was stood next to him – he was playing for Everton at the time.

"Hey Shay, how's it going?" he asked. I was a bit taken aback. I'd played a few games by then but no opposition lads had ever really said anything to me. "Good luck for the game," he said, with that big grin on his face. I remember thinking then that this was a classy gesture and that all the good things I'd heard about him as a man were probably spot on.

Six months or so after that match, Speedo joined Newcastle and he hit it off with everybody straight away.

He was ahead of his time when it came to preparing for games. Speedo was always on a protein shake here or had just come out of an ice-bath there. He was getting on a wee bit when he joined us but he was still as fit as it gets. We all looked up to him, his professionalism was outstanding and we all tried to follow his example. Nobody worked or tried harder in that Newcastle team than Speedo and he would put a real shift in, pouring everything into the 90 minutes for the team.

He would be absolutely wrecked by the time he came off the pitch but he set the standards for the rest of us. Everybody wanted to look as fit and as good as he did.

Al was the captain of the team but Speedo was a born leader, too. He was a natural figurehead, a man you would follow anywhere and whenever Al was injured, Speedo was the captain. He had such charisma and a big laugh that was contagious. It was this high-pitched, weird noise that seemed to come from nowhere and before you knew it, the entire room would be laughing along with him.

Speedo loved the dressing room and just being around the group. He was the heart and soul of Newcastle.

Speedo loved the craic, he was a good golfer and he loved the Portugal golf trips. Sometimes, we'd have a few beers and I'd be hanging the next morning – though Speedo never suffered with hangovers. He'd be as fresh as a daisy. It was the same at home in Newcastle. We used to go to The Diamond Inn and every now and again we'd have one too many – but the grin on his face the morning after would show he'd got away with it again. "Never had a hangover, never will," he'd say with that trademark grin on his face.

He was a great storyteller and always had a story or two about somebody. I used to ask him about Neville Southall and what he was like as a goalkeeper and he'd say that Big Nev would be laughing in Wales' training sessions because the squad could never beat him in shooting practice. Ball after ball would be flying towards him and Big Nev would keep them all out, laughing at the lads.

This one time we were in Portugal at Al's place in Vale de Lobo and a guy we were with called John Harvey invited me and Speedo back to his villa. We'd been to Montys and it was proper late when we headed back. I had a pair of these terrible white strides on and Al's house wasn't that far away – as the crow flies. But crows – and goalkeepers – never fly straight after a night in Montys.

If you went via the roads then you had to swing all the way around the place but, alternatively, there was this massive drainage trench, 10 foot wide, that you could cross.

"Fuck it, we can jump that," I told Speedo. "I'm not walking all around the road, no chance at all."

Speedo tried to speak sense.

"Horse, you've got absolutely no chance," he said. "I hope

you can swim!" That was all the encouragement I needed. Next thing, deep breath, fingers crossed and I set off. Let's just say there's a reason I'm not Ireland's long-jump champion.

I ended up about halfway across, waist high in shit and Speedo was just there, looking as pristine as ever, with tears rolling down his face. He couldn't speak for laughing his head off.

When my brother Kieran was over from Germany, he'd always come round to my house to see him and drop off one of his guitars. Kieran plays and Speedo was brilliant too. His fingers were always raw and peeling from where he'd been practising hard. He never failed to drop a guitar off for Kieran and then we'd all sit round after a game at my place.

The evening after a game is one of the best times of the week. The pressure is off, you can relax, get the day and the match out of your system and we'd sit around with a few beers. Often, we'd all start singing.

Me and Kieran would be into the *Wild Rover* or something Irish – Dad would be blasting out *Fiddler's Green*, a folk tune, while Speedo always preferred newer stuff – even if he couldn't sing! He played the guitar like a dream but I used to batter him for how bad his voice was. Good memories.

When I think about what happened to Speedo, it still seems surreal.

I'm still raw.

It's like I'm talking about somebody else, not somebody who was one of my best mates.

He always appeared so bubbly, so upbeat, so happy. I suppose it all stems from what blokes do; we keep everything in check, we keep our feelings inside, locked away, in house. *Everything is great, yeah I'm fine, nothing to worry about.* I just wish Speedo had reached out to somebody who could've helped him. I'm sure there's people in the Wales set-up, the doctor, somebody who would've been there for him.

I never, ever, ever thought he had any mental health issues or anything like that. He would genuinely be the last person in the world I would think would be struggling and that makes it even harder to get your head around.

Could I have done more, could I have said more, could I have been there more?

These are all questions that have gone through my head – the same as every other mate of his – but hindsight is cruel and cold and I shouldn't think too much about that, about why we didn't catch up more because it gets you nowhere in the end. I suppose if I'd known what was going to happen then things would've been different.

But there's no point in saying that really as it helps nobody and Speedo wouldn't want that either.

Just before his death, I saw him shopping in Selfridges in Manchester and even then he was the same old Speedo – laughing and being funny. We had a really good catch-up.

You know when you have a good mate that you don't see too often these days but you immediately click back in with? Yeah, that was me and Speedo. Five seconds in, we were back to what we'd always done, taking the piss, having the craic, being idiots together.

When we wished each other goodbye that day in Manchester, there's just no way I could ever imagine that would be the last time we would chat in person.

*****

# ONE SUNDAY

*Sunday, November 27, 2011*

Aston Villa were at Swansea and my phone went.

It was about midday on the day of the game and we were about to go into a meeting to talk about the match. Al's name popped up on the display and I answered, same as always.

He broke the shattering news to me and my first reaction, same as everyone else, was just total disbelief. "Fuck off, you're taking the piss," I told him – but it's not exactly something you joke about is it?

I was in complete and utter shock, on the spot. I just couldn't take in what he was telling me. "Are you sure, are you fucking sure?" I asked but he confirmed again what had happened.

I didn't break down, I just sat down. I literally didn't know what to say or think or do. I was completely gone.

I eventually rang Craig Bellamy and told him the news. He was the same, asking me if I was sure, if I was definitely, definitely sure that Speedo, our mate, was gone.

It was all so strange, like walking around in mid-air, like a weird dream that I just couldn't shake off. It was too early at that stage to even be devastated – you don't get to that stage until it's started dawning on you, and that was way off.

On the way into the team meeting, I grabbed our manager Alex McLeish and took him to one side. "I need a word," I said. "Gary Speed is dead." He just stood there, as white as a ghost. He addressed the squad and he was as shocked as me. To be honest, the rest of that day is a bit of a daze that I struggle to really remember.

By the time we got to the ground there was talk that the match with Swansea would be called off and I think that would've been the right thing to do looking back but, equally, we were professionals and, even in circumstances as horrendous as those, you have to be ready to do your job.

"Gary would want you to go out there today," Terry Gennoe told me. "I know this is emotional, I know it's awful but you have to go out and play. Speedo would want you to do that more than anything."

The way Alex got us focused that day, to get us to channel that emotion was incredible and he did remarkably well. No manager in their worst nightmare would have to prepare a team in those circumstances. *Player dying young* is not on any UEFA coaching course. Alex was having to follow his instincts, follow his emotions and try and get us ready in the toughest possible circumstances. He can be proud of himself that day, as can the rest of the Villa lads.

The match itself obviously didn't matter one little bit but, even then, I knew Speedo was so professional that he wouldn't want us to just give it away. I tried to use that as some kind of motivation to get through the 90 minutes.

I got through the warm-up and felt ok but when the minute's silence got going, I just couldn't hold on anymore. I'd done a hundred of these tributes in the past for other people, often older legends whose time had come, but Speedo was still a young man, he was one of my best mates and now we were stood here in silence for him.

The emotion began to bubble up and it had to come out. Even thinking about it now makes that rawness come back. There's a picture of me with a tear about to drop as I stand arm in arm with my team-mates.

That says it all.

# ONE SUNDAY

It was just a weird, weird day all round. The whole of the stadium seemed to be in shock and the match felt like a sideshow. Speedo had obviously retired from playing but Wales were on the up, they were doing brilliantly under him and the Swansea crowd were mourning one of their own.

He was an extremely proud Welshman; their most capped outfielder with 85 caps for a reason. He was happy to travel anywhere and everywhere in the world to try and get Wales into a major tournament as a player and it hurt him that he never managed to do that.

After yet another disappointing international break, we'd meet back up at Newcastle and you could see Speedo was a bit quiet, so we used to do what all good mates do; we took the piss out of him. "You're wasting your time," I'd tell him. "Stay here, go on holiday, go fishing – you're never going to make it." He'd just sit there and laugh it off and tell me where to go.

Before his passing, I'd spoken to Craig Bellamy about life under Speedo in the Wales set-up and he said it was going really well. He'd done so much to make them more professional. They now stayed in the best hotels, took the best transport, ate the best foods and had the best training facilities they could. He had the odd battle with the Welsh FA, but for the right reasons. He believed, rightly, that if you did all you could off the pitch to make your players comfortable then they will reward you on the pitch and it was paying off.

Speedo had been appointed Wales boss in February 2011 and we played them in his first match in the Nations Cup. I was captain for Ireland that night and we managed to win 3-0. I went looking for him afterwards and found him in the Wales dressing room. The match was instantly forgotten. We sat around for a bit and I started taking the piss. "Your job's already on the line, you could be getting the push!" That famous smile cracked out as he told me what he thought of me, the 3-0 defeat and plenty of things in between!

It was a shame Speedo couldn't take Wales to Euro 2016. I have a huge amount of respect for Chris Coleman and the way he has dealt with the situation after replacing his mate in charge. Chris has done an unbelievable job in very, very difficult circumstances. I'm sure they've used Speedo's passing as inspiration at certain times because he put the foundations in place for Wales' current successes.

We went to the funeral in Hawarden and I broke down again in the chapel, St Deiniol's. I just couldn't stop thinking about his two boys, Tom and Ed. He loved and worshipped his sons more than anything on earth, so he must've been in a really bad way to leave them. It's impossible to comprehend what was going through his mind.

When you come to the end of your career, there is a big void there for all players. For 25 years I've been told to report for pre-season training at 9am on July 5. *Don't be late.* Your entire life is structured, from what you eat and drink to how often you train. When that goes, it leaves a big gap that can be very difficult to fill. It's something you have to deal with.

Playing football gives you the biggest adrenaline rush you will have ever get and then in a second, it's gone. Forever. You can never get it back. Even the best and busiest players have to keep themselves occupied when they finish because there's no doubt you will miss the buzz and the craic of training and the thrill of walking out in front of thousands of people, young, fit and ready to show what you can do. What can replace that? I'm not sure anything can and maybe that added to his problems, who can say? We don't know if that was something Speedo was thinking about.

What I do know is that Speedo worshipped his two sons and his entire family. Speedo's dad, Roger, used to come out with us after games from time to time and he is a great bloke. Speedo had such huge respect and love for him.

One night, we were all in a restaurant in Newcastle and we decided to play the Cardboard Box drinking game. Basically, you get an open cardboard box, put it on the floor, then you have to bend over and pick it up with your teeth. The box gets ripped every time it is picked up, so it becomes smaller and smaller and smaller until in the end you are trying to balance and pick up this tiny bit of cardboard with just your mouth. I know, mature right?

Me and Speedo had had a few drinks and before you know it, we're both on our faces in this restaurant, chewing the carpet. Roger got up, as flexible as anything, bent over and picked up the last bit of cardboard, much to his delight.

"Call yourselves athletes!" he was shouting. "You've just lost to your old man!" Speedo and Roger were both loving it, laughing their heads off together.

It's moments like that that I remember most fondly about Speedo. His big smile, his love of laughter and a good time, his dedication to his family and friends and his complete and utter commitment and professionalism to the cause – whether that be with Wales, with Newcastle or with any of his other clubs. He was, is and will forever remain so deeply loved and deeply missed.

# 23

# WHEN TOMORROW COMES

IN all my time with Ireland, I would have to say Euro 2012 was one of the least enjoyable experiences.

We qualified for the play-offs again and the seeding for the draw meant we could only face Bosnia and Herzegovina, Estonia, Montenegro or Turkey. As you can imagine, I didn't fancy the Turks after what had happened before Euro 2000. In the end, we were paired with Estonia. I was delighted. Absolutely no disrespect to them but we had to fancy our chances this time around, especially as the second leg was at home.

Before the first leg, Robbie got us revved up in the huddle before the game. "Our fans didn't come all this way to watch us lose. We go at these and we keep going at them until it's done." I hate to use the phrase 'professional' but when it comes to the 4-0 win, that's exactly what it was.

Keith Andrews headed us in front and we just never looked back. They went down to 10 men, Jon Walters scored and then Robbie finished it with a couple and we were as good as through. At the Aviva Stadium, we drew 1-1 and that was enough, we were on our way. It was also a nice way to mark an anniversary. The match was 10 years to the day since we'd held on in Tehran to qualify for the 2002 World Cup.

We did a lap of honour at the end, the fans were going nuts, Robbie was dancing around with a big flag, a smile plastered all over his face, me and Dunney walked around arm in arm and the Duffer started kicking matchballs into the crowd. Even the Trap smiled and then said we could drink as much beer as we wanted! That tells you how happy everyone was. It was a return to an international tournament after a 10-year wait. I was obviously thrilled because I felt that the likes of me, Robbie and Dunney deserved to get another chance, especially after the Thierry Henry debacle.

Afterwards we all headed into town to a place called House. I'm not much of a dancer but after a few scoops I'm not scared of having a go. I think I had a go that night, much to my embarrassment the next day!

In the qualifiers, Dunney had been absolutely immense. The 0-0 draw against Russia in September 2011 is probably the match he will most be remembered for. Sean St Ledger was suspended and John O'Shea was injured so we needed Dunney to be at his best and he was just unbelievable. It was great for him to finally get some recognition for his country. He was always better than people gave him credit for – he would do anything to win a game.

Some nights when you're completely up against it, you

actually end up enjoying yourself. You feel a collective strength, a feeling that nothing will break you down. We definitely felt like that against Russia in Moscow. I was almost laughing to myself at times because we were under so much pressure.

On one occasion, Dunney saved my arse by somehow clearing one off the line with a superb block. He just seemed to be everywhere. In the second half he flew into one tackle and I don't know who he nailed more – himself or Yuri Zhirkov. He landed on the athletics track that surrounded the pitch, smashed his head open and needed four stitches – as well as a new top. Ireland being Ireland, there wasn't a spare shirt for him so he just had to wear a top with no number on the back.

The fourth official wasn't happy about that and kept barking at Alan Kelly, our goalkeeper coach, "NO NUMBER, NO NUMBER." Everything started getting a bit heated. It looked like another John Aldridge moment was about to unfold – what is it about Ireland and touchline officials?! – until Al had a moment of genius and remembered he had a felt-tip pen in his pocket that he used to fill in the substitute cards for the ref. He drew a '5' on the front and the same on the back but then tried to start colouring it in. "JUST GET ME BACK ON THE FUCKING PITCH," Dunney shouted at Al, bringing their little art lesson to a close. The fourth official just looked at Al, nodded and went, "Ooh very good." Here we are, the middle of a European Championship qualifier and the fourth official is busy judging Al's handiwork! Only Ireland, right?

I had a good match that night too, making some crucial saves on their weird plastic pitch to help us escape with a point. Although the media talked of the result as some outrageous fluke, that was doing a disservice to us, especially Dunney.

Dunney's famous nickname was 'The Honey Monster' mainly because of his giant frame but he's a canny player and he'd certainly come on since I'd first met him. Back in 2000 we'd toured the USA for the US Cup under Mick McCarthy and, yes, we went out every now and then. In this one bar it was my round and I asked Dunney what he was having.

"I'll have a pint of vodka and orange please," he said. *Ha ha, yeah, whatever. No, really, what are you drinking?* "I just said. A pint of vodka and orange." He's matured a bit since and it's more like a pint of red wine now. He's a connoisseur these days!

After qualifying, we were a happy group. But our good mood soon changed when we saw the draw for the tournament itself. Put it like this, we'd used all our luck up getting Estonia in the play-offs...

Croatia. Spain. Italy.

You couldn't ask for a tougher group. For me, Croatia were a better team than Italy but Italy went on to make the final; so what does that tell you about the job we had to do?

The build-up to the tournament wasn't ideal for me because I was struggling big time with a knee injury. I was chasing fitness and as any footballer will tell you, that's a horrible place to be. It eventually led to a situation where some questioned if I was fit enough to have played in the tournament. I can talk a bit more freely now about what happened.

Three weeks before Euro 2012 was due to start and on the second day of our training camp in Ireland, I hurt my knee and it was clear straight away that I'd done something or other that wasn't too good. I came down on it awkwardly and I felt something pop.

The next day I flew to London to see Andrew Williams, one

of the UK's best knee specialists. The press found out and it was all played low-key with the official line being that the trip to London was just a precautionary issue and that I'd be fine to return to Portmarnock once he'd given it the once-over.

He recommended plenty of rest and ice so I immediately started using this device called a Game Ready which is a compressed ice machine. It helps ice a joint to reduce swelling and pain.

I was battering this machine as much as possible — you can put it on low, medium or high pressure and I had it on high about seven times a day, desperate to get the swelling down. As a result, I ended up adding to the problem by damaging a nerve on the outside of my right knee. I then began trying to protect that damaged nerve by overcompensating and loading all my weight through my left leg, which soon meant my left calf felt like it was going to explode. It wasn't good.

We flew to Budapest for a warm-up match against Hungary and there was still no way of knowing how fit I would be by the time the tournament kicked off 10 days later.

Ahead of the game, I was put through my paces by Alan Kelly. We took care to protect my knee and calf, but even then we knew it wasn't 100 per cent. I worked every day with Alan. He was also keeping the Trap and Marco informed about how fit I was.

I knew I could trust Al with my life. We went back a long, long way by this time. After all, if he hadn't injured his back in 1996, I would never have got an Ireland look-in because he was class, so our entire careers were linked. We used to laugh a lot, mainly about how disgustingly untidy my side of the room was when we shared together and now, at this stage of my life and with plenty of issues off the field as well as on it, having Al around was something that definitely helped me.

The night before the match, Al gave me a basic kind of fitness test which at one stage involved him hitting 12 shots at me as hard as he could – 12 bullets – and I would have to save them all. Three volleys, three off the ground, three half-volleys and three headers.

Al was smashing the ball as hard as he could but my reflexes felt fine and sharp and also, mentally, it was something I wanted – to go into the Hungary match knowing I was as fit as I could possibly be.

There was a huge thunderstorm before the match which left the surface really slippy – not ideal – but in the end I couldn't have been happier with how it had gone. I made one reflex save from a deflected shot that was as good as anything I'd ever produced before which proved to me – and probably to Al and the Trap – that I was fit enough to play.

However, after leaving Hungary for Poland to prepare for the tournament itself, my left calf was still not responding to treatment properly, it felt like it was getting worse and two more scans showed it wasn't 100 per cent. By this time, the first match with Croatia was only days away so in the end, I went to see the Germany team doctor, Hans-Wilhelm Muller-Wohlfahrt, at the German team hotel, the Dwor Oliwski, near Gdansk.

Dr Muller-Wohlfahrt uses special injections to help people recover from injuries quicker. Usain Bolt and all the German national team use him if they are struggling and he's got loads of players up and moving again. His injections contain natural ingredients – it's all a bit of a secret as to what they are – but I was desperate to get back to training. I'd been to see him a few times while I was at Villa, he'd inject my back and knee and the soreness and stiffness I'd occasionally get in both would go.

There is some controversy around these injections and some national teams have probably stopped players from going but Dr Alan Byrne, the Irish team doctor, was unbelievably supportive. "Shay whatever you want to do is fine with me," he said.

Fortunately, we were only staying in Sopot, a 15-minute drive from the German hotel, so it wasn't far to go and to Muller-Wohlfahrt's great credit, he couldn't do enough for me. Just before the Euros he could easily have said he was just going to concentrate on German players but he did the opposite.

He basically had to smuggle me in to the hotel past security so nobody – including the media – would find out he was helping a non-German player. He then put his arm around me and said, "Let's get you fit, let's get you out there" and that meant a lot to me, so credit to him for doing that.

The injections started to work. The Trap wanted it playing down and he wanted to give me as much time as I needed to get ready. Ireland needed their most experienced players available and I was one of them.

I needed to play and wanted to play as a way of not only helping Ireland but I think I also needed to play for me. That might sound selfish but I still think I was the right man for the job anyhow.

I was desperate to train because I always feel that if you train then the rest takes care of itself. I'd spent 20 years training every day and always trying to improve and now, on the verge of a major tournament, there was no way I was going to leave any stone unturned if it meant it gave me a chance of getting back out there.

# SHAY

Some players would have ruled themselves out but there was no way I was doing that. I would do everything exactly the same tomorrow. Some fans might read the book and accuse me of being selfish and that I shouldn't have played but they've not been where I've been.

I felt I was fit enough to play – I wasn't crawling across the training ground – and mentally, I was fine. It was only my training that was a bit limited.

*****

By the time the Croatia match came around, the knee did feel better and I felt a lot more confident on it.

Not that it mattered in the end.

We started poorly against Croatia and it only got worse. We were 1-0 down in no time when Mario Mandzukic's header wrong-footed me and snuck inside the near post. I felt if I had been more set I would've had a better chance of saving it but I wasn't quite there and it kind of drifted in.

Sean St Ledger equalised, sneaking in from nowhere to head us level but we were not tight enough defensively. We didn't close Croatia down and Nikica Jelavic gave them the lead again.

At 2-1 we still stood a chance and the half-time message was to get tighter and press them more but in the second half Mandzukic scored another header after it had hit the post and bounced back in off my head. *Oh, for fuck's sake.* Talk about unlucky. The ball could've gone anywhere but it ricocheted back into the net and that set the tone. We were bottom of the group. It was the highest we'd get.

The Trap came in for some criticism after the opening match

but he was a bubbly character and he really didn't care about what anybody outside the camp said, wrote or thought about him. He just said and did what he wanted. Most of the time he had the media eating out of his hand, yet even he was running out of friends in the press and things took a turn for the worse against Spain in the second match. It could have been a cricket score to be honest. It just felt that everyone, including me, was a second late to every ball.

I don't know what the stats were and I'm not too keen to find out. David Silva delivered a masterclass that night. You could argue that if we'd got one back against Croatia then that might've changed things but that was never going to happen against Spain. In life, you sometimes have to hold your hands up and say you were totally outclassed. In the blink of an eye it was 4-0 and that was it, goodnight Vienna.

With about 10 minutes to go in that Spain match, the Ireland fans showed why they're the best in the world as this rendition of *Fields of Athenry* started. I think it began behind my goal. You could just hear it building and building. In the end it sounded like there were 100,000 fans in the stadium.

After the Spain loss we were going home and we thoroughly deserved to be. In the qualifiers for Euro 2012 we had conceded seven goals in 10 games, a tribute to the Trap and the defensive strength he had brought us. Where did that go when we arrived at the tournament? We had conceded seven in just two matches, not 10, and you won't last long in football doing that.

Being involved in a dead rubber for Ireland is a weird old week in itself. On the one hand you're going home no matter what happens but on the other hand you still have a stadium full of fans and a country back home to make proud.

We played Italy in the last group game and goals from Antonio Cassano and a late one for Mario Balotelli did for us again. The Ballotelli goal made the final score look worse because we were actually in that game more than any of the others.

I think the Trap was hurt, especially as we lost to his home country, and I don't think many of the lads in the squad for that tournament returned home thinking they had done themselves justice. I know I certainly didn't and it was time to have a long think about what the future held.

I was very torn about what to do. I was looking at lads like Brad Friedel, Edwin van der Sar and Mark Schwarzer and they had all stopped playing internationals in their late 30s in order to try and keep their bodies in better condition. It wasn't the playing that was the issue, that's only 90 minutes after all, but the hours travelling and arriving back on a Thursday before a Saturday will eventually catch up with you and I wasn't getting any younger.

I spoke to Paul Lambert about it at Villa and he said, "I don't want you coming back here wrecked because I'll need you for Saturday." That did make me think I'd be playing a big part for Villa in the 2012/13 season but as it turned out I was dropped – and that made life really hard. Giving up Ireland was about playing week in, week out in the Premier League – and then I never got a look-in! Paul didn't say I was guaranteed a place but that felt like a big hint.

There were several things racing around my head at the time and I couldn't really see a way through it. I had a lot of stuff going on off the pitch with my family and a divorce. I've always been a big family man and getting a divorce was something I never thought would happen to me. I was also still struggling to process the loss of Speedo, that was still very painful, and it just felt like I needed to simplify my life a bit, especially because the Euros hadn't gone well for me or Ireland.

I also looked at players in my position and in my head I made a list of positive and negatives about staying or going. In the end, the huge disappointment of the Euros meant it felt like it was time for someone else to take on the mantle.

Had we done well then I would've probably carried on but the thing is, there's never a good time to retire from international football. I thought I'd walk away and hopefully prolong my club career. I was 36 and I'd played 125 games which sounded like a nice, round number. I think Peter Shilton played that amount of games and he didn't do too badly did he?

I didn't really speak to anybody about it on a personal level. I think Dad and the rest of my family were shocked when I gave it up but you can only go on your gut instinct and mine was telling me something had to give somewhere.

I rang the FAI and spoke to Peter Sheridan. His Italian was excellent and I asked him to get the message across to the Trap without there being any misunderstanding or confusion. He rang the Trap, who then called me.

"Shay, I would like you to stay on," he said. "But I understand and respect your decision and thank you." He was disappointed after the Euros as well and maybe deep down he felt somebody else needed the gloves.

Sixteen years in goal for your country is a long time. Maybe Ireland needed a break from me as much as I needed a break from Ireland.

When we got back from Euro 2012, the football was well and truly forgotten as I travelled to Blessington in County Wicklow for the funeral of James Nolan.

James, like thousands of others through the years, was a football-mad, passionate Irishman whose support for the team on the pitch meant the world to us.

He was one of a big gang of close mates who'd made the trip across to Poland but he tragically drowned in the River Brda the night before the Italy match. He was only 21 and we heard so many stories about what a wonderful young man he was with plenty of friends and family.

I was in two minds about whether to attend the funeral because I didn't want to make it into a big media event with reporters there and everything else but, equally, I felt it was right that somebody from the squad was there in person to show our respects.

The service, in the Church of Our Lady, was beautiful. Nearly a thousand mourners were present and that said a huge amount about the kind of man James must have been.

May he Rest in Peace.

# 24

# GO RAIBH MAITH AGAT

IT was Roy Keane who got me back in the Ireland squad.

When he came to Aston Villa in June 2014, it was good to work with him again and, crucially, he was also Ireland's assistant manager. Martin O'Neill had replaced the Trap as Ireland boss in November 2013 and had asked Roy to come on board as well.

After a few months at Villa, we were having a coffee and messing about at the training ground when he just asked, "So are you going to come back then or what?" I thought he was joking. I laughed it off and thought nothing else of it. About a fortnight later as we did battle over a game of pool, he tried again. "Why don't you think about it?" he asked. "Sleep on it and let me know."

To be honest, I was thrilled by the idea that I could get back into the Ireland set-up but I didn't really think I deserved the chance. I wasn't playing regularly enough at Villa to warrant the opportunity. Nobody has a divine right to play for anybody, least of all their country, and I didn't think it was a possibility by this stage.

A short while after I'd initially retired I had actually thought about changing my mind. At the time, the Trap was still the boss and I spoke to Marco Tardelli. I just wanted him to know I'd come back if they thought it was a good idea but the Trap, to his credit, didn't exactly jump at the idea. I understand that completely and hold no grudge whatsoever. "Leave it with me," he said. "I have to give the new keepers a chance." I got that totally – if new goalkeepers never got a chance then I wouldn't have played against Russia back in 1996 would I? But I still wanted him to know I would help out if there was an injury crisis. Fast forward to the Trap leaving and Martin O'Neill coming in and it became a possibility again.

Roy was insistent that I could challenge for the No.1 place and if not, I could at least offer my experience to Keiren Westwood and Darren Randolph. It was pleasing to hear that Roy still rated me and eventually I said I was open to the idea. "Leave it with me, I will talk to Martin," he said. "Just give me a few weeks."

Eventually, Martin drove up from somewhere down in the south of England and we met at The Belfry, which is literally a five-minute drive from Villa's training ground at Bodymoor Heath. I'd only bumped into Martin once or twice in 20-odd years in the game but he was somebody I respected. He'd had a lot of success at Leicester City and Celtic and he was one of the big names in Irish football.

We shook hands in the foyer, settled down for coffees and started talking. "Roy has seen a lot of you recently," he said.

"He still thinks you're capable of coming in and playing for us. He tells me it's something you'd be keen to look at?" I told him I was certainly fit enough to play and would love to get recalled.

"You will have to trust me Shay," he said. "I won't bring you back in the side straight away as the others deserve their chances too. But we will certainly get you in to have a look at you. I wouldn't be sat here now if I didn't think you were worth playing at some point."

We shook hands and that was it. I headed out on loan to Middlesbrough, got some football under my belt which definitely sharpened me up, returned to Villa and then ahead of a friendly against Oman in August 2014, Martin announced his squad.

I was in it.

It felt amazing again to be back in the group and I got plenty of abuse for returning. "I thought I'd got rid of you for good," Robbie said, grinning. He was an injury doubt for Oman but he was there, same as always, ready to go at any moment. It was good to be in a changing room with him again.

I'd obviously got to know Robbie well over the years. He loves a sing-song on a night out. His dad used to sing in pubs in Dublin and he's inherited that. He thinks he's Ronan Keating but the truth is he couldn't hold a tune in a shopping basket!

On the pitch, as I've already said, Robbie never stopped running. He was a fighter. His will to win and energy levels were unbelievable wherever he played. Robbie has scored so many crucial goals and I know how much he loved playing for Ireland.

If I hadn't retired when I did, I might have finished with more caps than him but 134 is fine with me and he deserves great credit because Robbie really put the hours in to get back home and play for Ireland. When he was at LA Galaxy, he would have to fly into London and then out again to Dublin. But you could never tell because he was always running around at full pace.

Stephen Quinn, who is a really funny lad, had been rooming with Robbie in my absence. When I returned, he thought he was going to get kicked out for me. "Cheers lads, no, honest, cheers – I'll just get my coat," he said. "I hope you two are very happy together again, don't you be worrying about me."

Quinny is a right character. A few years ago we were all having a beer together after a game, nothing too mad, and he got talking to my partner, Rebecca. She mentioned that she had a Land Rover Defender and Quinny has one too. "Hey Rebecca, have you ever tried to have a drink in one of them?" he asked, sat on this stool.

Next thing, he started mimicking a Land Rover bouncing all over the place, the suspension ruined, his pint glass flying here and there until he eventually tipped his pint over his head. We just stood there laughing our heads off as one of Ireland's premium midfielders was dripping with Guinness, a big grin on his face.

The Oman game was only a friendly and was pretty tame but I really enjoyed being in the side. The old feelings came flooding back, especially during the anthems. This was the 126th time the hairs on the back of my neck were standing up. I'd been gone a couple of years but I felt like I was part of the group straight away and the thrill of playing for Ireland was as strong as ever.

I played a further friendly against USA in November 2014

but then missed the first four qualifiers as we beat Georgia, Gibraltar, drew with Germany (thanks to John O'Shea's late equaliser) but then lost to Scotland. That sounds quite impressive on paper but the group was so tight that the next match against Poland at home was crucial because we were in fourth place going into the game. I was one of seven lads to come into the side after the Scotland loss and we scraped a 1-1 draw thanks to Shane Long's injury time equaliser.

I was happy to be back in the side. Martin had been true to his word about giving me a chance to prove I could still perform. I felt I did ok against Poland, certainly enough to be in the squad on merit, rather than on past performances. I stayed in the squad for a friendly with England and then a 1-1 qualifier draw with Scotland.

During that summer of 2015 it was also time to leave Aston Villa for Stoke City. At the time, I was on the verge of signing for Middlesbrough because I'd genuinely loved my time there on loan. Aitor Karanka was a really classy manager and we got on well. All the staff and fans were so friendly and it really was a wonderful place to play football.

Villa were happy to release me and Middlesbrough seemed a good fit but then late on, Stoke made an effort to get me and, to be honest, it was too good to be true for where I was in life. Rebecca was six months pregnant and we were living in Cheshire. My two older children were settled in schools and Stoke was just 15 minutes away on the train. They were an established Premier League side and I knew Mark Hughes and half their squad.

I got huge amounts of stick on Twitter because I know some fans believe that players just go wherever there is more money but I can sit here now and say the two deals were absolutely identical in terms of length and wage.

They forget that behind a player is a man with family commitments. If you had two identical jobs on identical money and one was on your doorstep and the other was three hours away, what would you do? A lot of Middlesbrough fans claimed I'd 'betrayed' them by picking Stoke at the last minute but it wasn't as simple as that. It never is.

Mark Hughes rang me once I'd joined and we had a catch up. He was very clear about what he wanted from me at the club. "Shay, I want Jack pushing hard, every day," he said. "I will have no problems in dropping him for you if you are performing better. He needs to be pushed and I want you to come in and help us. You're not a cheerleader here, I want you in the side if you are needed." It was good to hear that Mark, like Martin, still saw me as being good enough to be No.1.

*****

I stayed in the Ireland squad and everything was great until we played Germany in October 2015.

In my early 20s at Newcastle I had a knee operation that removed nearly all the cartilage. Nowadays, they just trim it down and you're good to go very quickly but back then it was a bigger deal and I was bone on bone by the time we played Germany at the Aviva Stadium.

I had some bone spurs going on inside my knee joint and during the game one of them must've snapped or become inflamed because my knee just blew up. It was huge, full of fluid and swelling up by the second. I just couldn't move. I wanted to get to half-time and get it assessed but there was no chance. Some of our subs were warming up in bibs near to my goal and I knew I was in trouble. "Tell Martin I'm done," I shouted. "Get the others ready."

I was devastated to be stretchered off but we actually won the game which left us still able to qualify automatically so, despite my own pain, I couldn't have been happier for Martin, Roy or the lads.

That was also the night the Aviva Stadium finally came to life and replaced Lansdowne Road.

It's an immense stadium, so state-of-the-art and the facilities are incredible, unlike Lansdowne Road where you were lucky if you got a clothes peg and a hot water tap! But I thought we struggled to get the Aviva atmosphere going at first and it took until that Germany match before it felt like our home.

We lost to Poland 2-1 in the last qualifier which meant we finished third in the group. We drew 1-1 in Zenica in the first leg of a play-off with Bosnia and Herzegovina and then it was the Jon Walters show at the Aviva, a 2-0 win in the second leg sending us to Euro 2016.

I was going nuts when Jon scored both goals. I was thrilled for him. I'd got to spend some time with him at Stoke and we always got along really well. Yet it was only until about a month ago that I found out he'd also lost his mum at a very early age. I read it in the paper rather than him ever mentioning it in person. Again, men don't spend much time actually talking about stuff, do they? Our lips move a lot but we never speak about things that matter.

I was thrilled that Ireland would be going to Euro 2016 but my own chances looked limited to say the least because of my knee troubles. After returning to Stoke, I'd had an operation to have the knee flushed out but it didn't really work and I was soon back in trouble. One day as I walked around my house, it went again – badly.

I was in that much pain that I had to ring the club physio, Dave Watson, and team doctor Andrew Dent, and they had to race to my house. By the time they got there, I was lying on the couch, my knee three times the size it should be. Dr Dent managed to ease some of the pressure. They eased it again 48 hours later but every time I tried to do gym work or any exercise, it ballooned again until eventually I went back in for another operation.

The problem kept me out of action for five months. I thought my chances of going to the Euros had gone – before a huge twist of fate changed all that.

You never want to benefit from anybody else's misfortune but in the space of no time at all, it looked like I had a chance of becoming the No.1 at both Stoke and Ireland without having kicked a ball for months.

In March 2016, Jack Butland broke his ankle on England duty and Rob Elliott suffered a horrendous knee ligament injury when we drew 2-2 with Slovakia at home. Robbie was in a lot of pain. It was terrible to see him like that, especially so close to a major tournament.

I was actually there that night but in a shirt and tie rather than a goalkeeping kit because I was doing some punditry work. When someone starts shoving a microphone in your hand and makes you wear an earpiece then you know your career is coming towards an end. I popped into the dressing room to wish Martin, Roy and the lads good luck but I didn't want to hang around. I was aware they were trying to mentally prepare for the match and they didn't want me getting in the way.

When Jack got injured at Stoke, it seemed to be a great chance to prove my worth to the club and to Ireland but it didn't exactly go to plan as we got battered by Spurs and Manchester City. I also picked up a groin injury against City which kept me out for a month. I came back into the side for the last match of the season against West Ham United and made a great save to keep out a Diafra Sakho effort when we were 1-0 down and I also kept out Michail Antonio and Emmanuel Emenike with a double block as we eventually came from behind to win 2-1.

That made me feel great and I was pleased to show my worth to Stoke as that result meant we finished in the top half of the table, above Chelsea.

In the crowd that night was Seamus McDonagh, the Ireland goalkeeping coach. He was also watching Darren Randolph who was in goal for West Ham and in the friendlies before Euro 2016, Martin wanted to try out both of us to see who he felt was his No.1 for the tournament. I always felt that Darren was going to be his preferred choice but I felt fit again and was ready to push him as hard as possible.

Against Belarus in Cork, I picked up my 134th cap and became the longest-serving Ireland player by timespan. Robbie has played more games than me but the match meant I overtook John Giles.

I was tremendously proud to get that record. One day and one cap would've done me just fine, never mind 134 over 20 years. Although we lost the match 2-1, I still went to the Euros with half a hope I would be picked by Martin as his first choice.

Going to France gave me a great chance to spend some time

with Martin and Roy and observe how they interacted. I think their contrasting personalities worked really well. Martin is very calm and analytical with a quiet authority while Roy can have a bit of a temper and give you a rollicking if you need it. The two of them were an effective combination.

Roy would tend to take the small-sided games. On some days, Martin would just come and walk around the pitch or sit in one of the dug-outs and watch. Watch and watch and watch. You could feel him there, calculating, thinking and judging you. It was a brilliant way of reminding us he was the manager. It was something Fergie and Arsene Wenger used to do as well apparently – in a way it kept you on your toes more than if he was stood there with a whistle in his mouth.

Martin has this way of keeping his distance from the players and there is no doubt he enjoys that and relishes keeping them guessing. His mind is always alert, he seems to have eyes in the back of his head and you never know what he is really thinking.

He is ALWAYS the last on the bus on the way to training in the morning and ALWAYS last on the bus after matches. It is just another of his wee subtle reminders that the bus waits for him, not the other way around because *he's* the manager.

Martin doesn't shout or bawl to get his point across, he can throw you one look which is as effective as the Fergie hairdryer. With Roy as his assistant, he has no need to let rip. Roy will do that for him!

During the March international break before Euro 2016, Martin had called a meeting for the players and stated that under no circumstances whatsoever were players allowed to book their partners or families into the same hotel as the squad. We were in France to work, not to go on holiday.

Some time after the domestic season had finished, we arrived at our hotel as planned. Then one day, Martin gathered us together in this conference room and started to speak.

"Now, lads," he said. "I looked out of my window and there's a campervan in the car park. They're Irish lads because of the flags. And there's a couple of them staying in the hotel here."

*He was just warming up.*

"So I went and looked at the room list."

*He was getting to the point now.*

"I looked at the room list to see who these young lads were in the campervan and, no, it couldn't be, but there's nobody's families staying here is there?"

*This is what he was up to then.*

Martin had gone through the room list and found some decidedly non-French sounding names on the list.

The lads had checked their families into the lavish Trianon Palace Versailles under their real names! How many people called Long and Walters are staying in a luxury hotel on the outskirts of Paris? Ever met a Monsieur McGeady?

*He asked again.*

"There's nobody's families staying here is there?"

Slowly a hand popped up here and there and Martin was not impressed. "Jesus, what?" he said. "What are you thinking?" before walking out.

Robbie went to see him and he was raging at us all which, us being us, was the perfect chance for some fun. Robbie told Bobby Ward, who looks after the team's security, to bring one of the naughty schoolboys, Richard Keogh, up to see him. I was staying in the next room with an adjoining door to Robbie and was sat in Robbie's room with him, waiting for Keogh.

Finally he knocked on the door and came in, dead sheepish. He'd been really worried about his family being in the hotel and had already expressed his worries. "Shay, I'm not gonna play now," he said. "He's not gonna pick me is he?" He was ripe for the plucking.

We sat him down and Robbie started up.

"Me and Shay need to speak to you about what you've done," Robbie started. "I don't know how to break it to you about your behaviour but Martin is in the room next door so you have to go into Shay's room, apologise a lot and get this sorted out – otherwise you're going home." The sweat is pouring off him by now and he's the colour of a bottle of semi-skimmed.

"What, he's through there?" he whispered to us, panicking. "You're joking right? I can't speak to him now, I've fucked up here."

"Just do your best," I chirped up. "Just do your best, tell him how sorry you are and you'll never do it again. I hope that works for you, mate."

"What am I going to say? What am I going to say?" Keogh said, flapping big time.

"Well, you best think of something, you can't keep him waiting any more," Robbie told him.

Keogh got up, really slowly and nervously, looked back at me and Robbie and turned the handle into my room. He pushed the door open quietly and there was half the squad waiting for him. All the lads were jumping on the bed, screaming and crying laughing. I bet you could hear the noise back in Dublin. "You bastards, you fuckers!" Keogh was off on one now, laughing his head off as well, so relieved that it was all a big wind-up.

Despite the odd brighter moment, Euro 2016 did confirm to

me one thing that had been evident for a while with Ireland and that was the fact that the old ways of doing things were well and truly gone. Quinny would've been climbing the walls with boredom and itching to escape through a hotel window if he'd been away with us.

Football has just changed, rightly or wrongly, and that meant once training was over, you barely saw your team-mates until the next day's training session. Me, Robbie, Jon Walters, Stephen Quinn, Robbie Brady and John O'Shea might've gone for the odd coffee together – while John gave us yet another terrible horseracing tip or was boring us rigid about what horses he wants to train – but we didn't socialise together as a group much at all and that was a big shame.

It was hard to get to know some of the lads. Some players wanted to keep a low profile or hide away on their Xbox. Don't get me wrong, I'm 41 now, I didn't want to be out raving until 3am, but a round of golf together or a few beers in the hotel, playing cards, would've been great. The old Ireland were like a family but at Euro 2016, it was clear the social side had fallen away. One of Ireland's biggest strengths was gone.

*****

Martin is old school. He would only announce the team in the dressing room just 90 minutes before kick-off.

Even the day before the opening match against Sweden, when you kind of think you know who is going to start and who's missing out, Martin deliberately mixed up the teams at training so nobody knew. We had a coffee and tried to name 1-11 but nobody got it right.

Before the match, the nerves and adrenaline were flowing in the dressing room as we all got changed. There's always an edge and a tension in the air because nobody has a clue what's going on. You just have to prepare as best you can and we were all sat down when Martin walked in with a piece of paper in his hand.

"Right lads, the team is…"

*This is it.*

"In goal, Darren."

It's as I thought. Darren's is the first name read out. I knew from then on it would be his shirt to lose. I had totally prepared for him to be picked ahead of me and although there was, of course, a small part of me that was hopeful, he was the coming man and deserved my support.

Years ago, before we drew 2-2 with Holland in the 1998 World Cup qualifiers, Packie came and knocked on the hotel room door to tell me and Alan Kelly that Al would be playing that night. I was naturally disappointed but Packie wanted to tell us to our faces. One of us was always going to be gutted but that's football isn't it? Someone had to miss out and it was my job then – and it was my job now – to react the right way.

Chin up, support the No.1, get back out there.

"It's just another game," I told him. "Prepare the same as always, let's get going." Darren is a very cool, calm goalkeeper and nothing seems to faze him. If he makes a mistake then he forgets it straight away and that is the perfect mindset.

We had a job to do. We went outside and warmed up together. I tried to help him by getting him ready for the match. We were competing for the jersey but we all get on well and it was the same old story really: we were all professionals and patriotic Irishmen trying to do well for their country.

Martin said to me after the tournament that without the knee problem I would've had a good chance of playing but that's the way it goes, you can't control the timing of injuries, so I don't have any regrets. And Darren did himself proud.

Being a tournament back-up was new to me but I did miss the pressure of playing and preparing. For me, you want that intensity, you want the demands being made of you and with that missing it was a different kind of Euros for me. I was there almost as a cheerleader more than anything; using my experience around the group to keep us focused, relaxed and ready.

We drew 1-1 against Sweden and it was crucial to get a good result in that match because Belgium were next and I felt they were the most dangerous side in the group, as they proved when they beat us 3-0.

Almost straight away, Martin and Roy emphasised that it was gone. Done. Forgotten about. Italy was the cup final now. Bring it on.

Martin delivered a team-talk before the game, while Roy was more personal. He went around and had a word here and there, reminding people of their responsibilities and their jobs. There was no chest-beating or pulling doors off hinges, everything was pretty calm.

Seamus Coleman might be a quiet person off the field but he was brilliant that night and I'm told he delivered a real adrenaline-pumping talk to the lads in the huddle before the match which got everyone revved up.

But this wasn't like the gung-ho speech of me and Robbie before the Thierry Henry handball match. They couldn't fly out and go too early at Italy because if Italy scored then it would be harder than ever. We knew that we had to be patient, disciplined and take our opportunities when they presented themselves.

When Robbie Brady scored, we just went nuts! The raw emotion when the ball hit the net was incredible, it felt like Robbie Keane's goal against Germany 14 years earlier and although I wasn't on the pitch this time, it still felt special. I was soon on the field, dancing around with everybody else. Robbie Brady was obviously on cloud nine afterwards, his brother was in the crowd and he got very, very emotional afterwards.

I was one of the last out of the dressing room that night. I was checking my phone, taking my time with the shower and getting changed. Martin and Roy were also late out. They were flying, grinning and chatting non-stop about what had just happened. It was an awesome performance and result for the entire country.

France were next up in the last 16 and the lads just tried to recover as fast as they could. We had belief inside the camp that we could beat them. They might've been hosts but the message was, 'You never know lads.' We had grown after the Italy match but, unfortunately, it wasn't to be, as we lost 2-1.

Robbie Brady's early penalty gave us hope but one of the players of the tournament, Antoine Griezmann, scored twice and we were going home.

After the France match, I walked around the stadium, waved an Irish flag with my arm around Robbie and we both looked at each other. That said enough. We wouldn't be doing this again at a major tournament, ever.

I applauded the fans who had been as magnificent as always. I was determined to take it all in, to hear and see as much as I could, to spot people in the crowd who I knew from home and to just absorb it all for a final time. I knew then that this was it. Darren and Keiren and Robbie Elliott were good enough, fit enough and young enough to be Ireland's goalkeepers for years to come. Walking around the pitch at the end of a major tournament wasn't the ideal way to go out. But I'd had worse.

I spoke to Martin on the phone and let him know that I was going to retire, this time for good.

"I knew this phone call was coming Shay," he said. "Thanks for coming back and making us a stronger group."

Roy also sent me a complimentary text message, telling me I'd enjoyed a good career and could be proud of my Ireland efforts. I was happy with that and in the end I used Twitter to let people know I was retiring:

> It's every boy's dream to play football for his school, his local club, and maybe, in his wildest dreams, his country. To try and be as good at football as his father was before him and make his mother proud.
>
> I've been blessed that I was able to do this, from kick-abouts in the back yard at home in County Donegal with my brothers, to playing for St Columba's College Stranorlar, Lifford Celtic and then to making my debut with the Republic of Ireland aged 19.
>
> I'm one of the very lucky ones who got to wear the jersey for his country and wore the badge with pride 134 times. But now it's time to hang up the gloves and move from the onion bag to the terraces, where I'll be shouting the lads on as one of Ireland's biggest fans.

## SHAY

*So as I retire from Ireland duty to focus on my club career, I want to say a HUGE thanks to everyone who supported me all the way – my close family, friends and amazing fans.*

*I couldn't have done it without you, and all my great team-mates, managers and friends at the FAI.*

*Go raibh maith agat.*

Thank you indeed. That was some journey we went on, together.

# 25

# WITH OR WITHOUT YOU

*Moss Rose, Macclesfield, September 4, 2017*

*"Ha Ha! Unlucky slaphead!" Danny Whitaker, who has been at Macclesfield Town on and off for about 100 years, tries to get a header in at me but the ball just runs off his greasy bald head, giving me the chance to have a pop at him. Earlier he'd nutmegged me and said, "Keep your legs closed next time pal!"*

*It's been pissing down all morning, I'm soaked through, caked in mud and sand and I've had to use my own kit because the kitman Tony Watson hasn't got any spare goalkeeping stuff.*

*My old Newcastle team-mate Steve Watson watches from the sidelines, laughing. He is the Macclesfield Town assistant boss and asked manager John Askey if I could come and train with the lads while I'm without a club.*

*It's been 19 years since me and Steve last played in the same side together, a 2-0 win over Nottingham Forest with Shearer scoring both. Nineteen years. That makes me feel old. Christ, I am old. Twenty five years now I've been doing this. For a quarter of a century I've been out there every day, no matter the weather, no matter the circumstances or the minor knocks.*

*Stopping a ball from going into a net; it's been my life.*

*I'm as happy throwing myself around in the mud with these lads as I was attempting to keep Barcelona out all those years ago. The thrill of training, of diving around, of getting out in the fresh air and trying my best remains as strong as it's ever been.*

*What is going to fill this gap?*

\*\*\*\*\*

Ireland may have been at an end, but I started the 2016/17 as the No. 1 at a Premier League club.

It felt good to be first-choice at Stoke City. Jack Butland was struggling with injury and Lee Grant was in competition with me but I got the nod from manager Mark Hughes.

The season didn't start well. After a 1-1 draw at Middles-brough in the opening game, we had a terrible start defensively, getting smashed 4-1 at home by Manchester City, 4-0 to Spurs and 4-1 on the road against Crystal Palace.

Our luck was summed up by one match at Everton, where we lost 1-0. Leighton Baines took a penalty, I managed to flick his effort on to the post but it rebounded and hit me on the back of the head and went in. I got credited with an own goal the day after – the dreaded penalty curse strikes again!

I didn't think I was accountable for all of those goals but when teams are losing by three or four every week the other 10 lads on the pitch somehow get forgotten about by the media.

All of a sudden it was all down to me. I could handle that and cope fine with the pressure but in a team game it is never just the goalkeeper's fault, just as most goals are never solely down to one individual.

I was dropped for a Hull City tie in the EFL Cup for Lee and never got back in as he went on to be named player of the year after a wonderful season.

Being dropped was not ideal but Mark, unlike others who I've mentioned, at least had the bollocks to do it to my face in his office. Eddie Niedzwiecki was the first-team coach and his fingers are more bashed up than mine. It seems like they point in 10 different directions. If he saw you and asked you to follow him to Mark's office you knew you were in trouble. "Here's Curly Finger, here's the Grim Reaper," Charlie Adam used to say. "You're fucked now."

I enjoyed my time at Stoke. It was just like any other dressing room – full of banter. I'll miss all that when it's gone. I already knew the likes of Jon Walters, Stephen Ireland and Glenn Whelan when I joined, so that helped. We'd all have lunch together and the mickey-taking would start. Ryan Shawcross, the world's scruffiest man, would come in for some stick. He'd wear a tracksuit to his own wedding if he could. I'd come in wearing a shirt and jeans, normal gear, and he'd walk in looking like a chav. "Where are you off?" he'd ask, as if I was ready for some big night out. "You're allowed to wear normal clothes every now and then you know," I'd say. "Why don't you try it?"

Peter Crouch was a good bloke too. We'd spend a bit of time at the railway station together as we went home after training. He was the captain of 'The Monday Club', which was the group of players who sometimes weren't involved at the weekend or who only got a few minutes on a Saturday. When I joined The Monday Club I saw it as a chance to keep improving in one area especially; my Spanish. I'd try out a few phrases on Marc Muniesa and he'd stand there, taking the piss out of my accent. I got my own back plenty of times. He came to me one day and said, "I play tonight against Morrr-com-bye, where is that?"

"Do you mean Morecambe?"

Jack Butland is a very confident and self-assured character, he has a lot of self-belief and once we got to know each other we got on very well. I think he can definitely become England's No.1 and play for whoever he wants. Lee is a great bloke too. They used to take me on at head tennis first thing on a Monday morning but the pair of them had forgotten they were up against a pro who'd been doing this for 20-odd years. My team was called 'Dusty Carpet' because we'd never been beaten – "You know the drill, you know the dance lads, it's time for the Dusty Carpet." They'd be raging after.

As the season came to an end, it was clear that I was going to be released. I could see it coming and it was all very amicable. Mark, the chairman Peter Coates and chief executive Tony Scholes rang me and thanked me for my efforts and, just like that, I cleared out my locker, shook hands with the lads and headed off to the car, a Premier League goalkeeper no longer.

\*\*\*\*\*

I know that I have to finish at some point, I know the clock is ticking on my life as a footballer but I'm ok with that, I know it comes to every player and that it's something you've got to get used to and adapt to.

# WITH OR WITHOUT YOU

I take tremendous pride in myself for making my career happen. The trophy cabinet might be a bit light but I think everybody I played for, with and against, will all say that I gave it everything; I never ducked it in training, I never avoided the tough decisions, I never went missing when my teams and my team-mates needed me. I turned up every single day, ready to work. I'll take that.

The vast majority of footballers at the top level do not win the Premier League or a trophy, and some amazing players like Ryan Giggs never play for their country at a major tournament, so it all depends how you look at these things. Playing for Ireland and in the Premier League was everything to me and although I feel lucky, it wasn't good fortune in itself that either got me or kept me there and I take a great deal of satisfaction from that.

It took application, work-rate, ability and commitment. And sacrifice. I've missed birthdays, weddings, christenings – you name it – because I've had a game that day. I even missed The Bear's wedding because I was playing.

This is not a complaint; footballers have a wonderful life and we can let our hair down and have a few beers and enjoy the craic when the time is right. It's not totally regimented and I know a lot of people would swop with me in a heartbeat.

I have played for more Premier League managers than anyone else: Tony Parkes, Kenny Dalglish, Ruud Gullit, Bobby Robson, John Carver, Graeme Souness, Glenn Roeder, Nigel Pearson, Sam Allardyce, Kevin Keegan, Chris Hughton, Joe Kinnear, Mark Hughes, Roberto Mancini, Alex McLeish, Paul Lambert, Aitor Karanka, Tim Sherwood and Mark Hughes (again). In fact, apart from Bobby Robson on 198 occasions, only two other bosses – Graeme Souness and Mark Hughes – managed me over 50 times, and even that took two spells for one of them!

It's impossible to compare the managers I've had really but if I had to pick the manager who has had the biggest influence on my career I'd have to go with Kenny. Everyone needs a good start in their career and he showed unbelievable faith in me when I was young. When he took me to Blackburn and then Newcastle he was putting himself out on a limb, especially at St James' Park, and his belief in me made all the difference. As well as a manager, he's been a good friend. I sometimes scroll through my phone, see his name in the contacts list and think, 'How the fuck do I know Kenny Dalglish?!'

Bobby was also so important. He was a special manager of immense charisma and charm but still he ruled with an iron rod. You didn't last long at Newcastle if you thought you could outsmart Bobby and if I could change one thing about Premier League football, it would be that more local, homegrown managers were on the touchlines at our biggest clubs. Bobby had a direct link to Newcastle – the team and the area – and that made the fans dream and sing out loud which, after all, is what we are here to do.

It's been some journey. My career has seen the end of one footballing era and the start of another. I came in with pints and parties and I'm going out with pills and protein shakes. I've been in a dressing room with home-grown lads and one with players from all four corners of the world. I like to think I fitted in well wherever I've been. You need to move with the times, no matter what your job, if you want to survive. I count myself as a survivor.

# WITH OR WITHOUT YOU

The job of being a goalkeeper has changed plenty since I started. When I began, the back-pass rule was still in (as were flares) and then the six-second rule was introduced, which changed things again and placed more emphasis on being good with your feet.

Nowadays, all goalkeepers have to be able to play from the back. Once upon a time the goalkeeper would just try and kick it as far as he could but now you have to try and start attacks and spread the play yourself, as well as being another defender outside the box when it's needed.

I still work on my left foot every day because I was very right-foot dominant in my early days. People might ask what was up with my left peg and it wasn't too technical: I just couldn't fucking kick the thing! It's a lot stronger now and younger keepers work on both feet so they don't really have a weak side. Years ago, I used to run around the ball until it was on my right foot, otherwise I'd just ship it into touch and hope for the best.

The quality of delivery into the box has also changed beyond recognition. A lot of people hammer goalkeepers for their decision making. The standard of crosses and corners in the Premier League, helped by lighter balls that whip across more than ever, mean that goalkeepers have even less time to assess what they should be doing next. There's not a goalkeeper in the Premier League who wouldn't tell you the same.

Some players can also try and bully you in the box. I always push them away at the last second. There's no point having a WWE wrestling match with them because then you lose focus on the ball. A goalie like Jens Lehmann seemed to want to fight at every corner when players blocked him off.

Kevin Nolan was one of the worst opponents for trying to

ruin my afternoon. His arse – which isn't the smallest – would be shoved right into you, he'd be trying to stand on your toes and he had no interest whatsoever in the ball, his job was to just stitch me up. "Fucking hell Kev, you again," I'd tell him, trying to kick him out of the way. "Give it a rest eh?" He'd always give a little laugh and then try and stop me doing my job. Being a goalkeeper is tough enough without having to deal with that!

*****

I don't think I've ever felt truly secure and comfortable at any of the clubs I've played for. You never feel settled, especially as a goalkeeper. One mistake and you can be remembered for life for the wrong reasons. You're on a tightrope, watched by millions around the world. It takes one slip, one handling error, one swerve of the ball here or there and, bang, your career can be down the drain.

Nobody gets comfortable with that. Could you?

All you can do is prepare, work hard in training, do your best in the game and then repeat that process. Do that enough times and you've got a career. It's a game-by-game outlook, look no further than Saturday and hope everything goes your way.

I also think some self-doubt is a good thing, an important part of what makes a professional sportsman. Am I good enough? Was Saturday good enough? Will this Saturday be good enough? You look at some young kids now and they have more arrogance, but maybe a bit more self-doubt from time to time helps drive you on and keep you constantly striving for better.

One thing that has remained – and will forever be part of me – is the fact I despise conceding goals. The fury inside when I've let one in is as strong now as it's ever been. That's not always self-doubt – 'Should I have done better there?' – it's just something inside me, something that I think all keepers need.

Players are under scrutiny like never before and I think the media spotlight is making the job harder than it's ever been. On *Monday Night Football,* you never see Jamie Carragher or Gary Neville praising the goalkeepers. It's always, 'That was a nice height for the goalkeeper' or 'the striker should have done better.'

You know yourself if you've made a big mistake. The next day, the press will focus on the 'howler', and not mention the saves the goalkeeper made afterwards. After an error, I wouldn't bother reading the papers, I didn't need a reporter to tell me where I was going wrong.

These days, it seems that every time I turn the telly on, I am conceding to somebody. I switched the box on the other day and they were talking about Arsene Wenger's career. Then up popped the Bergkamp goal. I was sat there lying on the couch thinking, 'Of all the goals Arsenal have scored in 20 years, I have to pop up, don't I? Show something else!' Straight after the Wenger show – and I swear this is the truth – I switched on *Sky Sports News* and Rooney was getting linked with his eventual move back to Everton.

Which goal did they show? You guessed it, that screamer past me at Old Trafford in 2005! Surely he scored past someone else once or twice! "Ah lads, just get Shay's reel down, there'll be something on there we can use!"

That's just the keeper's lot in life. I like to think it takes a certain type of character to be able to handle life between the sticks. If you're a weak character, you wouldn't cope.

I don't have any big regrets and I don't spend any real time thinking about yesterday or what-ifs, it's the present that counts the most and what's coming next.

If I was to say I regretted anything, it would be failing to save that penalty against Spain and not staying at St James' Park a season longer. If I'd done that, I would've become Newcastle United Football Club's all-time leading appearance holder. But at the time, it wasn't right for me and there is no chance I'm going to spend the rest of my life worrying about that.

'What's next?' is the only question that needs answering. I've no divine right to any job, whether in football or outside it. I'm doing some media work now and I'm a novice at that so I want to improve and become better at it so the public stays interested in watching and listening to my views on the game I played for a long, long time.

As for Ireland, well, I'm just a fan these days, I wear the green jersey the same as anybody else and sing the anthem as loud as the guy next to me.

When Ireland played Austria in June, me and my son stood up in the living room during the national anthems. He had a big grin on his face and a straight back as the anthem was played. He might not have been born in Ireland but he won't forget his Irish roots in a hurry!

I'd love to go to more games with my brothers and mates, get stuck in with the fans and enjoy the craic. I'm sure that will happen. I always said during my career that half of me wanted to be bouncing in the stands and blaring out *Fields of Athenry* and there's plenty of time for that to happen.

*****

After the 2002 World Cup, I went on holiday and ended up in this restaurant in Cannes. A bloke walked past and I thought I recognised him.

*Fucking hell, it's Bono!*

I was way too nervous to go over and say hello but I had a couple more Heinekens and had nothing to lose. Fuck it. I got up, walked over to where Bono and his wife Ali were sitting and he spotted me coming. "Shay, how's it going?!"

*Bono knows me?*

*Bono knows my name?*

I nearly fell off my feet.

"Sit down, please, sit down and join us for dinner," he said. I tried to knock him back but he insisted. "Now sit down, please, and say hello to my friend Michael." It was only Michael Stipe, the lead singer of REM, wasn't it? "Hello mate," I said and shook his hand, like I'd known him all my life.

After a long lunch he asked me what my evening looked like but I was just heading back to the hotel with nothing planned. "Well, come out with us," he said. "We're heading for a few drinks."

Why not, I'd come this far. Fast-forward three hours and I'm on a dancefloor with Bono, swinging my hips, attempting to dance and generally having a great time. At the end of the night he gave me a scrap of paper and said, "Write down your number and we'll meet for a drink next week." This was mental. I wrote it down and then thought nothing else of it. About five days went by and I thought that was it but then I picked up a voicemail and it was the man himself. "Sorry Shay, I lost the piece of paper," he was saying. "But I got it from Mick in the end."

Mick? Mick who? Shit, does he mean Mick Byrne?! Bloody hell, he hadn't been talking shit to us for all these years, he really did know *U2*!

"So anyhow," this voicemail continued. "I'm around all week, so ring me back."

We spoke on the phone and Bono invited me up to his villa for lunch the next day. He also said he could get me into a plush hotel near his place if I needed somewhere to stay. Later that day, I rang him back and left a voicemail, asking if it was possible to book me into this hotel he had recommended.

The next day, I got to his villa, and he had given me the code for his gate so I walked straight in and up to where his pool was. His place is right on the beach and all these super-yachts were flying past. Me and Bono got talking and it was clear again that he hadn't got my voicemail about this special hotel he knew so he quickly rang the place but it was booked up.

"Ah, nothing to worry about," he went. "Just stay here." I tried to say no but he was adamant. "I insist, just go up the stairs, turn right and take any room you want."

Later on, I popped out to meet some friends while Bono stayed at home and then when I got back to his, I again tapped the code in the gate, walked to the pool and there was a bloke sat there with a cowboy hat on. "Shay, good to see you made it back," Bono said. "Meet The Edge." *What do I do here? Do I call him The Edge? Mr Edge? Mr The Edge? Edgey?* This was unreal. We sat around with a few beers as the sun went down, enjoying the craic and then went to bed.

In the morning, after breakfast, Bono came into the kitchen and wanted my opinion. "What do you think to these?" he asked, and started singing a song he was planning to put on an album. He played the track on a CD player and was then singing away to it. I'm sat in Bono's kitchen, – the actual Bono, in his actual kitchen – tapping my feet and nodding my head, as if I've got the first clue about what makes a good record. Bono and Ali couldn't have been more welcoming and down to earth.

It was an amazing experience. Later, I texted my brother Liam who started going mad that I'd spent the night at Bono's and he asked to speak to him.

"Bono, would you mind having a quick word with my brother?" I asked him and he was more than happy to do it. I rang Liam, put him on the phone and he went, "Bono, check your pillow cases, dressing gowns and duvets because anything not nailed down, he'll have stolen. He'll clear you out."

Bono stood there laughing his head off, the coolest Irishman on the planet. He was more than happy to join in as well. "Honest Liam, I only invited him for lunch," he said. "And now I can't get bloody rid of him."

*****

Staying at Bono's villa? It's mad isn't it? I've had some crazy adventures thanks to my football career. Believe me, I was as much in awe of Bono and The Edge as any fan.

I like to think that I'm still the same Shay as the one that grew up gathering spuds with jute bags tied around his knees in Lifford. I hope that people in the game would say I've pretty much remained a normal bloke. I'm genuine when I say that I'd have been just as happy working for Dad on the market garden all my life.

There's a lot of bullshit, noise and noisy characters inside the game – the sport just seems to attract them – but I've shut that all out fairly easily. I know one Premier League star – and he really is a superstar – who goes to training, returns to his house, which is behind a big set of gates, goes upstairs and plays on his Xbox for the rest of the day. That's it. He never goes for dinner with his family, never walks the dog, nips out for a pint of milk – nothing. Who wants that?

I still go to Sainsbury's and do the shop, I still nip to the pub down the road for a pint and when I was at Stoke, I still cycled to the train station on a Daisy Bell bike.

Just the other day two lads nudged each other and one went, "That's Shay Given!" and the other looked at him as if to say 'Is it fuck, why would he be riding that bike around here?'!

I don't need a chauffeur to take me to training and I don't get a first-class seat, just a standard train ticket. Why would I? I don't feel I need to be lifted and laid.

Nothing is more important to me than making sure my own children feel loved and I will support them all with whatever they want to do in their lives.

At home, I'm knee-deep in nappies or I'm cooking dinner, I'm on the school run and I'm always out in the garden playing football and netball or watching my kids smiling and laughing on the trampoline. I think some people reckon footballers don't have to change nappies or get sleepless nights but I can assure you this one does!

My children will be taught the same lessons I was as a kid, namely that hard work is the only recipe to success, no matter what they want to do. Football has given me a wonderful security but I won't let my children be spoiled by that and they will grow up knowing the value of a pound note, just as we all did. My eldest two wash my car and do other errands and if they want paying then they have to do a good job!

A few years back, I needed to pop home for a family party and a generous friend offered me the use of his helicopter to dash to Lifford for the day. It was very quick, very luxurious and very not-me! I landed in the back garden and you can imagine the stick I got. My brother Liam stood there, grinning and shaking his head. "Look at that," he said to me as I ducked under the blades and shook his hand. "He left in a tractor and came home in a fucking helicopter."

Having so many brothers and sisters is one sure-fire way of never getting above yourself. Good luck getting a big head in the Given household.

There's a saying we always use in our household. 'It's far from (whatever) you've been reared.' For instance, if I'd ever been stupid enough to go home in a flash car then it would've been, 'It's far from a Ferrari you were reared'! I'm thankful for that, especially when it would have been so easy to get carried away with some of the ridiculous doors that open for you when you're a footballer.

At home I'm just Shay, or 'Horse' or 'The Crab'. All the noise that comes with being a football gets switched off, it's just me and the family and I wouldn't want it any other way.

My only regret these days is that we don't get together enough. We are spread all over the place and all have so much going on. I think the last time we were all under one roof was my 40th birthday. We have a WhatsApp group that we fill every day with photos of our kids and the general craic that comes with a big family. We've even allowed Dad to join it recently but he just pushes loads of buttons on his phone and hopes for the best.

Dad was never the kind of father to praise us too much and it's only recently that he's opened up a wee bit more about Mum and my career. I know he's proud of me but it's never been a conversation we've had. I don't know who would cringe more, me or him, if all of a sudden he started saying how proud he was of me. Anyhow, he's got plenty more children and grand-children and he's equally as proud of them and rightly so.

The role Dad played in my career has been massive. In the early years it was his help that created some big opportunities. He didn't stand for any shit. He protected his boy as he knew best. I know he doesn't want any credit for that. In his eyes, he was just doing what dads should do – and what I try and do with my own four amazing children – and that is protect them and help them make the most of their lives and enjoy it as much as possible.

We were all were brought up the same, there were no half-siblings in our house. Dad and Margaret deserve huge credit for that. Margaret has been an incredible example for taking us all on board. She deserves a medal. Nobody has gone off the rails, there's been no drug or alcohol problems and we've all done well for ourselves. I suppose that goes back to the discipline and work ethic Dad instilled in all of us. We knew the difference between right and wrong, we knew there was a line we couldn't cross and we never did. I think that's so important.

In June 2006, I received the Freedom of Donegal which was totally unexpected but very special. I don't look back too much but I love Donegal as a place; I love going home, I love the people and the beauty of it. Everybody is so welcoming. It's a way of life to stop a stranger in the street and ask him how his day is. We are a friendly bunch.

# WITH OR WITHOUT YOU

A few years back, a lad called Micky Joe Harte represented Ireland in the Eurovision Song Contest. I know him, so when I was back home I told him to head to Lifford for a drink and a sing-song – and he turned up with an entire band!

My mates from back home, lads like Willie Curran, Donal Burns and Bungle are the same ones I've had since I was five years old. Me and Donal sat next to each other at school, he cried his eyes out on the first day and I've never let him forget it.

I go to Bannigan's for a pint at home – my brother Paul owned it a few years back – and it's just normal. Then we all head up to McCauley's Restaurant on Bridge Street, not far from the River Foyle, for steak and chips.

Dad and Margaret go in every Sunday, without fail. At the World Cup in 2002, I took him to some lovely restaurants but the answer was always the same, "It's nice son, but it's not McCauley's." In fact, he's there that often that when a helicopter flew over taking aerial photos of the place, there was Dad's car in the car park. The photo is now hanging up inside.

When I do return to Lifford, the memories of childhood come flooding back and there's obviously still a gap in my life that, unfortunately, no amount of international caps or good memories can change. That's the early loss of Mum.

Agnes Given, that grand-looking woman of just 41.

I've missed her all my life and I've spent nearly 40 years wondering what her advice would've been and how she would've guided me and protected me, the same as Dad and Margaret have. I still pray to her, her death still hurts and it's still wrong that she missed out on watching us all grow up and do well.

She missed out on grandkids and all the normal family stuff that people across the world get to do every single day. It's a shame I never got to know her as a real person but I do know one thing: I'll never stop looking up at her grave from Dad's home and I'll never stop trying to make her as proud of her son Shay as he is of her.

In a way, I think Mum's passing has been a driving force in my life. It's up to you how you react to the hand you're given. All I ever wanted to do was make my family, friends, Lifford and Ireland smile and be proud that one of their own was out there for them, doing their best every day.

I've been incredibly lucky to have played for so many fantastic teams and in front of such great fans; to have represented my country for 20 years; to have had four beautiful children and a wonderful partner in Rebecca. When I think back on my life and career, I cannot help but use the word 'blessed' to sum it all up.

My life's been a journey that I never even knew was out there, never ever thought could be mine. I'll always be grateful for the chances football has given me to make the best of myself and bring security and happiness to my family. It turns out that a size five football is actually a passport to a world I will never stop being thankful for.

I love the sport just as much now as I did as a kid and I always want to be involved; as a fan, a pundit or maybe even by still pulling on a pair of gloves. What the future holds is still to be decided and that excites me. The next game, the next week, the next challenge; whatever is on the horizon doesn't scare me. It never has. Bring it on.

All I can hope, all I can dream, is that the second half of my life is as good to me as the first one has been.

# ACKNOWLEDGEMENTS

MY family have played such an incredible, important role in my life and I owe them an enormous amount. Through thick and thin, good times and bad, they have always been there for me with unconditional love and support. Their help throughout my career has been so crucial. I've never lost sight of how fortunate I am to come from such a hugely loving background. From the freezing cold evenings in front of two men and a dog at Lifford Celtic to the fancy surroundings of playing on the biggest stage at the World Cup finals, the Givens have always been by my side, especially my dad, and I will never be able to thank them all enough.

My uncle, Packie 'Paparazzi' Keeney, also deserves a special thanks and mention for all his hard work collating some of the photos for this book although looking at them now, I'm not sure whether I should be laughing or crying!

The lucky ones get to meet their soulmate and I'm forever thankful for the day I met mine. Rebecca is a fantastic mother, partner and my best friend. It's not always been easy but she is always there, solid as a rock. It never ceases to amaze me how she tirelessly takes care of me and the children and nothing is ever too much for her. Caring for a house full of children and all that comes with it is not easy, but she makes it look that way. We're not the stereotypical footballing showbiz couple; you're more likely to find us walking to the park with the kids than walking up a red carpet. It's the simple life we choose and when you have love, nothing else really matters.

The people of Donegal and Ireland have always had my back and it's always been such an honour to represent them when on international duty. I hope they feel like I did them justice – I certainly played every match for my country with them in mind.

I met some special people along the way, especially the likes of Michael Bland, Ian McGuinness, Mark Devlin, Damien Taylor, Jack Leonard, Steve Johnson, John Stevenson, Steve Burns and Alan Beenshill. They have all been only a phone call away if ever I've needed them. Michael Kennedy has also always been there to lean on and to advise me and there have been a few periods in my career where I've very much needed and listened to his calm counsel and guidance.

I've played for a huge number of coaches throughout my career and I'd like to thank all of them. I've learnt something from each and every one of them, most good.

A special mention though has to go to Robbie White, Mick McCarthy, Terry Gennoe, Kenny Dalglish, Bobby Robson, Kevin Keegan and Mark Hughes. They all saw something in me that they liked and that they felt needed developing further. I hope I repaid their trust and I hope they realise how grateful I am for all they have done for me.

At my publishers Trinity Mirror Sport Media, I would like

# ACKNOWLEDGEMENTS

to thank Steve Hanrahan, Paul Dove, Claire Brown and especially my ghost-writer Chris Brereton who has been first class. I
could have used other writers to help me but I read some of his
previous work and I loved it. It's been a real pleasure going back
over everything, Chris has become a mate and I hope we will
continue to have a long friendship in the years to come.

Finally, I want to thank Agnes Given. We may only have known
each other a short while but she was my mother, you only get one
of those, and she is still dearly missed.

*Shay, 2017*